Approaches to the Treatment of Stuttering

Edited by Peggy Dalton

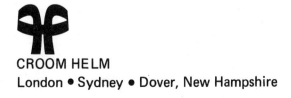

CROOM HELM

London • Sydney • Dover, New Hampshire

© 1983 Peggy Dalton
Croom Helm Ltd, Provident House. Burrell Row,
Beckenham, Kent BR3 1AT
Croom Helm Australia Pty Ltd, Suite 4, 6th Floor,
64-76 Kippax Street, Surry Hills, NSW 2010, Australia
Croom Helm, 51 Washington Street, Sydney
Dover, New Hampshire 03820, USA
Reprinted with corrections 1985

British Library Cataloguing in Publication Data

Approaches to the treatment of stuttering.
  1. Stuttering   2. Speech therapy
  I. Dalton, Peggy
  616.85'506   RC424

ISBN   0-7099-0837-7 (hd)
       0-7099-0824-5 (pbk)

Printed and bound in Great Britain
by Billing & Sons Limited, Worcester.

CONTENTS

CONTRIBUTORS

Carolyn Cheasman, B.Sc., L.C.S.T., Lecturer, Speech Therapy Unit, The City Literary Institute, London

Frances Cook, M.Sc., L.C.S.T., Chief Speech Therapist, Camden and Islington Health Authority, London

Peggy Dalton, M.A. L.C.S.T., Clinical Organiser, The Centre for Personal Construct Psychology, London

Rosemarie Hayhow, M.Sc., L.C.S.T., Lecturer, The Central School of Speech and Drama, London

Roberta Lees, L.C.S.T., Senior Lecturer, Jordanhill College of Education, School of Speech Therapy, Glasgow

Celia Levy, B.A. (Sp. Th. & Aud.), Tutor Organiser, Speech Therapy Unit, The City Literary Institute, London

Lena Rustin, L.C.S.T., Area Speech Therapist, Camden and Islington Health Authority, London

PREFACE

The scarcity of contribution from Britain in recent years to the vast literature on stuttering is regrettable. It is largely due to the fact that in this country we have nothing to compare with the combined research and therapy centres of, for example, North America. Most clinical work here takes place in hospitals, Health and Community Centres, where provision is made for treatment and the opportunities and facilities for research are extremely rare. There is, however, a great deal of interest and concern amongst speech therapists for the improvement of treatment for stuttering. Specialisation is increasing and courses providing a wide range of both practical and theoretical knowledge are constantly in demand.

A number of the contributors to this volume have developed approaches which combine both the structure and the flexibility needed to take into account the many facets of this complex problem. They may be said to represent the current trends in therapy for stuttering in this country. Rustin, for example, with Cook, describes her programmes for intervention with children evolved over the past eight years within the Camden and Islington Health Authority in London. Cheasman and Levy outline their work with adults who attend intensive and weekly group therapy at the City Literary Institute (the City Lit.) in London. Dalton discusses developments in the personal construct theory approach to stuttering combined with speech modification procedures which are taking place at the Centre for Personal Construct Psychology in London. All are involved in research or the preparation of case-studies, which will be available for publication in the near future.

The presentation at this time of detailed accounts of the therapeutic processes involved in these approaches comes in response to the demands of clinicians and students. We have attempted first to evaluate some of the published programmes which we have used and learned from, secondly to describe the modifications of these ideas evolved through clinical experience and thirdly to exemplify how these may be combined with newly developed procedures. Thus we hope to provide therapists with a practical basis for the planning and development of treatment for a wide range of needs. In addition, we hope that people who stutter and those who are concerned for disfluent children may find these chapters useful in their search for the most appropriate help for them.

The editor has wished each contributor to present her work in her own way and no attempt has been made to impose a rigid framework on the chapters which follow. Only one or two stylistic points have been agreed upon. It was decided to use the term 'stuttering', rather than 'stammering' since, although the latter is still more commonly used in Britain, the former is increasingly being applied here and is more often found in the literature. 'He' is generally used to refer to the disfluent person, as the greater number of people who stutter are male and a constant 'he/she', 'his/her's' etc. was felt to be clumsy and irritating to the reader. Similarly, 'she' is used with reference to the therapist, as the majority of speech clinicians working in this country are female, although we are aware that this is not universally the case.

Peggy Dalton.

1 INTRODUCTION

Peggy Dalton

Theories and Therapy

This book is concerned with current approaches to the treatment of stuttering. No attempt will be made to cover the theoretical background related to its causes or development. These aspects are discussed fully in such volumes as Van Riper (1982) and Wingate (1976). Therapy is devised, however, on the basis of the clinician's understanding of the nature of the problem. In this section, therefore, we shall look briefly at some of the ways in which contemporary workers define stuttering and the implications these definitions hold for the ways in which treatment is planned and executed.

Van Riper, for example (1971), states simply that 'a stuttering behaviour consists of a word improperly patterned in time and the speaker's reactions thereto' (p. 15). But his therapy, developed over many years, is founded on 'learning theory, servotheory and the principles of psychotherapy' (1973, p. 204). The steps involved in his complex treatment programme incorporate measures to deal with three major aspects of the problem as he sees them. The client is helped to unlearn old maladaptive responses to the threat and experience of fluency disruption and learn new and more adaptive ones. To counter the failure in the auditory processing system, which Van Riper proposes as the likely cause of the basic disruptions, stutterers are trained to monitor their speech by emphasising proprioception, thus by-passing the auditory feedback system. And psychotherapy, to bring relief from the psychopathology that he regards as so often surrounding the disorder in adulthood, is interwoven throughout all therapeutic interactions. Cheasman discusses Van Riper's treatment approach in some detail in Chapter 4.

Ryan (1974), also describes stuttering in terms of three components: a speech act, an anxiety component and an attitude component. To him, however, it is the speech behaviour which produces the anxiety and attitude problems and he therefore focuses his attention in therapy on the improvement of speech fluency. Approaching stuttering as operant behaviour, which is 'overt, has an impact on the environment and is controlled by its consequences' (p. 7), he seeks to control dis-

9

fluency by manipulating both the evoking stimuli and the consequences. The evoking stimuli take the form, for example, of instructions to 'speak very slowly and as fluently as you can', while the consequences may be 'very good', if the speaker is fluent, or 'no, don't do
that' if he stutters, both resulting in a decrease in disfluency. These
procedures are programmed in very small steps from one-word utterances to lengthy conversations, as outlined by Rustin and Cook in
Chapter 3. These authors evaluate the usefulness of such an approach in
relation to work with children. In Chapter 4 Cheasman comments on its
applicability to therapy with adults.

While Perkins (1979), also focuses on the speech act in his definition
of stuttering as 'dis-co-ordination of phonation with articulation and
respiration' (p. 105), his treatment programme is very different from
that of Ryan. He works directly on achieving fluency through management of the breath-stream in order to initiate voice with a gentle onset
and maintain airflow throughout the phrase. Though articulatory rate
is slowed in the early stages to facilitate co-ordination with phonation,
natural rhythmic patterns are introduced from the beginning as the
key to developing normal-sounding speech without loss of control at
faster rates. Unlike Ryan, Perkins does not see anxiety and negative
attitudes as being automatically altered with changes in fluency, but
unlike Van Riper, he does not include desensitisation or psychotherapeutic procedures in his programme. He estimates that 'even the most
diligent users of normal-sounding speech will likely require about five
years to feel as normal as they sound' (1979, p. 109).

A completely different view of stuttering from any of the above is
taken by Sheehan in his later work. In an earlier attempt to define the
problem (1958), he too included three components, similar to those
presented by Ryan. One describes the disfluent speech behaviour, the
second the fears and anticipations of speech failure and the third the
self-concept the person develops as a stutterer. But by 1970 Sheehan
had come to focus almost entirely on the psychological effects of
stuttering and described it as 'a disorder of the social presentation of
the self . . . not a speech disorder but a conflict revolving around self
and role, an identity problem' (p. 4). Not surprisingly, therefore, his
treatment is different again. He questions whether it should be referred
to as speech therapy at all, since 'the stutterer does not have to be
taught how to speak, or anything about speech, *per se*'. He prefers the
term 'specialised psychotherapy' to describe his approach, which
includes the client's accepting openly the role of stutterer, changing attitudes to effect a reduction of shame, hatred, embarrassment and even

'stuttering on purpose' (p. 19). Sheehan's Avoidance-Reduction Therapy is discussed in some depth in Chapter 5.

It will be seen from these few examples that contemporary therapy for stuttering can take widely differing forms, both in the emphases and in the procedures used to bring about the alleviation of the problem. Each of the authorities referred to has made changes in the light of clinical experience and with the advancement of knowledge through research and technological progress. Yet though they and others who work with such thoroughness and concern to improve their methods of treatment can claim success with many who participate in their programmes, no one has developed an approach which can be universally applied to all who seek help. Stuttering is clearly not one single disorder. It is important, therefore, for the working clinician to assess what each therapeutic approach has to offer and to choose those treatment stategies which seem most appropriate to a particular client's needs.

The Assessment of Stuttering

Throughout this volume it will be found that great emphasis is placed on the assessment of stuttering as a basis for such a choice. The next chapter is devoted to an exposition and evaluation of procedures for investigating both the nature of the disfluency and its effects on the speaker's attitudes towards communication and concept of himself as a person. It is stressed that analysis of the speech pattern forms only a part of our preparation for treatment. If we are to decide on a course of action to alleviate stuttering we need also to understand how disfluency is experienced by a child or an adult, how parents or other significant people react to it, and what part it plays in governing the person's behaviour as a whole. It is equally important to try to judge the extent to which changes in speech will demand other changes and take this into account before we launch into a fluency programme.

This exploratory stage is seen as going far beyond the gathering of information. Rustin and Cook in Chapter 3 show how, by means of their extensive interviews with children and their parents, they attempt to build up a picture of the young person they are dealing with and to understand fully the circumstances in which the child and those round him will have to work. They see this as a period when the rapport essential to a successful outcome is established with all concerned, and they base their choice of treatment as much on these factors as on the extent and severity of the child's disfluency.

Similarly, in Chapter 4, Cheasman stresses the importance of the diagnostic phase of the intensive courses at the City Lit. Here, adult clients are fully assessed and given the opportunity to explore the overt and covert aspects of their problem. Trial therapy procedures are followed to allow them to test out not only the usefulness of various techniques but their own reactions to them. An approach is chosen as appropriate to each person on the basis of his or her attitudes towards what is involved, as well as an analysis of the stuttering behaviour.

Chapter 5 includes a discussion of personal construct procedures, which can be seen to be therapeutic in themselves, as well as forming part of the assessment in this particular approach to stuttering. As the client goes through the stages of setting up his own repertory grid (Kelly 1955) and writes a sketch of how he sees himself in his current position, he may already begin to look at people and events from a new angle. Sharing some part of his outlook on life with another forms the beginning of a relationship which will prove of considerable importance if real progress is to be made. Here, too, the therapist is gaining knowledge of how the client functions as a whole and her initial plans for treatment will be based on her understanding of him as a person and the circumstances in which any course of action will be framed.

Lees, in her chapter on adjuncts to speech therapy, sees diagnostic potential in some of the methods used to alleviate stuttering through external agencies — masking, biofeedback and drugs. Noting the recurrent finding that while some people who stutter become at least temporarily more fluent while using these means, others are unaffected by them, she suggests that further research might bring to light subgroups of disfluency. This could contribute both to our understanding of a particular client's problem and our choice of the most appropriate procedures to mitigate it.

The Choice of Treatment

This book contains descriptions and evaluations of many techniques, programmes and approaches. These are, however, only a sample of the hundreds that are available. Responsible clinicians offering a specific course of treatment acknowledge that theirs is not the only method and that, while they have their successes, there are always those who cannot be helped through their programmes. Claims for instant and lasting 'cure', though attractive to the media and, understandably, to those who stutter or have disfluent children, are regarded with a distaste which comes from long experience and concern for the well-being of clients, rather than any threat to their own professional work.

An alternative to following one particular approach in treatment is for the clinician to equip herself with a wide range of skills and attempt through careful assessment to choose those procedures which seem relevant to the client in question. This is not a matter of dipping into what Sheehan (1970) has called 'the Smørgasbørd of stuttering therapy' (p.294). The clinician rather considers all aspects – the nature and severity of the disfluency, the psychological effects that the speech difficulty has produced, the context within which any improvement has to take place – and, with the client, sets up a balanced programme where due weight is given to each component. Eclecticism in one's approach to treatment is advocated by a number of contributors to this volume and it will be seen that this does not imply the woolliness often associated with the term. It is urged that all procedures used should be integrated into a course of therapy which has both structure and relevance and its purposes clearly understood by those involved.

The Structure of this Book

Although, to a large extent, each chapter of this book is complete in itself, there is some interdependence where topics overlap. To save reiteration, for example, Hayhow (Chapter 2) has focused in her discussion of assessment on the differential diagnosis of disfluency in the very young child and then turned her attention to adults. Since Rustin and Cook (Chapter 3) present their assessment of the older child as an integral part of their therapy, it was felt unnecessary to cover this ground also in Hayhow's chapter.

Cheasman and Levy (Chapters 4 and 6) include two aspects of the therapy carried out at the City Lit. In Chapter 4, techniques and programmes are discussed and in Chapter 6 the group context within which this work is undertaken is described. Levy, therefore, assumes that the reader will be familiar with any techniques to which she refers.

Grids and self-characterisations (Kelly 1955) are referred to both as aspects of assessment (in Chapter 2) and as part of therapy (Chapter 5). Again, to save duplication, Dalton has largely left the description of these procedures to Hayhow and it is important that those are read first, in order to make full sense of references to them in the later chapters.

The concluding chapter is in no way a summary of all that has gone before. Here, an attempt is made to address the major issues for the therapist who works with those who stutter. No single format is suggested as the answer to all treatment problems. There is no ideal clinician presented for workers in the field to model themselves upon. Only some suggestions are made with regard to training, the therapeutic relationship and the aims of therapy for stuttering.

References

Kelly, G.A. (1955) *The Psychology of Personal Constructs*, Norton, New York

Perkins, W.H. (1979) 'From Psychoanalysis to Discoordination' in H.H. Gregory (ed) *Controversies about Stuttering Therapy*, University Park Press, Baltimore, pp. 97-127

Ryan, B.P. (1974) *Programmed Therapy for Stuttering in Children and Adults*, Charles C. Thomas, Springfield, Illinois

Sheehan, J.G. (1958) 'Conflict Theory of Stuttering' in J. Eisenson (ed.), *Stuttering: A Symposium*, Harper and Row, New York, pp. 123-66

——— (1970) 'Role-Conflict Theory' in J.G. Sheehan (ed.), *Stuttering: Research and Therapy*, Harper and Row, New York, pp. 4-34

Van Riper, C. (1971) *The Nature of Stuttering* (1st edn), Prentice Hall, Englewood Cliffs, N.J.

——— (1973) *The Treatment of Stuttering*, Prentice Hall, Englewood Cliffs, N.J.

——— (1982) *The Nature of Stuttering* (2nd edn), Prentice Hall, Englewood Cliffs, N.J.

Wingate, M.E. (1976) *Stuttering: Theory and Treatment*, Wiley, New York

2 THE ASSESSMENT OF STUTTERING AND THE EVALUATION OF TREATMENT

Rosemarie Hayhow

The assessment procedures currently used with people who stutter are generally agreed to be inadequate. The aspects of the individual and his problem that are considered relevant to assessment are largely dictated by the treatment approach of the therapist. Since the treatment of stuttering seems to be developing in some interesting new directions it is hoped that in the near future more sensitive and clinically useful assessments will be developed and tried. In this chapter some of the theoretical issues and current procedures are discussed, firstly within the context of normal disfluency and early stuttering and then in relation to the assessment of speech and attitudes in the confirmed stutterer.

Normal Disfluency and Early Stuttering

There has been a considerable change in attitude towards the young disfluent child over the last fifteen years. This is due in part to the increase in information available on the development of linguistic skills and also to a change in our understanding of the parents' role in the development of disfluency. There is now more information on the development of fluency in normally speaking children and on the interaction of fluency with other communication skills (e.g. Zuckerman and Bernthal 1980; Wexler and Mysak 1982). The parents are no longer necessarily viewed as the major contributors to the child's disfluency, although the assessment of their influence remains an important issue (see also Chapter 3).

The differential diagnosis between normal childhood disfluencies and early stuttering is still problematic. Although differentiating between the extremes is relatively easy, the clinical picture is usually confusing, with children either manifesting a variety of 'normal' and 'abnormal' behaviours, or failing to demonstrate to the clinician the behaviours that are causing parental concern. Before indicating the specific behaviours, and the precipitating and perpetuating factors that

15

should be considered during assessment, an examination of the theoretical problems is needed.

Meyers and Wall (1981) raise three key questions to be considered in the differential diagnosis of normal childhood disfluencies and early stuttering: Are early childhood disfluencies essentially the same for all children? Is there a real difference between normal childhood non-fluency and early stuttering? and finally, If differences exist, are they quantitative or qualitative in nature? In an attempt partially to answer these questions the patterns of disfluency in young stutterers and normally disfluent children will be considered. The word *pattern* is used because of the relevance not only of frequency and type of disfluency but also the factors within the child and his environment that may exert an influence on his development of fluent speech.

Patterns of Disfluency in Non-Stuttering Children

Several studies were examined by this author in an attempt to determine the nature and extent of disfluency that can be considered normal at different ages. Some frequently recurring problems emerged, for example age ranges that are too wide and disfluency categories that are ambiguously described. Recorded disfluencies are rarely related to either social context or to the linguistic demands that the child faces. These problems make it extremely difficult to extract any clear picture of either normal or abnormal disfluency. In addition patterns of disfluency within individual children have not been recorded. Generally, different children are used at each different age level and so our understanding of the development of fluency is fragmented. The long-term study of patterns of disfluency within the same children would seem an extremely fruitful area for research. Language samples could be used not only to obtain a count of the number and types of disfluencies but also to note consistencies and changes from one occasion to the next. In this way different profiles of fluency development might emerge.

The few conclusions that can be drawn from the studies examined suggest some features of normal fluency development. For example, disfluency is more marked and less within the child's control between 30 and 40 months of age than at later stages. The mean level of disfluency for 30-month-old children varies from 6.5 per cent (Yairi 1981) to 14.6 per cent (Wexler and Mysak, 1982). These two studies identify *revision* as the most common type of disfluency, whereas in an earlier study, Metraux (1950) refers to *word* and *phrase repetitions* as occurring most frequently. Perhaps the most important finding however is that the average occurrence of part-word repetitions over all the studies is around 1 per cent and the average number of repetitions per instance of part-word disfluency does not exceed 1.5 per cent.

There is some evidence to suggest that linguistic complexity may influence level of fluency in young normally speaking children. Hayes and Hood (1978) found that five year olds demonstrated a significant increase in 'word repetitions, revisions-incomplete phrases and dysrhythmic phonations' (p. 86) when producing more complex sentences. Similarly in a study of three-to four-year-old children Zuckerman, Pearl and Bernthal (1980) conclude that ' . . . when grammatical constructions were relatively difficult for children, complexity affected the occurrence of disfluencies' (p. 67). This study supports the notion that disfluency should be considered within the context of the child's general linguistic development and that the level of disfluency observed may vary according to the demands that the situation places upon the child.

Patterns of Disfluency in Stuttering Children

There is increasing evidence to suggest that stuttering in children is not an homogeneous disorder. Several different approaches have been developed in the attempt to identify different disfluency profiles in stuttering children. These profiles may be either descriptions of different patterns of behaviour or clusters of different causal and maintaining factors, or a mixture of both. For example, Van Riper's (1971) 'tracks' are concerned primarily with behavioural patterns and their development over time. He reviewed the information from 300 case histories of child stutterers and identified four different tracks of development. The first two, by far the most common, will be described.

Track-one children gradually develop a stutter at 2½-4 years of age, after quite normal language development. They have long remissions and initially they repeat syllables without undue tension or frustration. Gradually the repetitions increase in speed and frequency until prolongations occur.The child also begins to avoid certain situations and develops tricks to deal with his disfluency. This pattern of development was observed to a greater or lesser extent in about half the sample.

Track-two accounted for about one-sixth of the sample and is characterised by gradual onset of disfluency in a child who has already caused concern because of a general delay in language development. Speech lacks the usual rhythm, articulation is poor and the child shows little awareness of his difficulty. This lack of concern on the part of the child continues as the number and rate of repetitions increases.

Prolongations do not become a feature. This group might well be described as clutterer-stutterers.

Support for Van Riper's notion of different tracks or profiles of stuttering is emerging from the literature. However, the relative distribution of the two tracks is being questioned. For example, Blood and Seider (1981) surveyed the concomitant problems of 1000 stuttering children under 14 years of age. Unfortunately it was not within the scope of their survey to provide detailed pictures of the children and so caution is needed in relating their results to Van Riper's tracks. Only one third were free from any other problem while over 40 per cent had one accompanying problem, and the remainder had more than one additional difficulty. Either 'articulation' or 'language disorder' or both occurred most frequently in combination with stuttering. These findings suggest that track-two may be more common than was originally thought. Alternatively there may now be fewer track-one stutterers since these are the ones most likely to benefit from the type of parent counselling that has traditionally been offered.

The notion that different stuttering children may be responding to different influences has been further developed by Riley and Riley (1979) who suggest a component model. Nine components were derived from factor analysis of data on 176 stuttering children aged between 3 and 12 years and from examination of the literature. The authors used the terms 'neurologic' and 'traditional' to subdivide the components which are shown in Table 2.1.

Table 2.1: A Component Model of Stuttering

Neurologic	Traditional	
	Intra-personal	Inter-personal
Attending disorders	High self expectations	Disruptive communication environment
Auditory processing disorders	Manipulative stuttering	Unrealistic parental expectations
Sentence formulation disorders		Abnormal parental need for child to stutter
Oral motor disorders		

Source: Riley and Riley 1979

Riley and Riley suggest that stuttering occurs when '. . . disorders in the various components of the child's system of communication are of sufficient magnitude to reach a critical threshold of fluency breakdown' (p. 281). This model aims to assist in diagnosis and treatment-planning rather than to describe different patterns of stuttering development. It seems likely that different combinations of significant components would result in different stuttering profiles.

Another interesting difference between groups of stutterers was found by Stromsta (1965), when he examined spectograms from 38 children, all described by their parents as stutterers. Twenty-seven of these children had spectograms characterised by abrupt phonatory stoppages and lack of formant transition during blocks. Twenty-four of the twenty-seven continued to stutter 10 years later, while only one of the remaining children was still stuttering. Further references to this type of investigation could not be found in the literature. Hopefully, with increasing interest in speech science, more work will be done in this area.

Comparisons Between Early Stuttering and Normal Disfluency

The previous dicussion has shown that the relationship between normal and abnormal disfluencies and the nature and extent of any differences are still not clearly defined. Also we do not know whether the factors responsible for the disfluencies are the same for both groups. Those who maintain that the nature of the disfluencies are the same for both groups, and that the differences lie in the amount of disfluency, also would maintain that the factors responsible are the same, but that the stuttering children have a lower tolerance threshold. This view is well expressed by Bloodstein's (1970) 'Continuity Hypothesis' which is based on the observation that:

> 'there are few if any aspects of early stuttering which cannot be found occasionally and mildly in the speech of most young children. Seen from this point of view, stuttering as a clinical disorder is largely a more extreme degree of certain forms of normal disfluency' (p.30).

Those who hold the opposing view identify important differences in the disfluent behaviour of the two groups. The possibility that different factors are responsible for the different types of disfluency becomes an important issue since a better understanding or normal disfluency will not necessarily increase our understanding of early stuttering.

Part-Word Repetition. Much of this controversy revolves around the syllable or part-word repetition. This is the disfluency that is most likely to be judged abnormal. In a previous discussion it was established that the average frequency of syllable repetition in non-stuttering children is around one per cent. Stuttering children show a greater range and average of this type of disfluency. For example Johnson (1959) reports a mean of 5.44 with a range of 0-33.6 and more recently Floyd and Perkins (1974) give a mean of 9.88 with a range of 7.28-14.32. Another important difference between the two groups is the apparent absence of the *schwa* vowel in the syllable repetitions of normally speaking children. Van Riper (1971) believes the presence of the *schwa* vowel in these disfluencies indicates the probablity of stuttering developing into a persisting problem.

Loci of Disfluency. So far this discussion has been concerned with similarities and differencies between *types* of disfluency. A consideration of *loci* of disfluency may also be relevant to assessment. Bernstein (1981) analysed samples of spontaneous speech from eight stuttering and eight matched normally-fluent children. Common loci for disfluency for both groups were 'and', which was used as a sentence lead-in much of the time, and the first noun phrase of the utterance. The disfluency seems part of the attempt to utter a sentence and occurs when the major processing demands occur. One significant difference did emerge between the two groups. This was the additional amount of disfluency the verb phrase attracted in the stuttering group. The author suggests that the stutterers are 'taking advantage of midsentential stopping points to contemplate the rest of the utterance as a whole' (p. 349). Bernstein proposes that stuttering may be precipitated by the demands of higher-level sentence planning processes, and not word, sound, or motor-gesture-specific considerations.

Bloodstein and Grossman (1981) also believe that early stuttering represents a difficulty in either the formulation or execution of syntactic units. In their study, it was more likely that function words were stuttered on than content words. All types of disfluency occurred at the beginnings of syntactic units, but only repetitions and prolongations of sounds occurred on the last words of phrase structures. They suggest that 'part word repetition or prolongation may represent hesitancy in the initiation of words, whole word repetition reflects hesitancy in the initiation of entire syntactic units' (p. 299). The examination of the loci of stuttering in an individual child may give clues concerning the nature of the underlying problem.

Environmental Factors. Inevitably, once stuttering begins to interfere with communication, the child and the people in his environment are likely to feel concern and try to help in whatever way seems appropriate to them. The ways in which they try to help will most probably be a reflection of the family's general philosophy of child-rearing and so may have implications beyond speaking. Some of the relevant family issues are identified in the assessment checklist, which follows, and Rustin and Cook (Chapter 3) discuss the family's role in treatment. As the child's awareness of his stuttering increases he is likely to experience difficulty in dealing with the communicative pressures that a more fluent child can cope with. For the therapist, the important area is not so much how this child's environment differs from that of a fluent child, but what the maintaining factors within the individual child and his environment may be.

Assessment Checklist. The checklist, which follows summarises the points that have been discussed so far and aims to assist the therapist in planning her assessment procedures. Time and sensitivity are needed if the therapist is to feel confident in her assessment of the child's speech and the significant precipitating and perpetuating factors in his environment. After this, more time will be needed if the parents are to be helped in modifying these factors. A single session to allay parents' fears is no longer considered sufficient if prevention of stuttering is the aim.

ASSESSMENT CHECKLIST

SPEECH ASSESSMENT

General Speech and Language Skills
Language development
Attention control
Auditory processing skills
Sentence formulation skills
Phonological development
Oral motor skills

Fluent Speech
Rate
Rhythm
Intonation
Breath control

Normal Disfluencies
Word/phrase repetition

Revision
Interjection
Pauses

Disfluent Speech
% Syllable disfluency
Number of repetitions per instance of disfluency
Schwa vowel present
Tempo of syllable repetitions
Tense pauses
Breathing disturbances
Prolongations
Disfluency chronic/episodic
Total disfluency

Concomitant Behaviours
Loss of eye contact during disfluency
Sudden movements of;
    Head
    Arms/legs
    Others

ATTITUDE ASSESSMENT

Factors Within the Child
Child aware of difficulty
Extent of awareness
Avoidance of speaking
Post-disfluency reaction
High self-expectations
Verbally competitive
Strives for perfection
Importance of verbal communication to child and family

Factors Within the Family
History of stuttering in family
Child labelled as stutterer
Child aware of parental anxiety
Parents' response to disfluency
Effect of parents' response
Child teased
Child given more or less attention when disfluent

GENERAL HOME ENVIRONMENT

Generally disruptive communication environment
Rapid conversations
Interruptions
Poor attention to child when speaking
No time for child to organise thoughts
Generally unrealistic parental expectations
High standards for behaviour
   for speaking
   for academic progress
   for emotional independence
Problems with family relationships
Parents inconsistent
Parents overcritical
Parents each have different expectations
Poor understanding of children's needs and abilities
Specific problems in management
Sibling rivalry

For other checklists see Cooper (1973) and Luper and Mulder (1964).

The Assessment of Stuttering Behaviour

The assessment of stuttering behaviour has two main functions: first to assist in diagnosis and treatment planning, and second, to evaluate the effects of treatment. The latter may be on either an individual level or concerned with groups of clients whose progress is evaluated for research purposes. The value of a diagnostic battery that would give clear indications of an appropriate treatment plan is apparent; the problem lies in the inadequacy of our understanding of stuttering and the tendency for all stutterers to be grouped together and made to fit the available treatment programmes.

In this section the aim is to review the main issues concerning the assessment of stuttering behaviour. The appropriateness of the various aspects of assessment to different age and severity groups is left to the reader's clinical judgement. There are no specific ages at which one can state that a certain procedure is applicable. The therapist must use her skill in assessing the individual stutterer's needs and abilities and then devise her own assessment battery.

A Representative Speech Sample

One of the biggest problems in assessing stuttering behaviour is obtaining a representative speech sample. At the beginning of treatment there may not be a vast range in extent of disfluency from one formal speaking situation to the next, yet after treatment this is no longer the case. A stutterer may be capable of totally fluent speech in any situation that reminds him of his new speech skills and then, in other circumstances, stutter as much as before treatment. This may result from feelings of pressure or conversely the feeling that fluency is not important and so the need to monitor speech is reduced. This should be borne in mind when selecting situations for initial assessment. Either one or two popular approaches may be adopted; one is to select a situation that is likely to remain consistently difficult regardless of the phase of therapy, the other is to sample a range of situations. Howie and Tanner (1978) record three minutes of a telephone conversation to a stranger, with the stutterer's knowledge, for initial assessment and then, without his prior knowledge, on subsequent occasions. The issue of covert assessment is discussed in a later section. The alternative is recommended by Boberg (1981) who obtains the following samples: three minutes of video-recorded conversation away from the clinic; three minutes of reading; two minutes of recorded conversation with a stranger outside the clinic and a two minute telephone call to an outside party.

The approach adopted will depend upon client and resources but whatever situations are chosen the general principle of controlling as many variables as possible should be adhered to.

What to Measure? It is now generally agreed that syllables should be counted rather than words, for the following reasons: words vary in length (differences in vocabulary, while affecting the amount of speaking, will not be reflected in a word count); the rhythm of speech is built around the syllable not the word and it is therefore much easier to count syllables as fast speaking rates; and thirdly counting disfluent syllables takes care of the problems that arise when more than one stutter occurs in a polysyllabic word.

Perkins (1981) points to one problem that persists when calculating rate of speech in syllables: although the overall speaking, stuttering and pausing times are measured, the rate of actual speaking is not measured. He discusses this in relation to the evaluation of rate control therapies but it is perhaps also relevant to initial assessment. He says:

'It seems apparent that the measure of elapsed speaking time, which for convenience will be dubbed *phone rate*, is preferable to syllable- or word-rate if one is concerned with rate effects on fluency. It can be easily calculated by depressing a telegraph key in time with each syllable spoken, which in turn activates an event timer and cumulative timer. Thus phone rate excludes duration of stuttering . . . and pauses between syllables. It is, therefore, a reasonably accurate measure of the speed at which speech movements must be coordinated. More practically it is the appropriate measure when using rate control strategies to maintain fluent speech' (p.151).

Although not widely used, the *phone rate* does seem the best measure and, once some normative data are obtained, could provide clinically useful information. Syllables are certainly the next best and Johnson's (1961) study provides a mean rate of 200±34 syllables per minute (SPM) for American male speakers. The rates of speaking for British males is taken to be much the same, while female speakers are known to be approximately 20 syllables a minute faster. An indication of the severity of moments of stuttering can be obtained from the rate of speech, although a description of the stuttering is also needed.

There is considerable agreement in the literature that repetition or prolongation of sounds, syllables and words, when accompanied by tension, constitute stuttering. The percentage of syllables *stuttered* (%SS) is the most usual measure of severity, although Perkins (1981) suggests that syllable *disfluency* is a better measure at the beginning of and during therapy, since it is easily identified and avoids the debate about whether the disfluency was really a stutter, or was normal. However, during maintenance therapy, when the goal is stutter-free speech, then he suggests that %SS is the better measure. Probably the most important thing is that the people who rate the speech samples agree as to what constitutes stuttering and that consistency across raters and samples is established.

Concomitant Behaviours

Severity of stuttering is most usually measured in percentage disfluency and rate of speech. An instance of stuttering is often referred to as the stuttering *moment*. This emphasis on the stuttering moment is strongly criticized by Webster and Brutten (1972) who maintain that the concept assumes stuttering is a unitary disorder. Furthermore:

'implicit in this line of reasoning is the assumption that all the specific behavioural elements of stuttering moments are acquired in the same way, have similar histories, and can be dealt with as functional equivalent responses. Thus if a patient said, "Now is the uh ta-ta-ta-time for all good m-m-m-men to (eye blink) (arm swing) come to the aid of their party." one could say that six moments of stuttering had occured and that all of the grossly different behaviours equally represent stuttering behaviour' (p. 556).

Brutten and Shoemaker (1967) hypothesised that, generally, repetitions and prolongations are involuntary behaviours resulting from the 'disorganizing effects of classically-conditioned negative emotion.' Other behaviours are seen as 'voluntary, instrumentally conditioned, escape and avoidance behaviours' (p. 30). Therefore the recording of only moments of stuttering may mask important differences among the more 'molecular' behavioural elements comprising the moment. Their two factor theory of stuttering is a development of these ideas.

In a detailed analysis of a single stutterer, Webster and Brutten (1972) found evidence to support the notion of the two different classes of behaviour and also that the stutterer was able to differentiate between his voluntary and involuntary behaviours. In a more detailed study, Prins and Lohr (1972) found further supporting evidence for the two-factor theory and suggest that stutterers could be given factor scores which, when considered along with other information, would have 'significant implications concerning the aetiologies and therapies for stuttering' (p.70). In line with the theoretical approach Brutten (1972) has devised a behavioural checklist that comprises 98 items containing many of the adjustments made by stutterers. This is completed with the stutterer and any further behaviours either reported or observed are added. In this way a full picture of the two types of behaviours is obtained. Should the stutterer not know if he has control of a certain behaviour then he can try it out during assessment.

Therapists using behaviour checklists (e.g. Luper and Mulder 1964; Cooper 1972) and therapy procedures concerned with the identification and modification of stuttering behaviour should consider the work of Brutten and Shoemaker, since modification of the two types of behaviour may require different approaches. Some clinicians see the analysis of concomitant behaviours as part of therapy and not assessment; for example Van Riper deals with the issue in the *identification* phase of his therapy programme (see Chapter 4). Those who use just frequency counts would probably argue that their treatment techniques are effective at removing both types of behaviours. Where treatment teaches a pattern of fluent speech rather than the modification of stuttering this may well be true, and so in this case the assessment of concomitant behaviours could be redundant.

Assessment of Stutterers' Fluent Speech at the Beginning of Therapy

As has already been discussed, the emphasis in speech assessment recently has been very much on the moment of stuttering and the abnormal behaviours that closely surround it. However, as long ago as 1957, Williams suggested that stutterers' speech be examined in its totality, and that therapy should be concerned with more than just the removal of stutters (e.g. Williams, 1971).

A review of the research comparing the fluent speech of stutterers with that of non-stutterers shows that differences do exist and that they appear to be fairly consistent (Adams and Runyan 1981). Differences in the fluent speech of the two groups have been analysed either perceptually, objectively or both. Excessive muscular tension in the orofacial region and an excess of air pressure above the glottis were recorded in the stuttering group in several of the objective studies. There were also consistent acoustic differences: the stutterer's vowels were longer; there was more variability in their fundamental frequencies; and they were slower in starting phonation for the transition from voiceless to voiced speech sounds.

In the perceptual studies there were several cues that listeners found useful in differentiating between the two groups, for example: slow speaking rate; abnormal pauses and hesitations, vocal tremor and low vocal intensity. Adams and Runyan say in summary that 'the stutterer's fluent speech can be slow, dysrhythmic, weak, tense, tremorous, or imprecisely articulated' (p. 203). Stutterers' speech, when marked by these characteristics, has been referred to by Runyan (1976) as 'tenuous'. He chose this term to convey the impression that fluency breakdown is imminent.

The authors hypothesise relationships between fluency, tenuous fluency and stuttering and suggest how the relationships vary according to the severity of the stutter. So the more severe the stutter, the more often his speech is at or above the threshold for perceptible tenuous fluency and therefore the more likely to result in stuttering. They suggest a continuous relationship between fluency, tenuous fluency and stuttering; so, for example, in the severe stutterer as he approaches a stutter his speech first demonstrates tenuous fluency, then the stutter, and then a gradual return to fluency through tenous fluency. If another potentially difficult word arises at this point then he will most likely stutter again, and so on.

The concept of tenuous fluency supports the clinical impression that stutters do not necessarily occur in speech, which is otherwise normal and often there are cues that stuttering is imminent. The assessment of the ratio of *normal* to *tenuous* fluency adds an important dimension to the assessment of stuttering severity and may well prove to have prognostic implications

Evaluation of Treatment

The second function, the evaluation of the effects of treatment, is of prime importance in any discussion of assessment procedures. The individual therapist with a small case load of stutterers will probably have neither the time nor the inclination to assess as rigorously as the research worker. However, an appreciation of the issues and controversies should help in selecting the most reliable assessment procedures for evaluating not only one's own therapy, but also the results of published therapy programmes and techniques. When some common assessment procedures are agreed upon by therapists with both clinical and research commitments, then it may be possible to reliably compare different treatment approaches and hence generate numbers large enough to draw some definite conclusions about the more effective treatments.

The need for some standardisation is well illustrated in a study by Andrews, Guitar and Howie (1980), who analysed the effects of stuttering treatments by searching the literature. They found 100 publications, only 29 of which gave sufficient information for useful comparison. They suggest that a minimum set of measures should be agreed upon for inclusion in reports of stuttering treatment: frequency of stuttering, rate of speech, a speech attitude scale, all to be completed pre-and post-therapy and six months after the termination of therapy. Mean, range, standard deviation and skew of pretreatment scores should also be reported. These are the minimum requirements for treatment comparisons. Much more information is needed in order to evaluate the effects of individual treatment approaches or programmes.

Representative Speech Samples. Problems of reliability in the assessment of treatment results have been highlighted by the apparent success of programmes using prolonged speech and gentle onset, taught intensively, and evaluated after the intensive phase and then at intervals during the maintenance phase of treatment. Since clients are taught to monitor their speech and this is then generalised to a variety of speaking situations, the assessment of speech should occur outside these contexts, that is, if one is to be confident that the stutterer is fluent in his life generally and not just in therapy and therapy-like situations.

There is some controversy over the issue of monitored versus un-monitored speech and this is discussed more fully in Chapter 7. This, to an extent, is related to the controversy described by Gregory (1979) in his discussion of the *speak-more-fluently* vs the *stutter-more-fluently* therapies. For some in the former camp the criterion for success, a year after the end of therapy, is stutter-free unmonitored speech. Whereas the other group emphasises ways of dealing with disfluency and so '. . . stuttering smoothly and minimal interference with the ongoing speaking behaviour whenever one speaks represents 100% success' (Williams 1979, p. 267). However, with both theraputic approaches, some assessment completed without the stutterers' knowledge would undoubtedly increase the validity of the end of treatment and follow-up data.

The need for covert assessment is most strongly argued by Ingham. For example, when discussing evaluation he says:

> 'Surely one principle concern in clinical research is to have confi-dence in the validity of the data measures — particularly when they suggest that treatment has been successful. Indeed any claims made for post-treatment fluency would be meaningless if this fluency appeared during an *aware* recording condition but not during an equivalent *unaware* recording condition.' (1981, p. 187)

Ingham acknowledges the ethical problems that arise during collec-tion of covert data and suggests that the client be told that covert recordings may be made at any time during the course of treatment and that he will have the opportunity to erase these recordings at the end of treatment. This approach should minimise the possibility of the client monitoring his speech more carefully in case it is being assessed, since almost constant monitoring would be required. Perkins (1978) offers a different solution. He suggests covertly recording the beginning of a telephone conversation and then letting the client know he is being recorded and offering to erase the recording if the client wishes. Ingham (1981) points to one advantage of this approach, if the whole conversa-tion is recorded, in that there would be data for identifying any re-activity effects associated with overt assessments.

The telephone itself presents some additional problems concerning the representativeness of any such sample. When Ingham (1975) compared overt and covert speech samples at three and six months after treatment, telephone conversation produced more stuttering than either talking to a stranger or to a familiar person. Since the majority of stutterers probably spend relatively little of their talking lives on the telephone this situation will not necessarily give an accurate picture of their general level of fluency. However having pointed to these problems it must be acknowledged that recording telephone conversations is a far more practical solution for many busy therapists, who most probably will not have the resources to collect face-to-face covert recordings.

Stutterers probably vary considerably in the extent to which they are affected by the knowledge of assessment. In an extremely detailed single case study Ingham (1981) found there was little difference between overt and covert assessment data. However in an earlier study with a larger sample, the same author (1975) found a significant difference between the two types of data. At three months post-therapy both syllables stuttered and rate of speech were affected. Three months later there was no longer a significant difference in the level of fluency under the two conditions, but speech remained significantly slower during the covert assessment. It is possible that the differences between the overt and covert assessments were minimised in this particular study, since all assessments took place within the author's work environment, which was also presumably where the stutterers' intensive course of therapy took place. Perhaps greater differences would be apparent if data obtained by stutterers' relatives or friends was compared with clinic material. This suggestion however returns us full circle to the ethical and practical problems.

While fully acknowledging the value of Ingham's contribution to the assessment of stuttering and treatment programmes, a nagging doubt remains in this author's mind concerning some of the implications of covert assessment. If the data so collected is to be truly representative of the stutterer's everyday speech then considerable time, money and deviousness needs to be invested in this area, and so the question of priorities is raised. Also, although one cannot entirely rely upon the stutterers' report of how fluent he has been, the assumption that he is not able to play a responsible role in this assessment is worrying.

Williams (1979) argues the case for quantitative assessments for comparison with self reports and for the recognition of client therapy goals, as well as those of the clinician. He suggests that until people who have stuttered 'can interact and talk with people the way *they want* to talk, at any time, to any one, *they* still have a problem of stuttering' (p. 268). Therefore he would argue that any assessment should take the stutterers' subjective report into account.

Perkins (1981) devised a speech performance questionaire that asked not only about fluency but also about the stutterer's use of speech control skills. Assuming that the responses to this type of questionaire are valid then

> 'at least 75% of the people we have seen are capable of sounding like normal speakers if they choose to use the skills they think are still available to them. The fact that over half these people use their speech controls only occasionally may have something to do with the fact that less than half of them consider their speech to be good, or think of themselves as normal speakers, more than occasionally.' (p. 155)

The type of information that Perkins obtains from his questionaire does seem to have value, not necessarily in supporting or replacing objective measures but in providing additional information. This information can be used to facilitate future treatment planning for the individual stuttering client and also to assist in modifying and improving the treatment programme for future clients. Assessing clients' attitudes towards the speech control skills that they are taught in therapy, and determining how and when they are used is a major problem for many therapists, some of whom have devised their own questionnaires. An effort to pool this information and generate more sophisticated and reliable questionnaires seems long overdue.

Assessment of Fluent Speech. Another important area for assessment after treatment is the quality of the stutterer's fluent speech. To some extent this relates back to the issues discussed in the last section; if a person is to find his new fluency an acceptable alternative to stuttering it must be normal in other respects. The importance of normal rates of fluent speech have been recognised for some time (e.g. Andrews and Ingham 1971; Ryan 1974). Yet there are other aspects of speech that are important, not just for the stutterer to feel confident that his speech is normal-sounding but also so that others will judge it as such. For example, the features of *tenuous* fluency described earlier should no longer be present.

Perkins (1981) stresses the importance of assessing those speaking skills which require successful management if fluency is to be maintained. He believes that the successful management of rate and phrase length, phrase onset and breath flow within the phrase and voice and rhythm should produce fluent, normal-sounding speech. He suggests that the well-trained ear is adequate assessment equipment. Although in general it is agreed that the speech therapist is trained to make these types of judgements, clinical experience suggests that therapists adjust to the speech of their clients and often have difficulty in being objective. Consequently the development of more objective measures of these aspects of fluent speech would be welcome.

A different line of inquiry offers considerable support for Perkins and his concern with the quality of fluency after treatment. Runyan and Adams (1978) sought to determine if the fluent speech of a group of 'successfully therapeutized' stutterers was perceptually different from the speech of normally speaking subjects. The stutterers were all considered to have been successfully treated by one of several different therapy methods (Van Riperian, metronome-conditioned speech retraining, delayed auditory feedback, operant conditioning, precision fluency shaping and 'holistic' therapy programmes). They found that none of the therapies completely removed all of the cues of *tenuous* fluency and all seemed to add some new features that differentiated the stutterers' speech from that of the non-stutterers. Those stutterers who had a mild level of disfluency before treatment were least often differentiated from the controls. It was the originally moderate-to-severe stutterers who retained some abnormal features. In another study (Metz, Onufrak and Ogburn 1979) the fluent speech of a group of successfully treated stutterers, who had all completed a modified version of Van Riperian therapy, was analysed acoustically. Vowel duration and the occurrence of voicing during stop consonant production increased significantly when pre- and post-treatment samples were compared. These seem to represent the over generalisation of devices taught to be used when stuttering is anticipated.

Runyan and Adams suggest closer collaboration between clinicians and speech scientists to

'conduct careful perceptual and objective assessments of stutterers' speech both prior to and then after therapy. The results of these studies would subsequently be used to (1) formulate a more refined description of the patients' fluent and stuttered speech; (2) construct comprehensive remedial programmes, and (3) determine if clients had achieved maximum gains in treatment.' (p. 37)

The assessment of the stutterers' speech after treatment and his attitudes towards it require considerable refinement before we can be confident that our therapy procedures are effective. Whether or not attitudes towards communication and stuttering should also be investigated is the concern of the next section.

The Assessment of Attitudes

The question of whether or not to assess attitudes is controversial. There are some who believe that the problems involved in this area of investigation are so great that resources are better spent refining the assessment of observable and measurable behaviours. Others maintain that the stutterers' attitudes towards his speech and therapy exert a powerful influence on his progress and therefore should be taken into account in diagnosis and treatment planning. The attitude assessments in current use are, on the whole, unsatisfactory. Their reliability and validity has either been assessed on very small samples or not at all. There is confusion as to what the scales measure, and there has been little research into their contribution to the understanding of stuttering, the planning of treatment, or the prediction of long-term therapy effects. In this section some of the current assessment procedures will be briefly discussed.

Stutterers' Attitudes Towards Communication

The S-24. The procedure to be considered is a shortened version of Erickson's (1969) S-scale, so called because it purports to assess *stutterers'* attitudes towards communication. The scale consists of statements, such as: 'I find it easy to keep control of my voice when speaking'; 'I often feel nervous while talking'; 'Even the idea of giving a talk in public makes me afraid'. These examples illustrate the general nature of the statements. The higher the score, the more disordered the attitudes towards communication are considered to be. The scored response varies from 'true' to 'false' throughout the scale, but the favourable response can be easily guessed by all but the most naive subject. In this author's experience most stutterers are happy to complete the scale as honestly as possible.

Andrews and Cutler (1974) re-considered the reliability and validity of the original items and assessed their suitability for repeated administration. Twenty-four items were selected because: '. . . they discriminated between stutterers and non-stutterers, showed a strong trend toward normalcy when improving in treatment, and proved reliable when repeatedly administered to non stutterers' (p. 135). Normative data was derived from the Andrews and Cutler study and this is shown in Table 2.2.

Table 2.2: Mean, Range and Standard Deviation for the S-24

	Mean	Range	S.D.	*n*
Non-stutterers	9.14	1-21	5.38	25
Stutterers				
Pre-treatment	19.22	9-24	4.24	37
Instatement of fluency	14.27	0-24	5.73	37
Post-treatment	9.11	1-18	5.18	37

Source: Andrews and Cutler 1974

These data suggest that attitudes towards communication do not become normal with the initial experience of fluency, but only once this fluency has been experienced in a wide range of speaking situations. Silverman (1980) sought to determine the appropriateness of the S-24 to women who stutter. She compared the scores, from one test occasion, of ten female stutterers with ten female non-stutterers and with ten male stutterers.. Silverman states that 'the scale not only differentiates women who stutter from women who do not, but also differentiates women who stutter from men who stutter' (p. 537). The first claim is predictable from previous studies; the second claim however seems contentious in view of the small samples. Moreover the stutterers are described as 'drawn from the same treatment population . . . ' (p. 534), a selection procedure wide enough to allow variables other than sex to exert an influence. If the two samples *were* more carefully controlled than the description suggests then the tendency for stuttering women to score lower than stuttering men has clinical implications. Silverman suggests that an end of treatment score of six or below might be a more suitable criterion for women who stutter than the ten or below suggested by Guitar and Bass (1978).

The relationship between attitudes towards communication (as measured by the S-24) and severity of stutter is not clear. Several studies have failed to find significant correlations between stuttering severity and S-24 scores (e.g. Andrews and Cutler 1974; Guitar 1976; Guitar and Bass 1978). However significant correlations were found between two measures of pre-treatment stuttering severity and the S-24 scores when Helps and Dalton (1979) used the scale with a slightly larger sample of stutterers. In an earlier study Helps (1975) attempted to assess the extent to which individual stutterers saw themselves as being like other stutterers, and whether or not this related to other assessment measures and progress in therapy. The possibility that this might be an interesting area for study was identified by Fransella (1968), when she examined the notion of *self concept* in the stutterer (see Chapter 5 for a further discussion of Fransella's work). Although the measures used by Helps were rather crude and would not be recommended for a larger study, they nevertheless produced an interesting correlation. She found that those stutterers who saw themselves as being most like other stutterers tended to score higher on the S-24. If this is generally true it would perhaps explain the conflicting results obtained when comparing symptom level with S-24 scores. A stutterer who is very aware of the abnormality of his stuttering behaviour may become skilled at concealing it and so have a relatively low symptom score and high S-24 score. Conversely a person with a cluttering/ stuttering type of speech pattern may have a high frequency of disfluency and yet be relatively unaware of the problem and so score low on the S-24. It seems reasonable that attitudes towards communication would be affected by how abnormal a speaker an individual feels that he is, rather than by the observable level of difficulty. Further research might identify different patterns of scores for different subgroups of stutterers.

Generally clinicians and researchers seem to have found the S-24 a useful scale, but one exception must be mentioned. A Norwegian translation of the scale (Preus 1981) was administered to 100 stutterers whose ages ranged from 16-24 years. The subjects failed to answer a great many questions and gave inconsistent answers to others. This inconsistency was apparent when responses to pairs of statements, dealing with similar attitudes, were compared, e.g.

11.   I often ask questions in group discussions, and
13.   I do not mind speaking before a group.

20.   I often feel nervous while talking, and
22.   I feel pretty confident about my speaking ability.

The importance of checking for consistency of response has not been mentioned in any of the earlier studies, but seems an important precaution to take before drawing any firm conclusions about the nature of a stutterer's problem. Another question has been raised by Ingham (1979) who accepts that the S-24 scores do not correlate with stuttering severity measures obtained in the clinic, but points to the lack of data 'demonstrating that the Erickson scores are independent of measures of speech in situations referred to within the scales questions' (p. 399). Guitar (1979) in reply, says that at the end of treatment his stutterers were achieving nought per cent disfluency in a wide variety of speaking situations and that sampling speech from each of the situations in the scale would be unnecessary. Ingham's point is an important one and will hopefully be pursued in some further study.

The Prediction of Therapy Outcome

Attempts to predict therapy outcome of intensive prolonged speech programmes for individual stutterers have not so far produced any definite results. Whether this is due to the lack of sensitivity of the presently available assessment procedures or due to failure to measure the pertinent aspects of the stutterer and his problem is open to speculation. A brief review of two studies will show the general direction of work so far published.

Guitar (1976) analysed the relationships between pre-treatment factors and final outcome in a group of Australian stutterers. His pre-treatment measures included the Eysenck Personality Inventory (Eysenck and Eysenck 1963), the Stutterer's Self Ratings of Reactions to Speaking Situations, (Johnson, Darley and Spriesterbach 1963), the S-24 scale and measures of stuttering severity. The Eysenck Personality Inventory (EP1) yields scores on two independent dimensions of personality: extroversion and neuroticism. The Stutterer's Self Ratings of Reactions to Speaking Situations (The Iowa) consists of forty speaking situations, and the stutterer is asked to rate each one on a 1-5 scale. First he rates each of the situations according to his tendency for *avoidance*, then according to his *reaction*, then the amount of *stuttering* likely to be elicited and finally the *frequency* with which he encounters the situation. Examples of the types of situations included are: 'Ordering in a restaurant'; 'Introducing one person to another'; 'Conversation with mother' and 'Taking leave of a hostess'. The average score for each of the four modes of response is calculated. The Iowa was designed to help identify areas for counselling and specific help. For therapy-planning all four modes would be used; Guitar concentrated on the first two (avoidance and reaction) in his study. The measures of stuttering severity included the percentage of syllables stuttered (%SS) and the syllables spoken per minute (SPM).

The intercorrelations between these different measures and then their relationship to outcome were looked at. Guitar found high intercorrelations between the three measures of attitude (avoidance, reaction and S-24), a finding supported by Helps and Dalton (1979) in a study using a similar battery of assessments. The latter study found other significant correlations between the pre-treatment variables, suggesting that the less extrovert stutterer is likely to stutter more severely, avoid stressful speaking situations and to have disordered attitudes towards communication. Stronger differences between the studies emerge when the prognostic value of the attitude measures is examined. Guitar suggests that the best predictor of outcome is pre-treatment attitude. Helps and Dalton however found that pre-treatment speech and EPI scores correlated more highly with final outcome. These differences could be accounted for by the different levels in fluency experienced by the two groups after treatment. Guitar's sample all achieved 0%SS in a variety of speaking situations at the end of the intensive treatment, whereas the British stutterers demonstrated a mean of 7.8%WS (words stuttered) at the end of the course. Twelve months later this sample was stuttering at much the same level, whereas the Australian sample had regressed slightly but was still more fluent, with a mean disfluency of 2.4%.

In a subsequent study Guitar and Bass (1978) 'tested the hypothesis that stutterers who do not show a normalisation of communication attitudes during treatment will have a poorer long term outcome in %SS than do subjects who show a normalisation of attitude' (p.397). To test this hypothesis they divided stutterers into one of two groups on the basis of their S-24 score at the end of the transfer phase of therapy. Stutterers in Group 1 had a score of nine or less and the scores of Group 2 members were ten or over. There was no significant difference between the levels of fluency for the two groups at this stage of treatment but when they were reviewed one year later Group 1 demonstrated an average of 0.85%SS whereas the average for Group 2 was 4.8%SS.

The end of transfer S-24 score was a marginally better predictor of outcome than change in score from the beginning of treatment to this stage. This suggests that the S-24 scale administered at the end of the intensive phase of treatment could be useful in planning further management. Guitar and Bass discuss the possibility that the Group 2 stutterer's symptom may have developed as a result of avoidance conditioning, and that relapse is likely to occur when the motor-conditioned response is suppressed, without deconditioning the concomitant anxiety. The anxiety persists and is followed by a recurrence of the original response. They find further support for this in a comparison of the pre-treatment *avoidance* scores for the two groups. Group 1 had a mean *avoidance* score of 2.01, while Group 2 had a mean of 3.07. This difference is highly significant.

In summary it looks as though the *avoidance* dimension of the Iowa and the S-24 do have a contribution to make. The *avoidance* score at initial assessment may be helpful in treatment planning and the S-24 score at the end of the intensive phase of treatment may indicate whether further therapy is needed. Attitude-orientated therapies should perhaps continue until an S-24 score of ten or less (possibly six or less for female stutterers) is achieved and the *avoidance* score is reduced to two or less. Until better assessments are designed and tried it would seem that these two scales are useful in that they partially assess an aspect of stuttering that is not necessarily closely related to severity of stuttering behaviour. The prediction of long term outcome of stuttering therapy on the basis of pre-treatment attitude measures is not as yet to be recommended.

One further procedure that deserves consideration is Brutten's (1975) Speech Situations Checklist (SSC). This is of particular interest because of its similarity to the previously discussed Iowa scale. They are similar in that they both deal with commonly occuring speech situations and require the use of a five point scale. They are different in that the SSC asks the stutterer to rate the amount of negative emotion that the different situations elicit. The negative emotion might be fear, tension, anxiety or any other unpleasant feeling. The impression gained from examination of the items is that the wording on the SSC is somewhat more open than on the Iowa and so possibly fewer *don't knows* would occur. A shortened version of the SSC has been suggested by Hanson, Dale Gronhovd and Rice (1981), to be used as a screening device to identify disfluent speakers who experience an abnormal amount of speech-related anxiety.

It is to be hoped that this review of some attitude scales and checklists has give some indication of the clinical value and limitations of this type of assessment. A different approach, potentially providing more sensitive measures, is considered in the next section.

The Assessment of the Personal Meaning of Stuttering

The two procedures to be discussed in this section are unlike the attitude measures so far described in that they provide a much wider context within which to view the clients' fluency problem. Both have been developed from the original work of George Kelly (1955).

Repertory Grid Technique. Repertory grids have been used as an assessment tool for a wide range of problems over the past twenty years. For example, schizophrenia (Bannister and Fransella 1966), mental handicap (Barton, Walton and Rowe 1976) and alcoholism (Hoy 1973). Their value as an exploratory procedure can best be understood within the context of Kelly's whole theory of personal construct psychology. However only an outline of the technique and its application to the assessment of stuttering can be attempted here. In Chapter 5, Dalton discusses Kelly's theory and illustrates the role of grids in the treatment of stuttering. She also describes the work of Fransella (1972), who was the first to apply Kelly's theory to stutterers. It is still too early to evaluate the contribution of this approach to the assessment and treatment of disfluency, but since it combines respect for self-report with objective analysis its potential cannot be ignored.

Repertory grids are essentially concerned with the relationships among constructs and among elements and their interrelationships. Constructs are discriminations, they may be conscious or unconscious, some can be verbalised relatively easily while others are more readily expressed through behaviour or other non-verbal means. The individual develops his own network of constructs which enable him to make the best sense of his world and to change and develop as his life experiences change. Kelly argued that we make sense of our world by noting similarities and differences, hence constructs are bi-polar, a property that makes them quite different from the notion of concept. When a man or a woman is construed as 'strong-willed', for example, the implication is that others are 'weak-willed', or whatever the particular construer's opposite might be. If he sees himself as a 'success', there must be some notion in him of what a 'failure' is like, and so on.

Kelly saw man as evolving for himself a whole system of constructs, forming sub-systems, net-works of constructs related to events of all kinds within the person's range of experience. He discussed different types of constructs in terms, for instance, of their hierarchical relationship to one another. Some are considered *superordinate* to others, which are *subordinate* in that they are included in the range of meaning of the first. For most people, for example, the construct *good* vs *bad* occupies a superordinate position with respect to a large proportion of their other constructs. For a new construct to be formed 'there must be a potentially superordinate construct which is hospitable to the new construct . . . it is thus that a system is formed' (1955, p. 479).

When using repertory grids for assessment and treatment-planning, elements are chosen according to the area of construing to be investigated. Therefore, if interpersonal relationships are the focus of interest then people with whom the client interacts will be chosen as elements. Alternatively, if the client's construing of speaking situations is the main interest, then the elements may compromise a range of different speaking situations. The constructs also need to be relevant to the area of investigation and this is best achieved when the individual is free to use his own constructs. These are most usually elicited by the consideration of ways in which two elements are alike and thereby different from a third. For example, the triad may be (1) *self*, (2) *mother* and (3) *close male friend*, (1) and (2) may be alike, in that they're both *responsible* when compared with (3) who is *irresponsible*. Alternatively the preferred grouping may be (1) and (3) who are both *open to others* compared with (2) who is *wary of others*. The triads are successively changed until a range of elements have been considered and a reasonable sample of constructs elicited. Constructs may then be 'laddered'. This procedure aims to work up the construct system from a lower to a higher level of abstraction and is illustrated in Chapter 5.

The elicitation of constructs can easily take more than one session since for some the task is difficult, while for others it is so interesting and absorbing that time is needed to discuss some of the issues as they arise. Usually the constructs selected for a grid will contain some elicited from triads and some from laddering. The elements will represent people in the client's environment and several different selves, for example, *as I am, as I would like to be, me as a stutterer, me when fluent*, and so on. Once the elements and constructs have been decided upon by therapist and client, each element is rated or ranked on each construct in turn. This data is then subjected to statistical analysis which with the development of the micro-computer has become more accessible to a wider range of people.

There are various computer programmes available for the analysis of grid data, but only one will be considered in this brief outline. The GAB (Higginbotham and Bannister 1981) programme has been chosen because of its availability and increasing popularity. The parts of the print-out most relevant to clinical work will be briefly described, to give the reader an idea of the sort of information that repertory grid technique can provide.

The print-out first deals with the constructs and then with the elements. A matrix of the relationships among constructs appears. This enables the therapist to see which constructs correlate with each other and which seem more separate. Next, the constructs are listed in order of their contribution to variance; broadly speaking the higher in the list the greater their *importance*. The cluster analysis follows; the construct that accounts for most of the variance is the central construct of 'component' 1, then all the constructs that are related to this construct at the 5 per cent level (two-tailed), or higher, appear. The leading construct of 'component' 2 is the construct that accounts for the next highest amount of variance that is not significantly related to the 'component' 1 construct and again the significantly-related constructs are listed with it. This continues until all the constructs have been considered. The programme then deals with the elements in exactly the same way.

Figure 2.1: 'Eric's' Grid: Constructs and elements plotted along the two central constructs derived from a form of cluster analysis

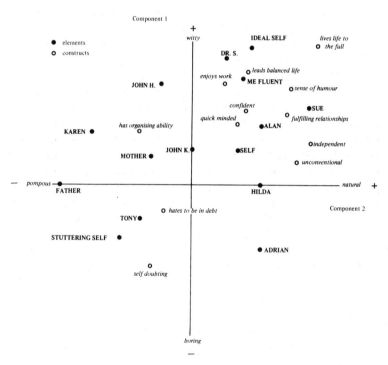

Note. Self elements were presented to client as *me as a stutterer, me as I'd like to be, me fluent* and *me now as a person*

In figure 2.1 the leading constructs of the first two components are used as axes in relation to which the other constructs have been plotted. By referring back to the original data the elements have been entered on this construct cluster diagram.

It must be stressed that this sort of data and analysis can only answer the questions that are asked of it. The area investigated is to an extent confined by the constructs and elements used. The more person-ally meaningful they are to the client the more potentially valuable the grid. It is then up to the therapist to ask question of the grid data. The therapist may want to know, for example, whether the client sees him-self largely in terms of his role as a stutterer or whether his view of himself as a person is more closely related to his ideal self, as in the ex-ample Figure 2.1. One would hypothesise that such an individual, who has a view of himself elaborated independently of his self as a speaker, would be better able to accommodate the changes involved in becoming more fluent. In 'Eric's case' (Figure 2.1) his view of self as fluent is positive, but this may not always be so. For example, while fluent speakers may be construed as having some desirable characteris-tics, they may also be seen as *insensitive* and *over confident*, which the client might not wish to become.

Some stutterers take a long time to get to know people well because of their preoccupation with their own speech and its effect on their listeners. In the illustrative grid several people are separated from the positive self elements and distant from the main construct dimensions. On this evidence the therapist might wish to explore more thoroughly the client's construing of people in his life, to determine whether or not there are problems in this area.

There is much more that could be said about the use of grids in assessment and the interested reader is referred to Fransella and Ban-nister (1977) for a full description and discussion of the variety of grids in use today. Grids were designed to help the therapist in understanding her client's view of the world and to assist in planning reconstruction in relevant areas. The validity of the technique can only be satisfactorily discussed in relation to therapy outcome and this still awaits further research. One important feature of grids is that they use the client's own words; they give the client the opportunity to tell the therapist how he views his problem and how it relates to his own personal philos-ophy of life.

Self Characterisation. A further method for eliciting constructs is the *self characterisation.* Kelly's (1955) instructions were carefully consi-dered to allow the client as much freedom as possible and to encourage an overview of the person rather than a cataloguing of faults:

'I want you to write a character sketch of Harry Brown, just as if he were the principle character in a play. Write it as it might be written by a friend who knew him very intimately and very sympathetically, perhaps better than anyone really could know him. Be sure to write it in the third person. For example, start out by saying, Harry Brown is . . . ' (p. 323).

The resulting sketch can be used to supply additional constructs for a grid or can be a part of assessment in its own right. The self characterisation can be analysed in terms of the major themes and the areas of the individual's experiences that he dwells upon. For example he may deal almost exclusively with his problem and write very little about other areas of his life. The constructs that recur throughout the sketch are likely to be important ones, likewise those where only one pole is named. It may be possible to gain some insight into the areas of experience to which the client is more sensitive or more able to make higher level discriminations. Maybe within the context of work considerable sensitivity is apparent and yet the client may rely on quite gross discriminations when attempting to understand other's feelings. Therapy might more successfully start in the area of work and gradually move towards the more hazy area of feelings.

Self characterisations can be used also as a record of change for both client and therapist. Many people find the experience of writing such a sketch of themselves enlightening and so wish to write other sketches to explore, for example, how they might be when more fluent. For a severe stutterer, self characterisation can offer a valuable opportunity to say some important things about himself which he would not otherwise be able to express.

During the writing of this chapter the author became increasingly aware of how much there is to say about the assessment of stuttering, much more than can be said in one chapter. Consequently there are some areas that have been ignored or only very briefly touched upon. However it is hoped that the reader has gained sufficient understanding and information to be assisted when planning assessment programmes for individual clients.

A question has been implied in much that has been written about both the theoretical issues and current assessments, concerning the homogeneity of stuttering. The notion that all stutterers are the same is once more being challenged. The assertion that there are sub-groups of stutterers calls for more sophisticated assessment procedures, based on a view of the whole person, rather than just his speech disorder. This in turn could lead to exciting developments in treatment approaches and techniques.

References

Adams, M.R. and Runyan, C.M. (1981) 'Stuttering and Fluency: Exclusive Events or Points on a Continuum', *Journal of Fluency Disorders, 6* 197-218

Andrews, G. and Ingham R. (1971) 'Stuttering: Considerations in the Evaluation of Treatment', *British Journal of Disorders of Communication, 6*, 129-138

Andrews, G. and Cutler, J. (1974) 'Stuttering Therapy: the Relation Between Changes in Symptom Level and Attitudes', *Journal of Speech and Hearing Disorders, 39*, 312-19

Andrews, G., Guitar, B. and Howie, P. (1980) 'Meta-Analysis of the Effects of Stuttering Treatment', *Journal of Speech and Hearing Disorders, 45*, 287-307

Bannister, D. and Fransella, F. (1966) 'A Grid Test of Schizophrenic Thought Disorder', *British Journal of Social and Clinical Psychology, 5*, 95-102

Barton, E. S., Walton, T. and Rowe, D. (1976) 'Using Grid Technique with the Mentally Handicapped' in P. Slater (ed.), *Explorations of Interpersonal Space*, J. Wiley, New York

Bernstein, N. E. (1981) 'Are There Constraints on Childhood Disfluency?', *Journal of Fluency Disorders, 6*, 341-50

Blood, G. W. and Seider, R. (1981) 'The Concommitant Problems of Young Stutterers', *Journal of Speech and Hearing Disorders, 46*, 31-3

Bloodstein, O. (1970) 'Stuttering and Normal Non-Fluency: a Continuity Hypothesis', *British Journal of Disorders of Communication, 5*, 30-9

Bloodstein, O. and Grossman, M. (1981) 'Early Stutterings: Some Aspects of Their Form and Distribution', *Journal of Speech and Hearing Research, 24*, 298-302

Boberg, E. (1981) 'Maintenance of Fluency: An Experimental Program' in E. Boberg (ed.), *Maintenance of Fluency*, Elsevier, Amsterdam, pp. 71-111

Bruten, G. J. (1972) 'Behaviour Assessment and the Strategy of Therapy' in Y. Le Brun and R. Hoops (eds.), *Neurolinguistic Approaches to Stuttering*, Proceedings of International Symposium on Stuttering, Brussels, pp. 8-17

—— (1975) 'Stuttering: Topography, Assessment and Behaviour-Change Strategies' in J. Eisenson (ed.), *Stuttering: A Second Symposium*, Harper and Row, New York, pp. 201-62

Bruten, G.J. and Shoemaker, D.J. (1967) *The Modification of Stuttering*, Prentice Hall, Englewood Cliffs, N.J.

Cooper, E.B. (1973) 'The Development of a Stuttering Chronocity Prediction Checklist: A Preliminary Report', *Journal of Speech and Hearing Disorders, 38*, 215-23

Erickson, R.L. (1969) 'Assessing Communication Attitudes Among Stutterers', *Journal of Speech and Hearing Research, 12*, 711-24

Eysenck, H.J. and Eysenck, S. (1963) *Eysenck Personality Inventory*, University of London Press

Floyd, S. and Perkins, W.H. (1974) 'Early Syllable Disfluency in Stutterers and Nonstutterers: A Preliminary Report', *Journal of Communication Disorders, 7*, 279-82

Fransella, F. (1968) 'Self Concepts and the Stutterer', *British Journal of Psychiatry, 114*, 1531-5

Fransella, F. and Bannister, D. (1977) *A Manual for Repertory Grid Technique*,

Academic Press, New York

Gregory, H.H. (1979) 'Controversial Issues: Statement and Review of the Literature' in H.H. Gregory (ed.), *Controversies About Stuttering Therapy*, University Park Press, Baltimore, pp. 1-62

Guitar, B. (1976) 'Pretreatment Factors Associated with the Outcome of Stuttering Therapy', *Journal of Speech and Hearing Research*, *19*, 590-600

—— (1979) 'A Response to Ingham's Critique', *Journal of Speech and Hearing
Disorders*, *44*, 400-405

Guitar, B. and Bass, C. (1978) 'Stuttering Therapy: The Relation Between Attitude Change and Long-Term Outcome', *Journal of Speech and Hearing Disorders*, *43*, 392-400

Hanson, B.R., Dale Gronhovd, K. and Rice, P.L. (1981) 'A Shortened Version of
the Southern Illinois University Speech Situation Checklist for the Indentifica-
tion of Speech-Related Anxiety', *Journal of Fluency Disorders*, *6*, 351-60

Hayes, W.O. and Hood, S.B. (1978) 'Disfluency Changes in Children as a Function
of the Systematic Modification of Linguistic Complexity', *Journal of Communication Disorders*, *11*, 79-93

Helps, R. (1975) 'A Study of Three Groups of Stutterers Undergoing Intensive
Group Speech Therapy', Unpublished M.Sc. Dissertation, London University.

Helps, R. and Dalton, P. (1979) 'The Effectiveness of an Intensive Group Therapy
Programme for Adult Stammerers', *British Journal of Disorders of Communication*, *14*, 17-30

Higginbotham, P. and Bannister, D. (1981) *The GAB Computer Program for the
Analysis of Repertory Grid Data*, High Royds Hospital, Ilkley, W. Yorks

Howie, P.M. and Tanner, S. (1978) 'An Intensive Behaviour Modification Treatment Programme for Adult Stutterers: Description of Procedures and Outcome', Paper presented to 1st. Annual Conference of the Australian Behaviour
Modification Association, Sydney

Hoy, R.M. (1973) 'The Meaning of Alcoholism for Alcoholics: A Repertory Grid
Study', *British Journal of Social and Clinical Psychology*, *12*, 98-9

Ingham, R.J. (1975) 'A Comparison of Covert and Overt Assessment Procedures
in Stuttering Therapy Outcome Evaluation', *Journal of Speech and Hearing
Research*, *18*, 346-54

—— (1979) 'Comment on "Stuttering Therapy: The Relation Between Attitude
Change and Long-Term Outcome" ', *Journal of Speech and Hearing Disorders*,
44, 397-400

—— (1981) 'Evaluation and Maintenance in Stuttering Treatment' in E. Boberg
(ed.) *Maintenance of Fluency*, Elsevier, Amsterdam pp. 179-218

Johnson, W. (1961) 'Measurement of Oral Reading and Speaking Rate and Disfluency for Adult Male and Female Stutterers and Non-Stutterers', *Journal of
Speech and Hearing Disorders* Monograph Supplement, *7*, 1-20

Johnson, W. and Associates (1959) *The Onset of Stuttering*, University of Minnesota Press

Johnson, J. Darley, F.L. and Spriesterbach, D.C. (1963) *Diagnostic Methods in
Speech Pathology*, Harper and Row, New York

Kelly, G.A. (1955) *The Psychology of Personal Constructs*, Norton, New York

Luper, H.L. and Mulder, R.L. (1964) *Stuttering Therapy for Children*, Prentice
Hall, Englewood Cliffs, N.J.

Metraux, R.W. (1950) 'Speech Profiles of the Pre-School Child 18-54 Months',
Journal of Speech and Hearing Disorders, *15*, 37-53

Metz, D.E., Onufrak, J.A. and Ogburn, R.S. (1979) 'An Acoustic Analysis of
Stutterers' Speech Prior to and at the Termination of Speech Therapy',
Journal of Fluency Disorders, *4*, 249-54

Meyers, F.L. and Wall, M.J. (1981) 'Issues to Consider in the Differential Diagnosis of Normal Childhood Nonfluencies and Stuttering', *Journal of Fluency Disorders, 6*, 189-95

Perkins, W.H. (1978) 'From Psychoanalysis to Discoordination' in H.H. Gregory (ed.), *Controversies About Stuttering Therapy*, University Park Press, Baltimore, pp. 97-127

—— (1981) 'Measurement and Maintenance of Fluency' in E. Boberg (ed.), *Maintenance of Fluency*, Elsevier, Amsterdam, pp. 147-78

Preus, A. (1981) *Identifying Subgroups of Stutterers*, Universitetsforlaget, Oslo

Prins, D. and Lohr, F. (1972) 'Behavioural Dimensions of Stuttered Speech', *Journal of Speech and Hearing Research, 15*, 61-71

Riley, G.D. and Riley, J. (1979) 'A Component Model for Diagnosing and Treating Children Who Stutter', *Journal of Fluency Disorders, 4*, 279-93

Runyan, C. (1976) 'Perceptual Study of the Speech of "Successfully Therapeutized" Stutterer', PhD Dissertation, Purdue University

Runyan, C. and Adams, M.R. (1978) 'Perceptual Study of the Speech of "Successfully Therapeutized" Stutterers', *Journal of Fluency Disorders, 3*, 25-39

Ryan, B.P. (1974) *Programmed Therapy for Stuttering in Children and Adults*, Charles C. Thomas, Springfield, Illinois

Silverman, E.M. (1980) 'Communication Attitudes of Women Who Stutter', *Journal of Speech and Hearing Disorders, 45*, 533-9

Stromsta, C.A. (1965) 'A Spectrgraphic Study of Disfluencies Labelled as Stutters by Parents', Thirteenth Congress of the International Association of Logopedics and Phoniatrics

Van Riper, C. (1971) *The Nature of Stuttering*, Prentice Hall, Englewood Cliffs, N.J.

—— (1973) *The Treatment of Stuttering*, Prentice Hall, Englewood Cliffs, N.J.

Webster, M.L. and Brutton, G. (1972) 'An Audiovisual Behavioural Analysis of the Stuttering Moment', *Behaviour Therapy, 3*, 555-60

Wexler, K.B. and Mysak, E.D. (1982) 'Disfluency Characteristics of 2-, 4- and 6-Yr-Old Males', *Journal of Fluency Disorders, 7*, 37-46

Williams, D. (1957) 'A Point of View about Stuttering' *Journal of Speech and Hearing Disorders, 22*, 390-7

—— (1971) 'Stuttering Therapy for Children' in L.E. Travis (ed.), *Handbook of Speech Pathology*, Appleton-Century-Crofts, New York, pp. 1073-93

—— (1979) 'Approaches to Stuttering Therapy' in H.H. Gregory (ed.), *Controversies About Stuttering Therapy*, University Park Press, Baltimore, pp. 241-68

Yairi, E. (1981) 'Disfluencies of Normally Speaking Two-Year Old Children', *Journal of Speech and Hearing Research, 24*, 490-5

Zuckerman Pearl, S. and Bernthal, J.E. (1980) 'The Effect of Grammatical Complexity Upon Disfluency Behaviour of Nonstuttering Preschool Children', *Journal of Fluency Disorders, 5*, 55-68

3 INTERVENTION PROCEDURES FOR THE DISFLUENT CHILD

Lena Rustin and Frances Cook

Introduction

Most of the research and literature on stuttering, as highlighted by Andrews, Feyer, Hoddinott, Howie and Neilson (1981), has been based on the adult population. However, many authorities agree that stuttering is a developmental disorder where multiple aetiological factors play a role in determining onset. Adams (1982) discusses the enormous changes occuring physiologically and psychologically in children at 2-7 years, when stuttering/non-fluency is most commonly noted. He proposes that the integration of all systems leading to eventual fluency depends on genetic and environmental factors. Myers and Wall (1982) (see Chapter 2) suggest a model of stuttering in terms of physiological, psycholinguistic and psychological 'microfactors'; Cooper (1976) also sees stuttering as the result of multiple co-existing factors, both psychological and physiological.

Although some research purports to demonstrate that as many as 80 per cent of non-fluent children will achieve normal fluency without intervention (Sheehan and Martyn 1967), recent developments in treatment programmes give strong support to the contention that the earlier the problem is identified, and the factors contributing to it understood the greater the chances are of success (Williams 1971; Cooper 1976; Shine 1980). We are concerned, therefore, to establish as soon as possible whether there is a fluency problem and, if so, determine the nature of the problem and consider the appropriate management/ treatment.

In this chapter, we shall begin by outlining the assessment and interview procedures developed by Rustin (1982) on which we base management and treatment decisions. Then we shall discuss a number of programmes specifically developed for children and evaluate their suitability for particular cases and circumstances. Finally, our own approach to therapy for children at various stages in the development of disfluency will be presented.

Assessment and Interview Procedures

In Chapter 2 Hayhow has discussed a number of issues relating to the assessment of the speech itself. Here we concentrate on the conduct of the investigative interview as a whole, as this procedure is believed to be an integral part of intervention, and requires careful preparation.

Facilities and Equipment

Two rooms are required, one for the parental interview and one for the assessment of the child. The rooms should contain as few distractions as possible and should be quiet. An important pre-requisite for the parental interview is a satisfactory seating arrangement, which should consist of a semi-circle of chairs for the parents and child, with the therapist seated centrally opposite them, so that eye contact can easily be made. If it is possible to have a further person to take detailed notes this both simplifies and speeds up the interview.

The equipment necessary for the assessment of the child's speech and language would be a tape recorder of reasonable quality, and a stock of suitable materials for eliciting speech samples from different age groups and abilities, e.g. books, pictures, toys, etc. The baseline assessment forms and standardised tests for phonological and language development should be carefully prepared in advance. A stopwatch and tally counter for the assessment of the speech behaviour are essential basic tools.

Parental Interview

The aim of the parental interview is to evaluate the family systems and structure. The specific questions are therefore directed at gaining a broad range of information in order to understand the disfluent child's place within this family structure and other factors which may provide further insights into the problem. It is preferable to have both parents, or caretakers, present. Although single parent families are common, where there are two parents, both should be requested to attend the interview. We use the following standardised interview procedure with the parents of pre-school and school children up to the age of fourteen.

First it should be noted how the family arrange themselves in the available seats in the clinic room. Some children hang back to allow the parents to make the decision of where they will sit, while others rush forward to take the central position. After the parents are seated the first question that is put to the family is: 'Does (child's name) know why he/she is attending here today?' The answer will tell the therapist

whether the family have put a name to the speech problem immediately. It is important that the therapist does not confront the child
by defining the problem as 'stuttering' at this stage. Indeed, it might
never be necessary to use the word 'stuttering' to describe the disrupted
speech; this is particularly applicable to younger children.

A description of the interview and assessment procedures is then
given to the parents; it is explained to them that the interview will take
approximately two hours and that during this time their child's speech
and language will be fully assessed in another room. The therapist
conveys the idea that the whole aim is to gather a detailed *functional*
analysis of the problem in order to design an individual intervention programme which recognises the special needs of that particular child, the
prevailing family concerns and lifestyle, and the therapeutic resources
available to meet these needs.

The parents are informed that the therapist will ask them many
personal questions and that there are no right or wrong answers. They
should answer the questions as truthfully as possible, but if there are
questions they would prefer not to answer, they have that option. It is
important that the parents see the interview as the piecing together of a
jigsaw. They should feel relaxed and comfortable about the ensuing
exploration. Throughout, the therapist should be careful not to suggest
blame, or engender feelings of guilt within the family.

The interview begins with a verbatim account of the child's problem,
as seen by the parents. Onset, frequency, severity and contexts are
carefully elicited. The ways in which the problem affects the family
and their attempts to deal with it are also explored. This gives the therapist information about how objectively the parents are able to see the
problem and how important it is in relation to family life. One finds a
great range of individual differences in reporting and it is interesting to
note how each parent may hold different views on the extent and
nature of the disfluency. From our experience we are beginning to
hypothesise that the less objectively the parents are able to describe the
problem, the less favourable the prognosis; Conture (1982) makes a
similar observation.

The interview moves on to consider a series of areas of the child's
functioning which may provide clues to the emergence of the stuttering, and hypotheses about its current maintenance. The information
gained about the onset of the problem should be continually born in
mind during the interview. The child's health is explored and looked at
longtitudinally; we are particularly interested to know the types of illnesses that have occurred, e.g. headaches or stomach aches, and

whether there are any recurrent illnesses, such as asthma. The parents are questioned about the child's vision and hearing, and notes made as to whether these should be investigated further or reports requested. Eating and sleeping difficulties are considered, as well as regularity of bowel functioning or other such problems.

The parents are asked to comment on the child's muscular system, e.g. co-ordination and laterality, and levels of concentration. The interview is carefully structured, employing open-ended questions so that the parents can settle gradually into the procedure. Information is gathered in successive stages and it is important to know what the parents consider to be the key issues. It is noteworthy that on such direct questioning two parents often differ both in recollections and in the importance they attach to particular details.

Apart from the problem in hand we would hope to find out how the parents view the child's speech development generally, by making comparisons with other siblings and asking for examples regarding the spontaneity of talking, to give insight into the communication systems within the family. At this point we often discover what the family thinks about 'conversation' in general, whether they lay some store on family communication or whether family members retire to private worlds whenever possible. Is intra-familial communication characterised by turn-taking, or constant interruption? Does the child have to fight for speaking time within the family? Closely linked with this evaluation is the exploration of emotional functioning. How does the child show his emotions, and how freely can he express them? We need this information to learn how the child shares his problems, expresses his needs and copes with the normal everyday worries that life offers. Any ritualistic or obsessional behaviours reported at this point are noted, as well as any habitual mannerisms or tics, whether associated with speech or not.

The parents' observation of the child's relationships is valuable. From this we gain additional information on the child's life style, and what he does independently or is encouraged to do in social interactions. Throughout the interview the format directs attention to matters within the family structure. Having established the number in the family and the child's position, his relationships with siblings are discussed. The parents are asked how they feel the child relates to them, and how affectionate they are as a family group. A useful additional factor is to discover the things the child does that irritate either or both parents and siblings, and how this is generally managed. We discuss the family relationships to find out how they react to each

other and which sibling each parent relates to more easily. This applies
to the parents together, as well as the parents with individual family
members. It is important to find out how much the father participates
in the child's care and household tasks. This leads on to discussion of
the rules and regulations within the family. There may be allocation of
daily tasks to individuals or few expectations of family co-operation in
household chores. Discovering who the disciplinarian is, and what the
usual forms of punishment are, will often tell a great deal about the
amount of structure present in daily family life. We check on any res-
trictions imposed on the child both at home and with regard to friends,
reading material and television.

Having evaluated how the child relates to the family we try to find
out how he generally gets on with the other children and the adults
he comes into contact with. The possibility that attachments have
developed with people outside the immediate family circle is explored,
along with evidence of any specific sensitivity or shyness which is
characteristic of the emotional disturbances of childhood and adoles-
cence. Temperament and personality characteristics are explored
through the parents' eyes. How does their child react to meeting new
people or entering new situations and how would he convey his
reactions? Awareness of normal psychological development helps the
therapist to ascertain whether the child's reactions are commensurate
with his age and understandable within his current psychosocial environment.

Exploration would extend, for the school age child, to his attitudes
towards school. We look for any evidence of school-related emotional
disturbance, such as anticipatory crying or school refusal. Anti-social
trends may emerge with the older child; for example behaviour problems, truanting or trouble with outside authorities, may need to be
discussed.

The parents' view of the child's progress at school should be elicited.
The literature tells us that parental expectations of a child are influenced by their own achievements and background (Johnson 1955; Van
Riper 1982; Conture 1982); we therefore include in our exploration of
the family structure the past social and educational history of both
parents. History of emotional or psychiatric disturbance is seen as
potentially relevant, and in particular we need to know of any stuttering in the family. Studies have demonstrated that the predisposition
to stutter could be inherited (Bloodstein 1981; Van Riper 1982) and
we feel that where such a history is present the families are at least
more sensitive to speech problems.

Information about home circumstances should be obtained, including accommodation, sleeping arrangements and general facilities, finances and the neighbourhood the family lives in. Valuable additional clues about family dynamics can be gained from this type of information. One particular family for instance were financially solvent, but because of the father's profession (minister), they were living in an exceptionally poor area where the children were never allowed out alone, and even when accompanied had been mugged. This had affected the degree of independence that the parents were comfortable in allowing their children.

Not only present circumstances but a complete developmental history should be obtained aiming to identify both the biological and social stresses which are associated with cognitive and social/emotional development. We look at illnesses and separations experienced by both children and parents. The developmental milestones are obviously important, as well as any fluctuations that have occurred during the developmental process.

Matters concerning sex education should be discussed. It is common for schools to deal with sex education and no mention is therefore attempted in the home. We are interested to know if the child asks questions about sex and how the parents answer them. This gives us another important aspect to the family communication systems.

Finally we ask the parents how they think their child's life would be different if he did not stutter. This information will tell us how much, from the parents point of view, the child's life is disturbed by his stuttering behaviour.

The interview is so structured that emotive questions are balanced with more factual issues. If the parents are at any time unsure of what is meant by a question, then giving examples may be helpful. It is also realistic to assume that during this interview the therapist is being evaluated for her clinical competence by the parents. It is a two-way exploration and the feeling of trust engendered during the interview will form the basis of future co-operation in the therapeutic endeavour.

Interaction between the parents is an important feature of the parental interview. We are concerned with the non-verbal communication between husband and wife, and take a close interest in their roles in the interview. A specific interest is also taken in the speech models being presented to the child, i.e. rate, clarity, spontaneity, etc. of parental speech.

On completion of the interview the parents are invited to ask questions before a summary is made. We should now be in a position to begin to understand the structure and life-style of the family, and the degree to which the parents are able to participate in therapy without disturbing their own equilibrium. In the event that other help is required, e.g. counselling, family therapy or psychological investigations, this would be discussed, and where possible, arranged.

Child Assessment

The following procedure is employed for all children within the range 3-14 years of age, but the length of the assessment, the equipment used and the depth of questioning of the child, must be pitched at a level appropriate for his age. In the very young child the investigation may be directed towards the differential diagnosis of normal non-fluency and the disfluencies characteristic of the young stutterer (Chapter 2). For the older child we are seeking information about the observed stuttering behaviour, as well as associated problems. The therapist seeks not only to analyse the disfluency, but also to investigate linguistic functioning comprehensively.

Speech Assessment. A tape recording is made of the child's speech based on the Fluency Interview designed by Ryan (1974). This includes samples of automatic and imitated speech as well as reading, monologue and conversation. The tape is analysed for frequency of stuttered words per minute (SW/M) and rate of words spoken per min-' ute (WS/M); from these measures a percentage figure is calculated (SW/WS x 100/1 = % SW). The *type* of stuttering behaviour is evaluated, using Ryan's classification system of whole word repetitions, part word repetitions, prolongations and struggle. Behaviours which may seem relevant, e.g. poor eye contact, avoiding words, circumlocution, started words or sounds, breathing changes, as well as concomitant physical movement, are noted.

During the speech assessment it will become clear whether further linguistic investigation procedures are necessary. The literature suggests that the disfluent child frequently has an associated linguistic problem (Riley and Riley 1979). Standardised tests and procedures are subsequently employed according to the age of the child.

Child Examination. During the assessment the child may be asked to play with certain toys to ascertain his neurological functioning in terms of laterality, motor co-ordination and constructional skills. A general description of the child's physical appearance and facial mobility is made. In the course of this part of the procedure the child should have built up a rapport with the therapist which enables further direct questioning to be pursued.

We are concerned with the child's attitudes to school, home, teachers, parents and friends. This offers an opportunity to note the child's overt anxiety level, reaction to questioning, state of body tension, spontaneity of talk, emotional expressiveness, attention span/distractability, gross activity level and any evident mannerisms.

The questions then put to the child is 'Do you know why you have come here today?' This will give us an idea of the child's perception of his communication difficulties. In the very young child the exploration may be done through play, but it is quite common for a four-year-old to be able to say 'I have come here today because my words get stuck'. One child graphically described that his 'blood gets too thick and stops him speaking'! Where the child is aware of the problem, and realises the significance of the interview, the discussion is extended to enable the therapist to estimate his motivation to participate in therapy. Young children can usually describe what they do to help themselves and whether what teachers or parents do either helps or disturbs the fluency.

The child is asked to describe the situations when the stuttering becomes worse, and when he is fluent; examples of typical contexts are sought. The therapist will want to know how well the child understands what happens at the moment of the disfluency. Conture (1982) feels that the more objective the child is about the actual behaviour called stuttering, the better the prognosis. How does the child envisage his life without a stutter, and are there any advantages in continuing this behaviour? It would be important to know of any disliked situations the child feels able to avoid because of his stutter (for instance, reading aloud in class).

Finally, it is necessary to ascertain the child's ability to monitor his speech, i.e. can he, on instruction, achieve fluency without modification of his speech behaviour, or can fluency only be achieved with some modification, or change in speech production? The child would be asked to say one word fluently, e.g. naming objects or pictures. If he was unable to do this, the therapist would model a one word utterance, instruct the child to say it with her (in unison) and then say it by himself, fluently. If this fails we would endeavour to produce fluency by modifying the speech patterns, as in 'smooth speech' where the rate is slowed, the consonant sounds 'softened', and the words joined together in suitable breath lengths. Short sentences would be modelled for the child, said in unison with him, and then the child instructed to say it alone. The therapist here is aiming to find the method which will be the least disruptive and allow the child's own natural fluency to predominate where possible. The child who can learn for himself the most effective way of controlling his speech is more likely to attain eventual fluency (Sheehan and Martyn 1967). His own opinions would be invited throughout this experimentation with fluency to discover which methods he found most comfortable.

Formulation of the Stuttering Problem

We now integrate the parental interview with the child assessment. From the child's assessment we can ascertain whether the speech problem is within the range of normal disfluency (Gregory 1979). If this is so, and intervention is not indicated, we would advise the parents, discuss management, and review progress within three months in order to confirm that the speech has not deteriorated. However, further investigations into such areas as phonology, linguistics or reading problems may be indicated. If therapy to correct these problems is necessary, we would suggest that a programme is designed which incorporates a fluency module. The information from the full assessment will now help us to match a programme of treatment to the individual needs of the child and family.

At the end of the consultation, the first task to be completed prior to the commencement of treatment is negotiated with the parents. Each parent is asked to spend a specific amount of time each day with the child, when he will receive their undivided attention. This could be 3-5 minutes (maximum). The frequency of these sessions is also agreed; for example, the mother's commitment might be six times a week, for 4 minutes a day, whereas father's might be three times a week, for 5 minutes. During this time the child is allowed to play a game with the parent, or any other activity of his choosing that promotes some interaction (not television). Parents are asked to record that the task has been done, and to note how their child responded. This is a positive exercise which helps parents to accept commitment to therapy, and should be evaluated by the therapist at the next session where records are completed.

Some Current Treatment Programmes

In this section we will outline some of the approaches to treatment that we have used, and indicate reasons for their adoption in specific circumstances.

Monterey Fluency Program

This programme was designed by Ryan and Van Kirk (1978). It is a strictly behavioural procedure and a therapist has to be trained by qualified instructors in its use. The approach relies on observable events, operational definitions, controlled manipulations of stimuli and responses, and the continuous collection of relevant data, which regulate the pace of progress through the various treatment stages.

The major assumption made by Ryan and Van Kirk is that stuttering is a *learned* behaviour. This does not deny that certain physiological or psychological factors may play a role in both the development and maintenance of stuttering, but these are not seen as the prime causative agents. Therapy therefore, is aimed at the *way* a person speaks. Anxiety and any negative attitudes towards speech are considered to be concurrent with, or the result of, the stuttering behaviour.

At the beginning of therapy, the stuttering behaviour is measured in terms of stuttered words per minute and type of stuttering. This gives a baseline for measuring change during the programme. There are three specific phases: establishment, transfer and maintenance. Establishment refers to the development of fluent speech in the clinical situation with the therapist. There are two alternative programmes to choose from; the GILCU (gradual increase in length and complexity of utterance), which is recommended for younger children and for those whose stuttering is mild to moderately severe, and the DAF (delayed auditory feedback) programme, for older students and for those with a more severe stuttering problem.

The GILCU programme employs a sequence of 54 steps. There are three modes of treatment: reading, monologue and conversation. Each mode is structured in the same way, commencing with one fluent utterance and progressing to five minutes fluency in each mode. It requires 10-13 hours to carry out the GILCU procedure, spaced over a three month period.

The DAF programme requires the use of a delayed auditory feedback machine, with at least six settings of 250, 200, 150, 50 and 0 milliseconds of delayed side tone. The student is taught a pattern of slow, prolonged fluent speech from an initial 40 words spoken per minute, which is gradually shaped towards normal fluency. There are 26 steps in this programme which include, reading, monologue and conversation, and requires 5-10 hours therapy time over a one to two month period. There is a built-in home practice programme for both GILCU and DAF. which may or may not involve the co-operation of the parents/caretakers. A schedule of reinforcement for each step and a token economy system is used for younger children and those with motivational deficits.

Transfer refers to the generalisation of fluency to other settings.The programme is the same no matter which method was used during the establishment phase. Here we need 10-13 hours for administration, over a three to four month period. The transfer programme may be tailored to suit the needs of the individual, so that different components are included or omitted, depending on the child's age and sophistication. The maintenance phase refers to the long-term follow up of the treatment. It comprises five steps, distributed over 22 months, and requires about three hours of the clinician's time. (See Chapter 7 for a fuller description of this phase.)

The Monterey Fluency Program can be used by all therapists, whatever their experience, provided that they have been adequately trained. It is structured in such a way that the therapist and client have mutually agreed aims, and all contingencies are accounted for. The client knows how long the therapy will last and acknowledges that there is a firm commitment on both sides. The emphasis in therapy is on building up 'talking time'. The young child with poor language skills benefits remarkably from this structured approach. Where there is difficulty in gaining parental involvement, for whatever reason, the programme can be run by the client and therapist alone. Finally, it is claimed no 'harm' can come to the client if other factors prove to be more of a problem than was initially hypothesised. The programme is sufficiently flexible to incorporate new sources of data continuously.

We feel however, that the Monterey Fluency Program is by no means suitable for all clients. Our assessment procedure described above will indicate whether the stuttering is accompanied by further emotional difficulties, which may need to be tackled first. This programme does not account for the occasions when parent conselling is needed, or changes in the family lifestyle indicated. There may also be problems for some therapists who find the programme too rigid and try to make alterations to suit their own methods of working. This will make the general evaluation of such programmes difficult.

We would consider this programme appropriate for stuttering children where little parental involvment is possible and where, because there are no other complicating factors, the stuttering behaviour can be tackled directly. It has also been found useful for children in the age range of 12-14 years. This age group can be difficult to manage in family therapy, as they are no longer children needing full parental support, nor are they adolescents who are able to take responsibility for their own difficulties. The clear structure of the Monterey Fluency Program, combined with the token economy system makes it a worthwhile tool in the clinical armoury.

Personalised Fluency Control Therapy

Cooper (1976) proposes four basic assumptions regarding the problem of stuttering in young children, and the roles of parents and speech clinicians in maintaining fluency.

(1)   Most stuttering behaviour is the result of multiple co-existing physiological and psychological factors.
(2)   Typical parental reactions in terms of drawing attention to, and suggesting means to alter disfluent behaviour, generally facilitate the development of fluent speech.
(3)   Very young children who stutter, exhibiting tension in the speech musculature and/or articulatory or phonatory struggle behaviour during moment of disfluency, can be taught to use fluency-initiating gestures (FIGS) efficiently and effectively.
(4)   The speech clinician has the responsibility of assisting the young stutterer in identifying, developing and reinforcing 'fluency-enhancing' attitudes and feelings.

The Personalised Fluency Control Therapy Program has been developed with these four basic assumptions in mind. Cooper is of the opinion that a stuttering programme is inadequate if it does not, at some time, assist the individual to identify and clarify his feelings and attitudes about stuttering and fluency control. Therefore, treatment is viewed in two classes; (a) learning from developing more accurate perceptions of the problem; and (b) learning from close observation of the motor speech act.

To enable the clinician to gain a clearer understanding of both the child's and the parents' attitudes, Cooper has compiled a series of checklists. Knowing the accuracy of the attitudes and perceptions that the parents have of fluency problems helps the clinician to correct misinformation, so that specific intervention which facilitates change in parental attitudes is achieved. The parents should be made to feel comfortable in discussing fluency, and fluency failure, and to be able to relax into offering appropriate suggestions. The assumption here is that the less anxious the parents are about breaks in fluency, the less anxious the child will become. Cooper suggests that through discussion with the parents, and with a growing understanding of the severity of the child's disfluency, it would be jointly decided whether the child would benefit from work on fluency initiating behaviour and attitude change.

The clinician, at this stage, works directly with the child. The child's attitude to his stuttering behaviour is investigated through the use of a simple check list as well as the 'stuttering apple', which graphically attempts to symbolise the stuttering behaviour. The core of the apple is the way the child describes the problem, e.g. the 'words getting stuck', and then the therapist encourages the child to identify any associated behaviours: the things he does *because* he stutters and the things he does *when* he stutters. The behaviours are noted in circles around the core of the apple. The apple is intended to be a focal point of communication, and should facilitate similar conceptualisation of the problem by both the clinician and the child. The apple then can be used to structure stages in therapy − 'eating' the 'apple' to its core!

Fluency Initiating Gestures (FIGs) are seen as those changes the child needs to make in order to initiate fluency. The therapist and child explore these together, generally in the presence of the parent. Using a graphic representation of a 'FIG tree' the fluency initiating gestures which appear to be the most efficient and effective for the child are selected and entered onto the FIGs on the tree. Examples of FIGs would be slowing down the rate/easy onset, smooth speech, etc. In this programme Cooper leaves the clinician the freedom to judge *how* and *when* the child should begin using FIG in various speech situations; the emphasis being on a gradual increase in the difficulty of the situations until the level of fluency is acceptable to the child and, more importantly, until the child experiences a feeling of 'fluency control'. Fluency is seen as a *by-product* of the feeling of fluency control. Finally, a main focus of the treatment package deals with the relationship the child has with the therapist. Cooper suggests that there may be a number of resistances to change which have to be dealt with for the success of the programme. He stresses the importance of *honesty* in this programme. If the child has not completed an exercise, he should have the confidence to explain why, and the therapist should be flexible enough to make the necessary changes.

We have found this programme useful when applied in a flexible way, selecting those sections which we feel are culturally appropriate. It is also suitable where parents are anxious to be part of the therapy process. Finally, where the child is able to derive benefit from personal exploration, and would not find this part of the therapy stressful, this approach can be very beneficial.

Gregory's Approach

Gregory has not published a complete programme for stuttering therapy, but several papers are available which portray his theoretical position (1973, 1979).

He states that from his clinical experience stuttering does not seem to be the result of any one specific factor, but will be related to the intrinsic characteristics of the child, and multiple environmental variables. These two categories of contributing factors are used in a frame of reference in differential evaluation and therapy.

Differential Evaluation. The first contact will be a telephone interview with the parents to discover what they consider to be the problem and to arrange a preliminary screening evaluation if necessary. The screening evaluation has four main parts:

(1)   An analysis of fluency, in which the frequency and severity of disfluency types are noted in monologue, play, play with pressure and parent/child interaction.
(2)   An analysis of parent/child interaction in which parental interactive behaviours, such as frequency of questions asked of the child and the pacing of a conversation, are noted.
(3)   An evaluation of speech, language and learning.
(4)   A case history, based on a developmental history form completed by the parents, and a discussion of speech, language and fluency development.

This evaluation process is extensive and Gregory gives useful criteria for selecting the most appropriate treatment strategy.

Strategy 1. Is described as 'Preventive parent counselling' for the child who is 'typically disfluent'. Here the parents are provided with feedback about speech and language skills and any areas that are considered particularly relevant for the individual child, e.g. attention span. Observations from the parent/child interaction are shared, reinforcing appropriate parental behaviours. Note is taken of behaviours that may interfere with further fluency development, e.g. correcting articulation errors, or rapid questioning. Factors from the case history may be dealt with if the clinician feels the parent's expectations are high, or not enough time is devoted to the child. The child will then be periodically reviewed (3-6 months).

Strategy 2 is described as 'prescriptive parent counselling' for the child who has a 'borderline atypical disfluency'. Here intervention is instigated immediately. The parents are helped to modify aspects of their interaction by teaching them to provide appropriate speech models. In addition, the parents are instructed to identify different types of disfluency, and to chart episodes of disfluency. This serves as a basis for discussion over the ensuing sessions (twice-weekly for 4 weeks).

The parents learn to observe the environmental conditions that disrupt fluency and to develop a problem-solving approach to modifying such conditions.

During the therapy session the clinician will model appropriate interactive behaviours and gradually the parents will become directly involved, learning to use more easy, relaxed speech, a slower speaking rate and a consistent approach in managing the child. Follow-up interactive analysis tests whether the parents have generalisation of the appropriate behaviours. There are monthly follow-ups, and a further screening evaluation three months post-treatment.

Strategy 3. This is a 'comprehensive therapy programme' for the child with 'atypically disfluent speech and complicating speech, language or behavioural factors'. The parents are involved in group counselling sessions (one hour per week), counselling during observation of the child's individual and group therapy sessions, and more formal feedback sessions as needed.

This strategy pursues five specific therapy objectives:

(1) To avoid creating or increasing the child's awareness of a speech problem.
(2) Increasing the amount of fluency the child experiences.
(3) Building tolerance to fluency disrupting influencies.
(4) Helping the child gain competence in all areas judged to be potential hazards to fluency development.
(5) Increasing the child's self confidence or self-acceptance in areas judged to have an impact on fluency.

Gregory emphasises the importance of parental involvement throughout the therapy programme. He uses group discussions, demonstration by the clinician, role play, child development studies, films and videotapes to convey the crucial role parents can play in shaping and modifying speech and communication.

Systematic Fluency Training for Young Children

Shine's approach (1980) to the treatment of stuttering in the 3-9 year population is radically different from the popular diagnosogenic theory (Johnson 1959). He suggests that the basic premise of this theory has been consistently contradicted in research literature (Wingate 1976), but that nevertheless therapists have avoided 'direct' work on stuttering for fear that drawing attention to the child's speech would exacerbate the problem (Shames and Egolf, 1976; Yonowitz, Shepherd and Garrett 1977; Adams 1977).

Shine suggests that the management of the beginning stuttering child should consider the following statements. Most children who begin stuttering at an early age have a 'constitutional predisposition' to stutter (Travis 1931), which may be genetic and/or may be associated with birth complications that result in neurolinguistic and/or motor programming disabilities, involving co-ordinative disruption of the physiologic speech processes.

It is argued there is no *conclusive* evidence that parents cause stuttering; they may promote it, but Shine says 'they are more likely to be responsible for the remission of stuttering' (Sheehan and Martyn 1967). He feels that stuttering is not learned, but, maintained by a continued 'dis-co-ordination' of the speaking physiology (Webster 1974). That is, the stutterer violates the physical rules of the speech mechanism by using repiratory, articulatory and phonatory patterns that are too forceful or aberrant. In the light of this theoretical position the assessment procedures include:

(1)   Physiological speaking processes including phonation, respiration and articulation-resonance.
(2)   Rate and severity of stuttering in detail.
(3)   Parent Interview.

Procedures. Shine recommends a minimum of two 40-50 minute sessions per week.
(1)   *Establishment of Environmental Program.* Here a 'significant' other (e.g. parent) is trained in identifying and scoring stuttered words.

This person is then required to collect data in the child's environment, during at least two periods each day – a total of 15-30 minutes. This information is used to determine progress. The individual who has been trained will gradually be brought into the therapy sessions and trained to manage each new 'fluent' activity. These activities are then transferred into the home environment.

(2) *Fluency Training.* The child is taught to use an 'easy speaking voice', that is, one in which rate and intensity are significantly decreased. The goal is to modify the speaking variables that are compatible with fluency, and incompatible with stuttering, e.g. vocal fold tension, hard glottal attacks. Length and complexity of utterance are also controlled and manipulated as part of the clinical procedure.

There are five main phases in this programme:

(a) Picture identification prestep.
(b) Development of speaking variables compatible with fluency.
(c) Fluency training during highly structured activities.
(d) Fluency training during conversational speech and generalisation to other environments.
(e) Maintenance involving periodically scheduled evaluations for at least one year (Shine 1980).

Shine feels that it is crucial that one establish an effective and efficient token economy system in which tokens are administered on a prescribed schedule for fluent responses.

This programme has similar features to the Monterey Fluency Program, but is not so highly structured. There is more parental involvement and there is freedom for the therapist to use her own initiative and imagination in choosing relevant activities. No formal training is necessary to adminster this programme.

Rustin's Approach

The following management strategies have been evolved over the past eight years by Rustin (1978, 1982b). We are currently in the process of evaluating the short- and long-term effectiveness of these procedures with the various age groups that will be mentioned.

Modification of the Child's Environment through Parental Involvement. This type of programme would generally be appropriate for the younger child with a mild or moderate difficulty, who has a great deal of fluency and little concern or awareness of it as a 'problem'. The aim is to facilitiate an increase in fluency by:

(1)   Preventing changes occurring in the speech behaviour towards the more severe end of the scale.
(2)   Avoiding the child becoming aware that the stutter can be used productively.
(3)   Circumventing the development of a self-image of being a stutterer, with all the limitations on life which such a view implies.

We are concerned with finding ways of changing the behaviours that may be contributing to the stuttering problem. Each part of the programme is laid out in careful steps tailored to meet the individual needs of the child. Each step must be carefully evaluated before the next step is attempted; moving too quickly will almost certainly result in failure. The parents must be positively reinforced for each success, and progress should be charted to record both rate of improvement and uncover further problem areas. Simply advising the parent to 'spend more time' with their child, without specific suggestions as to what tasks and goals to pursue, can cause more anxiety than was originally present. Where clear, unequivocal objectives are stated, to be carried out within an agreed structure of treatment, there is a much greater probability of encouraging positive change in the child's behaviour. Parents are shown how to promote and reinforce fluency, whilst coping with episodes of disfluency as they arise.

The first strategy employed for all parents is to teach them adequate observation skills. One is aiming to teach objectivity in assessing their child's communicative competence, as well as the patterns within the family as a whole. Throughout this programme the therapist should bear in mind that as soon as a parent begins to use these skills of observation, changes will start to occur. These skills, once grasped, will be quickly assimilated, but there are times when the therapist may have to model the behaviour she wishes the parents to observe. Observational tasks could be applied to the following areas:

(1)   Communication patterns within the family, including turn-taking.
(2)   Fluency promotors and disruptors.
(3)   Consistency in management of the child.
(4)   Degree of independence and self reliance.
(5)   Ability to problem-solve.

It is emphasised that the changes we seek are to help a specific current problem, and no guilt should be attached to any previous management strategies.

From the parental interview it will be understood how conversation turn-taking operates within the family structure. The child who stutters may have a particular problem in getting into a conversation: he may not be quick enough to make his point before the next person interrupts; he may become anxious if no-one listens, or, in some circumstances, discover that his stuttering may serve a useful purpose in attracting attention. We would proceed to discuss the notion of turn-taking as a basis of any interaction, and the need for the parents to consider how this operates in their household.

A first step in therapy might be for a conversation to be set up with the clinician and parents which is tape recorded for a few minutes — preferably on video. On replaying, the clinician will point out how the focus of attention in an adult conversation will change. Together they will examine pauses, the time given for replies, the types of questions, how a person takes his turn, and the signals used to show that someone is ready to contribute. The parents would then be asked to observe a situation at home, and report to the therapist on the strategies and patterns that exist in their family.

The next discussion would look to how the disfluent child copes on his own, and whether there are changes that could be made. An example from our own experience is a child who was reported to have great difficulty breaking into the conversation with older siblings at the end of the school day, when each had the day's events to relate. Through discussion, the mother and therapist devised a strategy whereby only one child was allowed to speak at a time, and the time was carefully allocated. Often the observation is made that once the stuttering child has broken into the conversation, he proceeds in a monotonous fashion. A different strategy would be tried here because of the importance of developing normal conversational skills in the child. It might be that the mother or father learns to notice the signals the child uses to indicate that he wants to join in the conversation, allows him in, and gives him the time to assimilate and express his thoughts. The family may be involved in actively changing strategies, and be allowed to voice their opinions of the advantages and disadvantages of these facilitating activities.

Parents are taught now to make correct observations regarding fluency and stuttering. Parents are often more able to observe stuttering behaviour than the periods of fluency. The original speech assessment tape can be used to demonstrate just how much fluency their child already has, when compared with the number of disfluencies. The parents' initial task will be to start to observe on specific occasions how much fluency the child has, *not* the amount of disfluency. The activities would be agreed by the parents and therapist. For example, a parent may be asked to observe the child's speech three times daily before the next therapy session, and to have recorded the information as follows: the observation time would be limited, e.g. to one minute and the child's speech would then be rated on a scale, e.g. 0-5, with 0 being no stuttering observed (that is, fluency observed). Initial activities would be suggested where the child is most likely to be fluent. Such information may have been obtained from the parental interview. The therapist would try to reinforce the parent for completing the various observational tasks accurately.

A discussion would follow from the findings and the next step carefully selected, which in this case might be to look at three new situations. The therapist's role is to reinforce parental involvement, and pave the way for change without the need for further therapeutic instruction. Dramatic changes, however, are sometimes not to be sought, as they can often result in other disruptions.

Patterns will be emerging which have a bearing on the child's disfluent periods. Normally these may be found to be associated with stress, anxiety, conflict, insecurity, tiredness, illness, encounters with strangers, etc. However, circumstances surrounding fluency will now be noted: perhaps in the one-to-one situation, in the morning, at weekends, when the child has no pressure on him to speak quickly. The parents are now learning *how* fluency may be promoted for their child.

We believe that stuttering is influenced by almost any significant factor in the child's life, and that there are often positive changes to be made towards greater security, independence and self-reliance. No guilt should be felt by the parents; the disfluent child could be 'at risk' for developing a more severe problem if parental distress is heightened. The type of intervention suggested here seeks to prevent this happening.

We aim to promote a stable and consistent background to help the child to *predict* the outcome of his actions with a good degree of accuracy. From the parental interview we would learn about the rules and regulations in the child's life, the structure he is used to, and the way life is organised for him. The parents and therapist will be able to seek out the areas which may be productively modified to bring about, where necessary, a more stable and secure background. Parents should be urged to keep promises, whether of a punishing or rewarding nature.

Children, as well as adults, are constantly confronted with conflict situations which, depending on how they are approached, may either be resolved with little difficulty or exacerbated.

Good problem-solvers tend to show better social adjustment when dealing with these problems than those with limited abilities in this area (Spivack and Shure 1974). Stuttering children could be placed in even greater conflict, and therefore our programme is actively trying to teach problem-solving skills to both the parents and children. We commence by looking at areas of difficulty which may appear unrelated to the stuttering problem. For example, a child of 6 years was very slow at eating; his mother found this very trying and, to hasten the procedure, more often than not fed him herself. The mother recorded the frequency with which this happened and the consequences, and came back to the clinic feeling that this was a problem which she had found difficult to resolve. In discussion certain alternatives were elicited:

(1)   Stop helping and let him go at his own speed, clearing up around him if necessary.
(2)   As above, but this time offering incentive for hurrying.
(3)   Starting him before the rest of the family.
(4)   Continuing as before.

These ideas were looked at for their advantages and disadvantages, and mother chose to 'experiment' with the first. For several days the child found himself left at the table alone while the rest of the family departed and mother started clearing away. It now became the *child's* problem, and he resolved this, without assistance, by finishing his meal in line with the rest of the family. His mother became more relaxed and was clearly reinforced by the success of her strategy.

This serves as an example of early problem-solving, to be followed by a series of exercises leading towards the management of the disfluency problem. The choice of exercises is governed by information abstracted from the parental interview. Throughout the procedures mentioned for identifying areas of change in the environment, it must be borne in mind that one of our aims is to prevent the child becoming aware that stuttering can be *productive*. An integral part of our approach is, therefore, to establish with the parents that it should be more rewarding for the child to be fluent than non-fluent. Parents are encouraged to pay more attention to fluency than disfluency — to listen to *what* the child is saying, not to *how* it is being said. It may be necessary to balance the extra time required to carry out these tasks in order to avoid new stresses occurring within the family.

Summary. The child's speech environment is subjected to a detailed functional analysis in order to detect anomalies in turn-taking, speech models, problem solving and 'locus of control' in stuttering. Parental involvement is aimed at identifying and modifying these features. Specific hypotheses about the stuttering problem are deduced and systematically tested through further investigations and specific forms of intervention. The child's progress towards normal fluency is monitored through the parents, who are encouraged to acquire a clear understanding of their goals.

Direct Clinical Intervention with Parental Involvement

We shall now describe clinical intervention procedures for the moderate-to-severe younger stuttering child, where he is becoming aware of a speech problem or fearing certain speech situations.

The same skills of observation and experimentation in the home, in order to produce an environment free from speaking stress, are the first aim, as in the previous section. The programme then changes, in that we look more closely at the parents as adequate speech models. The disfluent child with a more severe problem needs to be given time to organise and assimilate his thoughts, language and speech mechanisms.

One of the ways of assessing the effective speech environment is to set up a play situation between mother and child, and video tape (or sound record) for subsequent analysis. The therapist records the frequency and types of interactions, the questions, the time given to reply, the latency of response, the interruptions, statements, rephrasing and the rate of speech for both mother and child. The therapist selects aspects of the interaction for discussion, both positive and negative. Criticism is again sensitively avoided. Tasks are set to ascertain whether modifying a particular type of interaction does have an effect on fluency.

We have noticed, for example, that a common error on the part of the parents is a rapid succession of questions during play, 'look at this boy, what's he doing? where's he going? what's he wearing?'. This may be causing problems for the disfluent child in terms of rate of speech and lack of time to assimilate and formulate a reply. We would therefore seek to teach the parents better listening skills; accepting silence until the child has properly formulated his reply. This will in turn slow down the rate of interaction, and reduce perceived speaking pressures.

Whilst the speech environment is being modified to promote fluency, the actual speech of the stuttering child is dealt with in a more direct manner by either:

(1)   Increasing the fluency already present, or
(2)   Shaping the stuttering behaviour towards an easy, smooth, flow of speech.

Both intervention procedures use small sequential steps with a built-in schedule of reinforcement. Progress is recorded and charted for each phase. Intensive therapy has been found to be effective for the early establishment of fluency in the clinic. The number of weekly sessions can then be reduced to allow for the transfer of fluency into daily life.

(1) *Increasing Fluency*. It seems from our own work, as well as from using alternative programmes (e.g. Monterey Fluency Program), that this type of therapy is usefully designed around the gradual increase in length of utterance. The child is instructed to use the shortest utterance, usually one word, and gradually increase this towards phrases, sentences and eventual conversation. This relates to the findings that the disfluent child may have specific sequencing deficits and by working in small stages we are giving the child the necessary time to assimilate incoming information and to produce good speech. The child learns to gain control of his speech by himself; the less *direct* instruction the child is given by the therapist, the more quickly the child will be encouraged to monitor his own fluency. The child is rewarded for achieving prescribed fluent utterances. Charting should be appropriately designed for the age of the child and may include star charts, graphs, wall charts or tokens with back-up reinforcers.

When the prescribed goals of fluency have been achieved in the clinical setting, home tasks are set with the agreement of both the child and his parents. These are recorded by the parents and subsequently evaluated by the therapist. Transfer of fluency to other situations is very much related to the regular use of the fluency enhancement procedures and to the environmental changes that are happening in parallel. The parents become skilled in looking for fluency, and elaborate the occasions which produce fluency whilst minimising the periods of non-fluency.

(2) *'Smooth, Easy Flow' of Speech*.   The parental management proce-

dures and schedules of reinforcement are similar to those in the preceding section. Here, however, therapeutic intervention modifies and shapes the child's speech production. It is unusual for the younger child to need intervention at this level. The teaching methods and programmed exercises will be covered in detail when we discuss the next age group, but there are some specific points which should be considered:

(a)   General communication skills, e.g. listening, attention, normal use of breath-flow may have to be included in the programme.

(b)   Focusing on connected speech rather than on individual sounds or words.

(c)   The use of 'cue' words for the desired speech technique should be consistent, e.g. 'smooth speech'.

(d)   The use of imitation, unison speech and modelling helps the child to develop fluency without testing his linguistic competence.

Van Riper (1973) in his *Treatment of Stuttering* gives some extremely practical ideas for the child who has difficulty in initiating speech. He demonstrates how speech may be paired with gross motor activities, or the emphasis in clinic diverted from real speech to nonsense speech in play contexts.

Direct Intervention Only

Occasionally parental involvement and environmental change are presently inadvisable or simply not feasible. The child who is brought to speech therapy in this instance for his stuttering problem will be given direct help to achieve fluency in the clinic. The aim will be to give the child *one* stable environment where either his normal fluency can be enhanced, or he can be taught easy, smooth flow of speech. An example of this was a child who was stuttering badly and the parents were in the process of separating. Clearly we were not in a position to alter this unhappy situation, but arranged for the child to be seen more frequently to enable him to maintain some fluency, even though this was limited to the clinical setting. We feel that in times of stress children should be seen more intensively, rather than deferring until the crisis has passed.

Summary. In addition to the functional analysis of the speech environment, intervention is aimed directly at modifying the stuttering behaviour; initially in the clinical setting, with a gradual transfer to the home with parental co-operation where possible.

The Management of the Primary School Stutterer with Parental Involvement

Our intensive programme of therapy has developed as a result of a substantial increase in the numbers of young stutterers being referred to us for therapy. The procedures were evolved from those initially developed for use with the adolescent stutterer (Rustin 1978). One major difference which is apparent from the outset between these two groups of young clients, is the fact that adolescents are relatively autonomous in their decision making, whereas younger children are more dependent on their parents and influenced by parental perceptions of the need for treatment. In view of this distinction, we decided to seek a high level of parental involvement in our treatment design by requiring at least one parent to attend the therapy course with their child.

This programme is designed to be used over a two week intensive daily period, but may of course be adapted where these resources are not available. The aim is to teach the child to use specific techniques to control disfluency, together with extensive training in social skills and specific problem-solving exercises in order to encourage the child to generalise fluency. Parents are also trained in the fluency techniques and participate in group discussions of the implications that having a child with a stutter has for the family. Parents explore issues of managing specific situations and observing their own, and the children's behaviour, in the areas described in the previous sections.

Structure of the Course. The children attend on a full-day basis for two weeks during the Easter or Summer school holidays. There are usually 6-8 children per treatment group, which is run by three speech therapists and three students. The parents attend a separate daily group run by two speech therapists. Children are accepted provided one parent can attend on a daily basis and the children are able to read and understand English. (Their reading age can be slightly low) The speech assessment described earlier is carried out on each young client to obtain a baseline measure of current fluency.

Techniques for Children. Younger children (7-9 years) are taught relaxation through games (Trower, Bryant and Argyle 1980): for example, pretending to be a tin soldier and then a rag doll. The exercises are discussed so that the child understands *how* his body feels when it is tense, and exploring different situations that might evoke these feelings.

This will be contrasted by eliciting situations where they feel more relaxed. The older age group (9-14 years) are taught a standard form of muscle relaxation (Mitchell 1977). All children are supplied with a pre-recorded tape for daily home practice.

Smooth speech consists of breath stream management, rate control, soft contracts, flow and normal intonation. A token economy system is used to reinforce success in each stage of the programme. Initially the children are taught at a slow rate (30 words per minute); gradually the rate is increased in stages to 100 words per minute, using materials and exercises appropriate for each child. We select reading materials, pictures, topic cards, etc. to use to enable the child to practice smooth speech in each stage of the programme. It is important, particularly at the initial stages, to establish the *quality* of the technique before moving on to the next stage. Where a child has difficulty in achieving smooth speech, a delayed auditory feedback machine would be used. The main errors to be corrected are poor breath control, syllabic beats, hard contacts or the over-slurring of the 'soft contacts', and monotony.

Children are taken individually for smooth speech training and then practice simple smooth speech tasks within the group. Once the children have mastered the smooth speech, they are required to exercise their fluency in games, role play, social skills training and problem-solving exercises (Trower *et al* 1980; Cartledge and Fellowes Milburn 1980). At the end of the course children are given a tape recording of themselves using smooth speech at the various rates, a handout with suggestions for daily practice and suggestions on how to manage if their speech deteriorates, as well as a homework schedule.

Parents Group. The same detailed case history as was outlined for the pre-school stutterer is obtained from the parents prior to the course in order to detect any further individual problems or difficulties which may have implications for therapy.

Parents attend a daily group and, if necessary, can be seen individually. The parental group begins with a discussion of the aims of the course and an explanation of the roles of the children's and parents' groups. Parents are taught the technique of smooth speech, and the systematic muscle relaxation procedures which their children are undertaking. Their role in assisting their children to develop and practice these techniques is stressed in each session. Time is devoted to exploring the management of the stuttering child and discussing how the family can assist in this problem. Problem-solving techniques are used within the group, both through discussion and role play. Homework is set for both parents and children, to be recorded on homework sheets.

During the second week of the course parents and children learn to work together on a variety of exercises. Whenever feasible we encourage siblings to attend as well, in order that they can become more aware of both the problems that are faced by their brothers and sisters and how they can help. As we identify problems and difficulties over two weeks, we provide individual sessions for both children and their parents in order to tackle specific features of each case.

Transfer and Maintenance of Fluency. Each child is systematically followed-up in order to determine the benefits that have resulted from the intensive programme, and to chart progress in achieving consistent fluency control from the use of the various techniques. The aims are for *generalisation* of fluency into all situations in the child's life. The smooth speech technique is a stepping stone in the child's regaining of his own natural fluency.

Children are usually seen weekly following the course, and then the whole group is recalled some six weeks later for assessment of their speech and feedback on their transfer of fluency. During the weekly therapy transfer tasks are undertaken, e.g. taking the child out on assignments. The school is visited to discuss how the child will transfer his fluency into this situation. Homework tasks are set for both parents and children and record sheets brought to the clinic on a regular basis. The parents group is recalled a few weeks after the course to review how the child is transferring his fluency at home.

Parents report that they find working in a group beneficial to both the management of their stuttering child and dealing with other problems within the family. They are pleased with the increased confidence the child develops during and following the intensive course. The parents seem to become more relaxed in dealing with the disfluency, which has its own benefits, and feel more able to deal with a relapse, which they have been taught to expect. We have noticed that relapse in children who have attended these intensive courses seems of a shorter duration than that seen in traditional weekly treatment. Finally, parents are set homework tasks on a regular basis, e.g. praising their child so many times a day for fluency, encouraging mastery of specific problem situations, etc.

Summary. An intensive therapy programme is described for children aged 7-13 years which emphasises parental involvement. Techniques used include relaxation, smooth speech, social skills training and problem-solving exercises. These are taught in a structured way using a token economy reinforcement system. The individual needs of the child are catered for both within the group setting and through individual sesssions. We see parental involvement as an integral part of the therapy process. Transfer and maintenance of fluency are managed on an individual basis, with a periodic re-assessment of the group as a whole. This approach to the treatment of the disfluent child is currently being evaluated on both a short- and long-term basis. Clearly the approach outlined here is costly both in terms of the necessary treatment resources and the demands made on the families. Adequate evidence is required to justify this approach and it is hoped that such information will be available in the very near future.

References

Adams, M.R. (1977) 'A Clinical Strategy for Differentiating the Normally Non-fluent Child and the Incipient Stutter', *Journal of Fluency Disorders, 2*, 141-8

Adams, M.R. (1982) 'Fluency, Non-fluency and Stuttering in Children', *Journal of Fluency Disorders, 7*, 171-85

Andrews, G. (1981) 'Stuttering: A Tutorial', *Australian and New Zealand Journal of Psychiatry, 15*, 105-9

Andrews, G., Feyer, A.M. Hoddinott, S., Howie, P. and Neilson, M. (1981) 'Stuttering: A Review of Research Findings and Theories Circa 1981', Paper presented to the Annual Convention of the American Speech-Language-Hearing Association, Los Angeles, California

Bloodstein, O. (1981) *A Handbook on Stuttering*, (3rd edn), National Easter Seal Society, Chicago

Cartledge, G. and Fellowes Milburn, J. (1980) *Teaching Social Skills to Children*, Pergamon Press, Oxford

Conture, E.G. (1982) *Stuttering*, Prentice-Hall, Englewood Cliffs, N.J.

Cooper, E.B. (1976) *Personalised Fluency Control Therapy: An Integrated Behaviour and Relationship Therapy for Stutterers*, Learning Concepts, Austin, Texas

Gregory, H.H. (1973) *Stuttering: Differential Evaluation and Therapy*, Bobbs-Merrill, Indianapolis

——— (1979) *Controversies about Stuttering Therapy*, University Park Press, Baltimore

Gregory, H.H. and Hill, D. (1980) 'Stuttering Therapy for Children', *Seminars in Speech, Language and Hearing, 1*, 351-63

Johnson, W. (1955) 'A Study of the Onset and Development of Stuttering' in W. Johnson and R.R. Leutenegger (eds.) *Stuttering in Children and Adults*, University of Minnesota Press, Minneapolis

——— (1959) *The Onset of Stuttering: Research Findings and Implications*, University of Minnesota Press, Minneapolis

Mitchell, L. (1977) *Simple Relaxation, (the Physiological Method for Easing Tension*, John Murray, London

Myers, F.L. and Wall, M.J. (1982) 'Towards an Integrated Approach to Early Childhood Stuttering', *Journal of Fluency Disorders, 7*, 47-54

Riley, G.D. and Riley, J. (1979) 'A Component Model for Diagnosing and Treating Children Who Stutter', *Journal of Fluency Disorders, 4*, 279-93

Rustin, L. (1978) 'An Intensive Group Programme for Adolescent Stammerers', *British Journal of Disorders of Communication, 13*, 85-92

—— (1982a) 'Management of the Primary School Stammerer with Parental Involvement', *Northern Ireland Speech and Language Forum Journal, 8*, 15-19

—— (1982b) 'Early Intervention in the Treatment of Stuttering', *Northern Ireland Speech and Language Forum Journal, 8*, 7-14

Ryan, B.P. (1974) *Programmed Therapy for Stuttering in Children and Adults*, Charles C. Thomas, Springfield, Illinois

Ryan, B.P. and Van Kirk, B.(1978) *Monterey Fluency Program*, Monterey Learning Systems, Palo Alto, California

Shames, G. and Egolf, D. (1976) *Operant Conditioning and the Management of Stuttering*, Prentice-Hall, Englewood Ciffs, N.J.

Sheehan, J.G. and Martyn, M.M. (1967) 'Spontaneous Recovery from Stuttering', *Journal of Speech and Hearing Disorders, 21*, 313-16

Shine, R.E. (1980) 'Direct Management of the Beginning Stutterer', *Seminars in Speech, Language and Hearing, 1*, 339-50

Spivack, G. and Shure, M.B. (1974) *Social Adjustment of Young Children: The Cognitive Approach to Solving Real Life Problems*, Jossey Bass, San Francisco

Travis, L.E. (1931) *Speech Pathology*, Appleton-Century-Crofts, New York

Trower, P., Bryant, B. and Argyle, M. (1980) *Teaching Social Skills to Children*, Pergamon Press, Oxford

Van Riper, C. (1973) *The Treatment of Stuttering*, Prentice-Hall, Englewood Cliffs, N.J.

—— (1982) *The Nature of Stuttering* (2nd Edn), Prentice-Hall, Englewood Cliffs, N.J.

Webster, R.L. (1974) 'Behavioural Analysis of Stuttering: Treatment and Theory' in M. Calhoun (ed.), *Innovative Treatment Methods in Psychopathology*, J. Wiley, New York, pp. 17-61

Williams, D.E. (1971) 'Stuttering Therapy for Children' in *Handbook of Speech Pathology*, Appleton-Century-Crofts, New York, pp. 1073-93

Wingate, M. (1976) *Stuttering: Theory and Treatment*, Irvington, New York

Yonovitz, A., Shepherd, W.T. and Garrett, S. (1977) 'Hierarchical Simulation: Two Case Studies of Stuttering Modification Using Systematic Desensitization', *Journal of Fluency Disorders, 2*, 21-8

4 THERAPY FOR ADULTS: AN EVALUATION OF CURRENT TECHNIQUES FOR ESTABLISHING FLUENCY

Carolyn Cheasman

There is already a vast literature on techniques for 'getting stutterers fluent'. Indeed in recent years, with the development of fluency techniques and refinement of operant procedures, attention has focused on the problem of maintaining the new behaviour. Many therapists have become almost blasé about the earlier stages of therapy: 'It's easy to get stutterers fluent but how do we help them to stay fluent?' is a common cry. By sampling different therapeutic approaches, this chapter aims to provide more food for thought about selection of techniques for promoting fluent speech. These techniques will play a vital part in long-term outcome. The premise is that stuttering is one name given to many problems. To be too simplistic about any stage of the work with such complex problems could be premature or naive.

Speak-More-Fluently Versus Stutter-More-Fluently Approaches

There are many varying approaches to the treatment of stuttering. In order to discuss differing methods of establishing fluency, Gregory (1979) proposed a broad dimension which divided therapies into the speak-more-fluently versus the stutter-more-fluently schools. Followers of the speak-more-fluently approach advocate that therapy should aim to *replace* stuttered speech with fluent speech. This usually, but not always, involves teaching a fluency technique with explicitly described features. For advocates of the stutter-more-fluently approach fluent speech is *not* the only goal of therapy. They believe the stutterer should come to know his stuttering better, both overtly and covertly, in order to be able to change it. Usually direct attention is paid to helping the stutterer reduce his negative feelings and avoidance of stuttering before he is taught ways of modifying his speech towards a fluent, or more fluent pattern. The dimension is a broad one and extremists on both sides are rare. Many clinicians who follow speak-more-fluently principles do now pay attention to modifying the covert aspects of the problem. Both groups use largely behavioural techniques. The crucial difference is that for the stutter-more-fluently group controlled stuttering may be a goal of therapy. Fluent speech is not the only aim.

Establishing Fluency

The term 'establishment of fluency' has become increasingly meaningful with the development of the speak-more-fluently approach to therapy. Establishment refers to the phase of therapy where fluent speech is established in the clinical situation. It has been contrasted with the transfer and maintenance of fluency by workers such as Ryan (1974) and Florance and Shames (1980). It has become increasingly clear that to *establish* fluency is relatively easy, to *transfer* it to situations outside of the therapy room and then maintain it over time is frequently difficult (Perkins 1973c; Helps and Dalton 1979; Ingham and Andrews 1972). For such approaches, successful establishment is evaluated by the development of total or near total fluency in the therapy room. Fluency may be spontaneous and/or controlled depending on the nature of the therapy programme.

When examined in the context of the stutter-more-fluently approaches, the notion loses some of its meaning. For some workers of this school there is less or no contrast between establishment and transfer of fluency.

First, the whole notion of fluency is less clear-cut. The speak-more-fluently therapies aim to establish spontaneous and/or controlled fluency as opposed to stuttered speech. Stutter-more-fluently clinicians including Bloodstein and Van Riper aim to develop spontaneous and 'controlled' fluency but would also see modified, easy stuttering as a goal for some clients. Here, the criterion for successful establishment is the development of modified, easy stuttering. 'Our immediate aim, is not fluency, even if the stutterer can momentarily achieve it, but only a pattern of stuttering that is milder, simpler, less conspicuous, and less impeding to speech' (Bloodstein 1975, p. 82).

Secondly however, as stated, the whole notion of establishment and transfer as separate issues is less appropriate. Whilst therapy often involves practising different techniques in the presence of the clinician before attempting to use them in other situations, their application in these situations usually goes on in parallel with their learning in the therapy room. Transfer is thus seen as an integral part of establishment and 'development' of fluency is possibly a more fitting term. Sheehan, an extremist in this group, goes further; 'Transfer is a fallacy. It really does not happen. To the extent that there is a transfer problem, the therapy has been deficient' (Sheehan 1979, p. 191). It is apparent that the criteria by which success is evaluated for the two approaches cannot be identical.

Speak-More-Fluently Approaches

Since the advent of syllable timed speech (Andrews and Harris 1964) the world of stuttering therapy has been flooded with therapies aiming to replace stuttered speech with fluent speech. The ease with which stuttering lends itself to manipulation within the therapy room has led to many cries or hopes of 'Eureka!' Sheehan (1980) comments, 'Stuttering has a deceptively simple responsiveness to any novelty whatsoever in the alteration of the stimulus environment' (p. 394).

It certainly is possible to replace stuttered speech with fluent speech. Gregory (1979) offers an excellent review of the speak-more-fluently approaches in his Introduction, covering the delayed auditory feedback (DAF) approach (Goldiamond 1965), the use of masking and rhythm (Cherry and Sayers 1956; Brady 1968), Perkins' work on the replacement of stuttering with normal speech (Perkins 1973a, b; 1974), Precision Fluency Shaping (Webster 1974; 1975), Systematic Programmed Instruction (Ryan 1974), Wingate's work on 'learning the melody of fluent speech' (1976) and Schwartz's Airflow Technique (1974, 1976).

Clinicians who use such approaches work on the development of fluent speech by focusing on manipulation or modification of the speech pattern. However, it is now generally recognised, even by the most extreme practitioners in this group, that in most cases some direct work on modifying attitudes and feelings about speaking is necessary or, at least, worth investigating. Ryan (1979) suggests that the future best programme in fluency training may involve giving clients special training in attitude, of the type which is well described by Shames and Egolf (1976, p. 145).

Fluency Techniques

From the mid-to-late 1970s most therapists in the UK treated stuttering almost exclusively with fluency techniques. This section will describe the main ones currently in use.

Syllable Timed Speech (STS). Until the mid 1970s syllable timed speech, as described by Andrews and Harris (1964), was the major fluency technique in use in the UK. Clients were taught 'a form of speech from which all stress and syllable contrasts were removed.

They were taught to speak syllable by syllable, stressing each syllable evenly and each to a regular rhythm' (p. 156). Research has shown that despite an initial dramatic increase in fluency most stutterers are unable to maintain this, either in the short or long term (Ingham and Andrews 1972; Helps and Dalton 1979). It should be said however, that these studies also show that, as with most stuttering therapies, some stutterers have become and remained significantly more fluent as a result of being taught STS.

It may seem strange to include an account, however brief, of STS, as currently it is rarely taught. However, it is hoped that some important lessons have been learned from its use. Ingham and Andrews (1972) in their evaluation of the short term effectiveness of STS found two major areas of difficulty; the technique was difficult to master in a short time and, more importantly, clients were most reluctant to use it outside of therapy sessions. (This latter point was also seen as most significant by Helps and Dalton (1979).) Perkins (1973a) summarises the problem thus,

'if a new speech pattern is not weighted with indigenous satisfaction, the stutterer will not retain it. To make it permanent, he must like it so much more than his old pattern that he will work continuously to maintain it' (p. 285).

He goes on to say that satisfaction is mainly determined by the speaker's judgement of the normalcy of the new speech pattern. Although, as will be shown in Chapter 7, Perkins would say there is far more involved in the maintenance of fluency, this is a crucial point.

As a technique for eliminating disfluency STS could be said to be effective. However, if one of the criteria for establishment is normal-sounding fluency then, for most clinicians and clients, STS does not meet the requirement.

Slowed Speech/Prolonged Speech. Goldiamond's experiments in the 1950s and 1960s showed that when stutterers were subjected to DAF, many became either completely fluent or else had easy, repetitive or prolonged stutters as opposed to hard blocks. There has been much research attempting to explain the effect, leading to the speculation that auditory feedback in stutterers is disturbed. So far there is no definitive answer to the phenomenon but interest has also centred on the pattern of speech produced under DAF conditions. Speech becomes slow with prolonged syllables and is often slurred. It seemed that, for whatever reason, modifying the speech pattern in this way led to fluent speech. Various techniques have evolved from this finding and have been researched by Perkins (1973a, b, 1974) and Wingate (1976) in America, Howie, Tanner and Andrews (1981) in Australia and Helps and Dalton (1979) in Britain.

Helps and Dalton (1979) describe the introduction of prolonged speech into their work with adult stutterers attending intensive courses at the City Literary Institute in London. Their research showed that the technique was effective in establishing a normal-sounding speech pattern in the clinic. The speech pattern, although at its slowest rates sounding very similar to DAF speech, was in most cases able to be taught by modelling and imitation of the therapist without the use of a DAF machine. The technique has since been modified in various ways, and will be described as currently taught. However, the rationale is essentially the same and is based upon much theoretical and clinical research. Now called slowed speech, the technique is introduced to clients as a collection of features. These are described below and each can be seen as a separate fluency technique in its own right.

(1) Prolongation. One of the most prominent features of DAF speech is syllable prolongation resulting in reduced rate of speaking. Perkins (1973a) says that most stutterers begin therapy 'attempting to speak at rates considerably in excess of their abilities to co-ordinate phonation with articulation' (p. 286). Stunden (1965), in his doctoral study, found that stutterers differ from non-stutterers on word association tasks administered under time pressure. Sheehan, referring to this study says the stutterer develops a 'built-in, internalised time pressure system as part of his role conflict' (Sheehan 1970, pp. 316). (See Chapter 5 for a full discussion of this role-conflict theory.) Although Sheehan is fervently opposed to control techniques, this illustrates how opinions from both sides of the controversy can be used together in a constructive manner.

If stuttering is seen as a dis-co-ordination of phonation, respiration and articulation whilst trying to speak at normal rates (Perkins, 1973a), it follows that slowing down the rate at which these processes are co-ordinated will facilitate fluency. The client is taught to speak at approximately 45 syllables per minute (SPM) by prolonging syllables (average speaking speed is 200 ± 40 SPM (Andrews and Ingham 1971)), hence the syllable rate is slowed by slowing the rate of articulation. Few stutterers stutter at this extraordinarily slow speed. Speech is then shaped towards normalcy by gradually decreasing the amount of prolongation. Clients work through speeds of 60, 80, 100, 120 and 180+ SPM. Although for research purposes it is more valid to assess rate in SPM, it is now felt that it may be more clinically appropriate to work in words per minute. Putting emphasis on counting syllables may increase the problem of some clients who develop a rhythmic pattern of speech reminiscent of STS. Perkins (1979) emphasises the importance of developing a natural rhythm to speech even at the very slowest rates. Our experience would support his view that clients who speak with slow monotony go on to speak with fast monotony and, because this is usually unacceptable to them, go on to drop speech controls altogether. Perkins suggests that the best way to facilitate natural rhythm is to concentrate on teaching the client to shorten unstressed syllables, rather than teaching him to stress syllables or pay attention to pitch and loudness, which leads to artificial inflection.

(2) Pausing. As Sheehan notes, many stutterers appear to have an 'inbuilt, time pressure mechanism' often resulting in actual fear of *any* silence in their speech. It may be unimportant whether this silence is due to stuttering itself or a pause for thought or breath; speaking may become a desperate battle to keep on talking at all costs. The underlying philosophy of 'I'd better keep talking while the going's good' seems to be a common one. Such a philosophy is obviously incompatible with the development of a relaxed non-urgent speech pattern. Any therapy aiming to facilitate co-ordination of the speech processes usually involves 'taking the pace out' of speaking. Also, from a speech production point of view it is obviously necessary to take in air in order to speak at all!

It is important that the client learns to pause to take in air *in a relaxed manner* when he needs to breathe. At the slowest rates this often results in loss of meaning. The overriding need is to help the client feel he can speak without wanting to rush. Relaxed pausing is incompatible with urgency. Pausing also gives some people a hard-to-define feeling of control; as though now *they* are choosing when and how they will speak rather than feeling that something else is propelling them ever forward. Pausing is an aspect of normal fluent speech and it seems that, for many clients, it is the most important feature of the technique.

(3) Flow. Flow is described as a characteristic of fluent speech. Although there are breaks for thinking, breathing, revising, etc., speech is essentially a flowing, fluent process. Words are not spoken as isolated

units. Stuttering with tension, especially blocking, obviously disrupts this flow. Clients are asked to deliberately focus on 'running the words together' and to start thinking in terms of phrases rather than word-by-word. The initial sounds of words often have a great perceptual significance to stutterers and any move away from thinking about speech in this fashion is felt to be positive. Flow *within* words is also emphasised to develop the transition from sound to sound.

(4) Light/Soft Contacts. Here the aim is to teach a way of articulating sounds using less pressure than is used during stuttering itself and, initially in therapy, using less pressure than is used by a fluent speaker. It is particularly relevant to the articulation of plosives. Soft contacts give the speech a slurred quality and facilitate the flow aspect of the technique. It is again important that this feature is shaped towards normality as therapy progresses, otherwise the client may have slurred 'drunken' sounding speech, which is generally unacceptable.

(5) Continuous Voicing. Some therapists incorporate continuous voicing as an additional feature of the technique. Here all the voiceless sounds are voiced, thus removing one of the co-ordinations necessary during speaking, i.e. switching voicing on and off, and also facilitating flow. Despite being an excellent way of reducing stuttering, continuous voicing is no longer taught as a matter of course at the City Lit. It gave speech a grossly abnormal quality and as a result people were reluctant to use it outside of therapy. Unfortunately it was difficult to teach clients to omit the voicing whilst wanting them to retain one or more of the other features. Possibly because of its great perceptual significance, both auditorally and proprioceptively, some people reported they could not use slowed speech if they did not use the voicing. For eighteen months now, we have taught the technique without continuous voicing, and have been happier with the short- and long-term results. Voicing is occasionally introduced if an individual appears to need it. Our aim in teaching the technique in this way is to help clients to see it, not as just one technique which can be used rightly or wrongly, but as a collection of techniques which can be individualised to their own needs.

Each client has his own individual stuttering problem and it is for this reason that slowed speech is taught as a composite technique, with each component able to stand on its own as a fluency technique in its own right.

Perkins (1979) specifies three conditions that must be met before the therapist can hope for long-term fluency.

(1)   Speech must sound normally expressive for the person concerned.
(2)   The skills for attaining fluency must be under voluntary control.
It should be possible to describe these skills explicitly.
(3)   These skills should not be apparent when used.

Our work has shown that slowed speech can meet these criteria. It
could, therefore, be evaluated as successful as a technique for establishing fluency with many stutterers. However, it is apparent that much
more is involved in whether clients will go on to develop their fluency
outside of the therapy room and maintain it after therapy has finished
(see Chapter 7).

Most advocates of the speak-more-fluently approach would agree
that Perkins' criterion of normalcy is a critical and essential first step.
Slowed speech can be shaped to normal-sounding speech, is easily
taught, and is usually easily learned. Like everything else in stuttering
therapy it is not *the* answer. Not all clients can use it to establish
fluency; some fail to transfer this fluency and many still fail to maintain their fluency over time. However, as a weapon in the therapist's
armoury of techniques, it has an important place and should not be
discarded because it is not the ultimate technique; neither should the
client be discharged because he is unable, for whatever reason, to make
use of it.

Schwartz − Air-Flow Technique (Schwartz 1974, 1976).   Schwartz's
technique is based on his 'discovery' of the Airway Dilation Reflex
(ADR) and his further conclusion that it is the anticipation of, and
reaction to this which is the core of all stuttering behaviour. The ADR
is a dilation of the nostrils, pharynx and larynx which takes place prior
to vigorous inhalation. Schwartz goes on to say that in the infant the
throat is susceptible to kinking and the ADR could act as a kind of pro-
tective mechanism, causing dilation of the muscles involved. He postulates that the stuttering child, preparing to speak, interprets the build
up of air pressure behind the adducted vocal folds as being the result of
a kink. The reflex fires, the folds abduct and the child is speechless.
So, if the child perceives the folds to be in an 'about to speak' position,
he responds by pushing them together to 'beat the reflex'. This is called
a laryngospasm and any struggling is said to be a reaction to this, the
real heart of the problem.

As he developed this theory Schwartz went on to observe that former stutterers showed tiny airflows before they speak. This, he said, would ensure an opening of the vocal folds prior to speaking. Clients are therefore instructed to initiate phrases with a *passive* air-flow to ensure an open glottis. Following the passive air-flow the client is instructed to say the first syllable slowly. These are the keys to the technique, leading to the mnemonic 'PFSS', 'passive flow, soft and slow'. 'I now realised that if a patient adhered to the passive flow technique and slowed the first syllable after the flow, he could not stutter even if he wanted to . . . here, for the first time, was a specific and clear-cut prescription for fluency' (Schwartz 1976, p. 91). Unfortunately this is not the first time that such a claim has been made.

Schwartz has been criticised and dismissed by many workers in the field of stuttering therapy as much for the way in which he presents his theory as for the theory and therapy itself (Gregory 1979; Sheehan 1980). He cites no references to the literature in his book, extravagantly titled *Stuttering Solved*, and presents no data other than anecdotal case studies.

However, if one looks beyond this, it can be seen that there are links between air-flow technique and other, more substantiated therapeutic strategies. The passive air-flow and slowed rate of articulation of the first syllable facilitate the co-ordination of respiration and phonation. Although many would dismiss Schwartz's idea of the laryngospasm as being the core of all stuttering Van Riper (1971) states 'we have seen many stutters whose closures were never laryngeal' (p. 133)), many do believe it is the dis-co-ordination of respiration and phonation which are the motor determinants of stuttering (Perkins, Rudas, Johnson and Bell 1976; Adams 1974). There are obvious similarities between Schwartz's technique and aspects of slowed speech as described above. He emphasises the need to develop a normal sounding speech pattern and is aware of the need for follow-up therapy.

It is difficult to evaluate his therapy in the absence of any research. There is no doubt that, as with all therapies, it has helped some people. But it does not appear comprehensive enough to help many of our clients. Slowing only the first syllable would certainly not be sufficient to help many people maintain co-ordination of the speech processes through the phrase and hence remain fluent. It also seems doubtful that the client with strong word or phonemic fears would find the technique helpful. It may be most effective with the client who has particular difficulty initiating speech and who has no highly developed sound fears. Also, it does not appear to have any devices for handling, con-

trolling or modifying stuttering should it occur; it is sold in such a way
that this possibility is not countenanced. The philosophy being, 'if you
do it, it will work'. If the client stutters it is because he is not doing
it properly. (See Schwartz (1976) for his descripton of misuses of air-
flow.)

To be evaluated as successful, a technique must show itself to be
useful when used by a variety of therapists. There remains a question
that Schwartz's methods may be successful in his hands becuase of his
own charismatic qualities. Possibly many stutterers could be helped by
aspects of the technique but for most it simply is not enough.

A Fluency Technique in Use. Howie, Tanner and Andrews (1981)
describe a programme illustrating the clinical application of a fluency
technique. The name of their technique, Smooth Motion Speech,
emphasises that smooth, continuous transitions are equally, or even
more important than just prolonging static sounds. Its characteristics
are slow onset of phonation, continuous air-flow and movement of artic-
ulators through each utterance, and extension of vowel and consonant
duration. It does not employ continuous voicing.

Establishment and transfer of fluency take place over a three-week
period of intensive therapy. Clients are treated in groups of six. The
technique is taught at a speed of 50 SPM using clinician instruction and
modelling. (This overcomes the weaning problem that may occur if
DAF machines are used.) Speed is built up to normal in five SPM steps.
At each step the client must show zero per cent stuttered syllables
(SS) in a 45 minute rating session. The programme allows for no
gradual decrease in stuttering. Stutter-free speech is required from the
first rating session. Flexibility of speed is allowed within ± 20 SPM of
the target. By the end of the first week most clients show zero per cent
SS, at normal speaking speed, within the clinic. Throughout therapy
sessions measurement is continually taking place and continuous feedback is provided on digital display units in front of the client. Token
rewards are no longer used since it was found that their absence did not
adversely affect progress through the programme (Howie and Woods
1978). Clients receive immediate and contingent information about
their speech and small monetary rewards are used to confirm the
correctness of their speech.

The transfer phase of therapy consists of 25 graded speech assignments. Each one must contain 1400 syllables of stutter-free speech at
200 ± 40 SPM. Thus there is gradual generalisation of newly-acquired
speaking skills to situations of increasing difficulty. At the same time,

clients are undergoing *in vivo* desensitisation to specific fears about speaking situations. Detail of these procedures is not given. Then follows a maintenance programme of nine weeks daily, formal speech practice, real life assignments and weekly self-help groups.

In this research, outcome was assessed by percentage disfluency and speed of speaking. Attitudes to oneself as a speaker were measured by the revised form of the Erickson (1969) Scale of Communication attitudes, the S24 (Andrews and Cutler 1974). Two studies are reported and the second includes maintenance data on 43 clients at 15 months after the course.

The first study, involving 36 adult clients, showed that by the last day of the intensive course stuttering was virtually eliminated, speaking was within the normal range and negative attitudes had decreased from a level typical of adult stutterers to within the normal range. After two months of maintenance stuttering had increased slightly, but not significantly, to a mean of 2.2 per cent SS (t = 1.75: p > 0.05), there was a slight but non-significant decrease in speech rate (t = 1.35: p > 0.05) and virtually no change in communication attitudes (t = 0.72: p > 0.05).

The second study showed that at 15 months post-treatment speech rate and attitudes were still within the normal range but mean stuttering frequency (3.9% SS) indicated some relapse. Speech was assessed in a non-clinic setting by a stranger. There was also covert assessment of a telephone call, i.e. assessment made without the client's knowledge. It is interesting to examine some of their findings in more detail. Twenty one out of the forty-three were at least 85 per cent improved over pre-treatment stuttering frequency; 97 per cent reported improved speech; 86 per cent reported increased confidence; 86.4 per cent reported adequate fluency or better; 56.7 per cent reported dissatisfaction with their present speech. Most clients reported needing to pay attention to their speech more than one tenth of the time; 25 per cent reported its needing constant attention if they were to be fluent. There were signs of relapse in 30-60 per cent of subjects, depending on the stringency of the criterion for normal fluency.

These findings are comparable with many similar treatment programmes (Andrews and Ingham 1972; Perkins, Rudas, Johnson, Michael and Curlee 1974; Helps and Dalton 1979). The authors' suggestions are of interest to clinicians working with fluency techniques either on an intensive basis or as therapists working with clients in the maintenance phase following up intensive therapy. They talk of the need to investigate a more supportive and structured follow-up therapy, of weaning clients more gradually from the cues for fluency present during intensive treatment, of focusing on changing speech attitudes and of possibly isolating severe stutterers as a sub-group requiring special, more extensive treatment.

Evaluation. The major criterion of success for the establishment phase of a speak-more-fluently programme is determining whether the client speaks fluently within the clinic. There is little doubt that this programme meets this requirement. Also, importantly, clients are speaking at normal speed. The authors note that assessment of normalcy of speed could be important in evaluating the outcome of therapy. There is no such assessment in this paper but they report that, to date, research shows little evidence that naive listeners assess the speech pattern of treated stutterers as abnormal. Perkins (1979) feels strongly that clients generally will not continue to use speech controls if they perceive their new speech pattern to be abnormal. It is felt that some clinicians who teach slowed speech have put too much emphasis on developing correct technique and fluent speech at the expense of normalcy. Therapists should always ask themselves the question, 'Would *I* be prepared to go outside and speak like this?' It is our experience that a few clients will choose to speak fluently rather than stutter severely by employing very obvious speech controls, if they feel that these are the only options. They are, however, very much in the minority.

There is no self-report data for the establishment and transfer phases of the Howie, Tanner and Andrews programme. However, the S24 scores indicate that therapy had brought about substantial positive change in attitudes towards communication. The clients, as a group, felt much happier about speaking. It is agreed that this is an important criterion in the evaluation of a programme, both in the short and long-term.

The self-report data given for 12-18 months post-treatment is of interest. It would seem to be important to know the criteria clients use in saying whether they are satisfied with their speech. One wonders whether the zero per cent SS criterion used in the establishment and transfer phases of the programme leads many clients to also be satisfied with nothing less than total fluency in the long term. Given that stutterers as a group already have abnormally high standards for their own fluency (Knepflar 1972) this could be important. It would certainly seem vital to allow for normal non-fluencies when assessing zero per cent SS. As it is at times difficult to distinguish normal non-fluency and stuttering one could again question the desirability of the criterion of zero per cent SS. It could be that by so doing an essentially 'stuttering' attitude towards speaking could be reinforced.

As with most speak-more-fluently programmes, emphasis is placed on measuring outcome of therapy. The clear presentation of various data is most helpful in evaluating the programme. The stages of therapy are clearly described, facilitating use by other clinicians and enabling clients to have clearly specified goals at any one stage. As a means for establishing clinical fluency the programme is mostly successful — as the basis of a long-term therapy programme it helps a significant number to retain a high level of fluency. Therapists are also referred to Boberg (1980) and Florance and Shames (1980). These clinicians work with similar programmes and incorporate some additional features of interest.

Boberg's programme includes sessions set aside exclusively for self-assessment, where success is contingent not upon quality of speech, but upon accuracy of assessment of speech and disfluency. He also introduces a technique called cancellation. The client is instructed to stop speech as soon as there is any struggle behaviour. He then has to say the word correctly and repeat it correctly several times. This is designed to replace a presumed reinforcing event, completing the sentence, by a punishing consequence. (Cancellation here is somewhat different from that described in Van Riper 1973.) Boberg's clients are also taught to adjust their rate of speech if they anticipate stuttering. They have to complete successfully two therapist-directed sessions of rate change, followed by two self-directed sessions. This may be important for many clients using rate-control techniques.

Florance and Shames have introduced a four-stage procedure for developing self-responsibility and self-reinforcement. Clinicians will recognise the importance of both of these to successful therapy. These workers teach their clients to employ various speech controls and have the interesting idea of allowing clients to reward themselves with unmonitored speech for using monitored speech. Their work has supported the notion of Bellack (1973) and Rozensky (1973) that there are high and low self-reinforcers and that low self-reinforcers need more external support during later phases of therapy. (See Chapter 7 for further discussion of both self-responsibility and monitored versus unmonitored speech.)

Operant Conditioning and Programmed Instruction

Some workers, particularly those who follow the speak-more-fluently approach, adhere to the principles of operant conditioning in their work with stutterers. The applications of the principles have become so diverse that it is sometimes difficult to say that they are related. However, there is a common thread uniting them, namely a belief that certain kinds of responses (operant responses) will occur more or less often depending on the consequences they generate. It is the consequences of the response which are deemed to be of greatest importance. As the consequence depends entirely upon the behaviour it is said to be a 'contingent' event. So, for the operant conditioners, a behaviour will increase or decrease according to whether the contingent events are desirable or not and hence the behaviour is modified by manipulating its consequences. In the case of stuttering it is said that fluent speech can be increased, or stuttered speech decreased, by the consequences they generate (Figure 4.1).

Figure 4.1

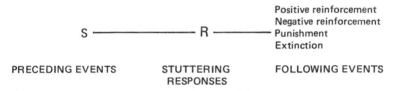

Source: Conditioning in the Stuttering Therapies: ed. Malcolm Fraser, 1970

Stuttering responses (R − see above), included such behaviours as syllable, repetitions, blocks, prolongations, etc.; secondary behaviours, e.g. eye closing and jaw jerking; and topics of conversation reflecting attitudes towards speaking. The operant conditioners usually avoid descriptions such as starters or postponements which interpret the function of a behaviour rather than simply describe it. The emphasis is on overt, observable and measurable behaviour.

Positive and negative reinforcement both increase the frequency of the reponse they follow. Positive reinforcement might be the therapist smiling or saying 'good' after the client has said a word fluently or reported going into a feared situation. Negative reinforcement involves taking away a response to increase a behaviour, e.g. if a child is afraid to speak to his teacher because of a certain reaction, the teacher might be asked to stop responding in this way in the hope that the child would speak to the teacher more. It is obviously crucial to know what event positively or negatively reinforces a behaviour for the individual concerned. A response should not be said to be reinforcing until it has been seen to increase the frequency of a behaviour. Extinction refers to the removal of a reinforcer to weaken or extinguish a response and is frequently ineffective as a technique for modifying stuttering. Though many workers would agree that certain factors in the environment may operate to maintain stuttering, it is usually far too complex to simply remove one and expect any change. Punishment serves to stop or decrease a response.

For the operantly-oriented clinician it is usually the overt stuttering response which is the problem to be changed. They would often not deny that the stutterer's feelings, fears and attitudes are a part of the problem, but they believe that changing the overt stuttering behaviour to fluent speech will result in the covert stuttering 'behaviour' going away, being replaced by a fluent speaker's attitudes to speech or ceasing to be significant. The operant conditioner then fits his basic principle into a 'programme'. There are a variety of programmes for developing fluent speech but they too are all based on common principles. There is no reason why operant principles should not be applied to the *speech modification phases* of stutter-more-fluently approaches as these also use largely behavoural techniques. This tends not to have been the case, possibly because these clinicians pay more attention to the *person* as opposed to the *response*. The principles of programmed instruction will be outlined as described by Costello (1977).

Successive Approximation. The programme starts with learning a response which is within the learner's ability and which is related in some way to the final target response. The learner then proceeds through many small, hierarchically arranged steps (successive approximation). As a result the learner is usually able to achieve each step with relative ease.

Active Participation. The learner is required to make many overt responses in any one session so is actively involved and the instructor (therapist) is able to record data.

Immediate Knowledge of Results. Various forms of immediate feedback are given to the learner.

Mastery Learning and Self-Pacing. Learners do not proceed to the next step until they have mastered the previous one. Programmes usually have criterion tests built in which must be passed before moving on to the next stage. Each learner then moves at his own rate.

Fading Stimulus Support. Initially, correct responses are made more probable by using many models and cues. Gradually these are faded until, at the end of the programme, the response is evoked by 'natural' stimuli.

Concept Learning Through Varied Repetition. The programme should aim to 'evoke the response' by presenting as wide a variety of stimuli as may be naturally encountered.

Approaches already described may use similar behavioural techniques and the difference between these and operant approaches may be seen as largely a difference of degree. For programmed instruction every stimulus, response, reinforcement schedule and criterion for pass at each step is clearly specified. The principles are illustrated by Ryan's programmed therapy for stutterers (Ryan 1974, 1979).

Rustin and Cook discuss this approach in relation to work with children in Chapter 3. Here it will be evaluated with particular reference to therapy for adults.

The Monterey Fluency Program. Ryan and his co-worker Van Kirk, have now produced data on a considerable number of children and adults who have successfully completed the establishment and transfer phases of their programme. Such publication makes it more possible for us to evaluate their contribution. Principles of operant conditioning can thus be seen to be successful in teaching clients 'clinical fluency' and helping them to transfer these skills to outside situations. Programmes are economical on therapist time, taking 20-30 hours over a two year period; the bulk of the therapy comes in the first six months. (Establishment takes 5-13 hours depending on client and programme; transfer 10-13 hours over three to four months.) The programme is less suited to group therapy however, as it requires constant monitoring by the therapist. Ryan acknowledges the importance of developing a normal sounding speech pattern for use outside of the therapy room by incorporating a rate programme into the DAF Programme. This is for clients whose speech sounds slower than normal. It is used at the *end* of the transfer programme and so it appears that clients are expected to transfer fluency even if speech sounds abnormal.

There is no assessment data on feelings and attitudes towards speaking. Ryan works under the assumption that helping clients to change their speech does change their attitude (Martin and Haroldson 1969). He assumes that verbal statements about oneself represent attitudes and presents some analysis of self-report data for *children*. He describes his data as inconclusive and suggests that for at least some of the children some direct work on 'attitudes' may have been helpful. One suspects that with adults, where usually the covert aspects of the problem are far more developed, this percentage would be larger.

The transfer programmes are felt to be particularly useful to clinicians working within the speak-more-fluently model, where the transfer of fluency is a key issue. They are clear, explicit and carefully graded. If working within such a model it is important to have a very carefully graded series of transfer activities. However, Ryan does not grade his transfer assignments according to the hierarchy of difficulty for the person involved, e.g. it is *assumed* that, within Series F of the transfer phase (talking to strangers), it is harder to converse fluently with strangers in shops than with friends. Transfer may be facilitated if transfer programmes could be individualised whilst retaining their other characteristics. And so, working on the principle that if a model is to be used it should be done as efficiently as possible, for many clients it appears that operant methods are an excellent way for establishing and transferring fluency. The GILCU programme in particular is most useful with children, who often respond well to operant methods and token reinforcement. Also, the methodology in general makes clinicians aware of the effect that their own behaviour can have on modifying their clients behaviour.

It must be remembered that Ryan's data refers to the clients who have completed the transfer phase of therapy. Completion implies successful completion. It also refers to completion of the transfer phase of the *therapy programme* which is not synonymous with transfer in the fullest sense. This leaves some important questions. What of the clients who do not complete the programme? What of those who cannot even begin it because their rate of stuttering in the fluency interview was less than the three stuttered words per minute (SW/M) stipulated as a criterion for acceptance? Do the maintenance checks merely ensure that the client can pass the maintenance checks? What is needed, as with all stuttering therapy, is some individual investigation of the clients who do well in the long-term, in real life, with this approach, and of those who fail at various stages. It appears that as a group, children do better than adults, but we need more information that this in order to select a therapeutic regime.

Ryan believes that as professionals we should seek the ideal goal for our clients. For him, this is fluent speech but is this ideal realistic? At present it seems that what is realistic is intimately related to the client himself. For a fuller review of operant conditioning approaches see

Fraser (1970).

Stutter-More-Fluently Approaches

This group of therapies, developed largely from the work of Bryngelson, Johnson and Van Riper, have declined in popular usage in recent years. The wave of fluency techniques which grew in the 1960s and 1970s led, until recently, to a state where many British therapists were able to offer their stuttering clients only one option in therapy, i.e. a fluency technique. An evaluation of research and self-report data from therapists and clients would however indicate that, despite helping some greatly, there was still dissatisfaction from therapists and clients alike with what speech therapy had to offer adult stutterers.

Therapies in this group approach stuttering as more than just an overt behaviour to be removed or controlled. Feelings and attitudes towards speaking and stuttering, and the consequent avoidance of the problem, are seen as being equally or more important. (At least, they are seen as an integral part of the problem.) Sheehan's (1970) analogy of the stuttering iceberg is useful here. Only part of the stutter is visible with the *major* proportion hidden. The ratio of course varies, but Sheehan's belief is that for most adult stutterers the majority is 'below water'. His avoidance-reduction therapy and role therapy is based on this model of stuttering and is discussed in Chapter 5.

Many of the workers who aim to replace stuttering with fluent speech would not deny the covert aspects of the problem. They believe these will change by concentrating on the disfluencies of speech. The controversy has led to heated debate. Ryan (1979) quotes Mowrer (1977), 'speech-language clinicians deal only incidentally with psychological problems (depending on their training) but mostly with the speech act, stuttering' (p. 145). Whether or not they do, the important questions are first, should they? and second, can one in any case distinguish stuttering from 'psychological problems'? Sheehan (1980) from the other side of the divide says,

'defining stuttering as a fluency problem borders on professional irresponsibility. It ignores his feelings about himself. It ignores the significance of stuttering in his life . . . It ignores the principle that just because an individual person stutters, that is not necessarily the chief problem with which a clinician need be concerned.' (p.391).

Currently the chief advocates of the stutter-more-fluently approach are Bloodstein, Sheehan and Van Riper, although some of the work of Williams and Gregory could also be included here. Although their therapies differ one can trace their common philosophy back to Travis.

'The primary concern of speech correction is the person . . . It is not enough to know what sort of a speech defect a person has. In addition, one should know what kind of a person has a speech defect. The speech defect has no particular meaning apart from the person who presents the defect. We are not interested in speech defects but in speech defectives.' (Travis 1936, p. 1)

Van Riper echoes his words: 'speech correction is but one small area in the field of clinical psychology, and the speech correctionist who thinks he deals with stuttering rather than stutterers, will find discouragement at every turn.' (Van Riper 1939, p. 62).

Bloodstein (1975) describes the goals of this school of therapy. He says it is appropriate for his 'phase 4' of the development of stuttering. Phase 4 is typical of adult stuttering but may be found from the age of 10 years, and similarly it does not apply to all adults who stutter. His approach consists of carefully planned observations and experiences leading to the achievement of two major objectives which are the reduction of anxiety about stuttering and the modification of the stuttering behaviour. Bloodstein presents an account of his own therapy programme but acknowledges that Van Riper has developed the most comprehensive range of modification techniques. A summary of Van Riper's therapy is presented here to illustrate the basic principles of this school of thought. For a full account readers are referred to Van Riper (1973).

Van Riper's Programme

Identification. Therapy begins with the client 'identifying' the overt and covert aspects of his stuttering. For Van Riper, if the client is to change what he does it is important that he comes to know *exactly* what it is that he does when he stutters. The stuttering pattern is broken down into its component parts. Starting and postponing devices, sites of tension and release mechanisms are examined analytically. The phrase 'stuttered word' as used by Ryan has little meaning here. Each client has his own individual collection of stuttering behaviours. He has to 'collect' the stuttering to be identified and so is actively involved in therapy from the beginning; this process tends to de-mystify the problem. Stuttering is often seen as a curse which descends from outside. Instead of saying 'I just get blocked', the client comes to realise it is he himself who performs a series of behaviours, incompatible with fluent speaking. He starts to take responsibility for his stuttering *and* for his fluent speech. Therapist and client also examine *why* the client performs these various behaviours, leading on to the analysis of the covert aspects. The calm and clinical analysis of an often feared and hated problem in the presence of an accepting and understanding therapist frequently leads to reduction of anxiety./As such, identification becomes part of the second stage of therapy: desensitisation. 'For once, the experience that he has always avoided is sought and described. The untouchable can be touched.' (Van Riper 1973, p. 247).

Identification must follow a hierarchical sequence. Van Riper suggests identifying fluent words first, followed by the short easy stutterings which are to become a primary target of therapy, then an analysis of avoidance behaviours, then the postponing and timing devices, moving on to the core behaviours, the tremors and fixations and finally the feelings resulting from the experience. The client does not move on until he can calmly identify the behaviours belonging to one stage. At no time is he asked to change or modify his behaviour. Van Riper recommends starting with reading, moving on to conversation and the telephone, and then going into situations outside of the therapy room with the client.

Desensitisation. Here the aim is to reduce the client's negative feelings about stuttering. Van Riper describes two types of stimuli in stuttering, those which govern avoidance and those which govern escape. Desensitisation aims to disassociate the responses from the stimuli. If the client can become toughened to his stuttering and if he can learn that he does not need to panic when he anticipates stuttering, the eventual modification of the problem becomes easier. For Van Riper, the primary emotions of stuttering are fear, shame and frustration. In this phase the aim is to reduce shame, weaken fears and develop tolerance of communicative frustration.

In relation to this aspect of Van Riper's work, Williams (1979) describes four specific stuttering fears. These are: fear of being found out to be a 'stutterer'; fear that having started a word he will be unable to finish it; fear that one instance of stuttering will precipitate an 'avalanche' of stuttering; and fear of feeling out of control of one's behaviour. The classification seems useful in designing a desensitisation programme.

There are many desensitising techniques and the therapist must choose those most suited to the individual client. A summary of Van Riper's procedures is given here.

Calming the Client Down. Here a hierarchy of situations is established, commencing with the easiest situation, the aim being for the client to remain as calm as possible *whilst* stuttering. Signs of calming are less forcing, decreased panicky avoidance, less disturbed breathing and self-report of feeling calmer.

Testing Reality. Based on the principles of disconfirmation, the areas to be tested are, first, is the client's stuttering as severe and frequent as he reports? and second, do listeners always manifest the reactions attributed to them?

Eye Contact. Developing eye contact during moments of stuttering can be a very powerful desensitising device. The client can test the validity of his fears about listener-reaction as well as putting listeners at their ease. Also, he openly demonstrates acceptance of the fact that he stutters.

Self-Disclosure. The clinician helps the client stop pretending he is a fluent speaker. Talking about stuttering and therapy to friends and colleagues can be important here.

Voluntary Stuttering (Pseudostuttering or Faking). Here the client is asked to deliberately stutter on *non-feared* words, commencing with easy prolongations or repetitions. The experience of stuttering and yet feeling in control is again a most powerful desensitising agent.

Freezing. Freezing is a technique for developing tolerance of communicative frustration. At the sign of blocking, prolonging or repeating, the therapist signals for the client to freeze articulation (or continue to prolong or repeat) for as long as the signal lasts. The length of freezing is gradually increased to increase tolerance.

These are but a few of the procedures which can be used. Desensitisation is an on-going phase of therapy and cannot be worked through and completed in a neat compartment. It should be approached boldly but sensitively in careful steps and above all it should not be rushed.

Modification. It is in this phase of therapy that Van Riper has been most creative and again his techniques are too numerous to describe here. What is presented is a breakdown of the modification programme sometimes described as block modification.

The first stage is called *variation* and here the key word is change, not necessarily to fluency, but the aim is for any change of highly stereotyped behaviour. For example, if the client always postpones stuttering with 'er', can he go 'oh' or 'oo'? By varying seemingly uncontrollable behaviour, some of the feelings of helplessness are lost. Change in a broader sense, i.e. changing aspects of style of living, may also be experimented with.

The client then moves on to learn a new, fluent form of stuttering. The aim here is to teach him to stutter in a way which will not cause him frustration nor lead to listener penalty.Van Riper has used the phrase *fluent stuttering* to describe the end product. Words are said with sounds in the normal sequence and with smooth transitions rather than sudden shifts. The stutterer is committed to saying a word rather than pulling back. The key is approach, not avoidance. Having reduced some of the negative feeling the client is now in a position to work on speaking more fluently. Van Riper describes three phases to modification, commencing with post-block correction (cancellation), moving on to in-block correction (pull-outs) and concluding with pre-block correction (preparatory sets). These, he suggests, are not just mechanical devices, but in many cases serve a deeper, psychotherapeutic purpose. Cancellation may be seen as a kind of self-confrontation. Pre-sets and pull-outs may be likened to the client in psychotherapy gradually taking responsibility for, and becoming actively involved in changing his behaviour.

It is not possible to give any adequate description of these techniques here. Van Riper, aware of the issue of maintenance of fluency, also describes a stabilisation phase (See Chapter 7). Therapists who wish to use this type of therapy are urged to read Van Riper themselves. Clients following such a programme frequently benefit from reading *Self Therapy for the Stutterer* (Fraser 1979).

Evaluation

The notion of establishment of fluency is less meaningful here. Transfer is built into the programme from the moment the client starts identifying and the goals of therapy include the development of fluent stuttering. There is little recent research on this work. Van Riper (1958) reported that about 50 per cent of his sample had very fluent or essentially normal speech, largely free from fear and avoidance, five years after therapy. This was reported as being encouraging but indicated that further work was needed. Since then procedures have been broadened and changed considerably and there is a need for these later procedures to be researched and for detailed results to be published. Until this happens his theories and techniques will be subject to the criticisms that they are unsubstantiated or have only been successful when used by Van Riper himself. The therapy has been described by some of the opposing school as aiming to develop 'happy stutterers'; they stutter just as much but do not care. This is patently not the case, as evidenced by the detailed modification phase. The aim is to develop clients who do care less about stuttering and who as a result of this, coupled with the use of modification techniques, are able to speak very fluently. Many therapists will recognise that some of their clients who have done well on a fluency technique still need to cope with the feelings associated with stuttering when it does occur, in order to use their technique more effectively.

The regime is less economical on therapist time and probably is less suited to short, sharp intensive courses. It is very demanding of clients, especially in the early stages, and is more demanding of the therapist's understanding of stuttering and of people, and hence of her therapeutic skills generally. As such it may be daunting or stimulating. If therapists can allow for some anxiety there is no doubt it is more interesting and challenging. Interest of the therapist is not the best criterion for selecting a therapy programme however, and clearly she should choose that which is best for the client.

Cooper (1979) and Williams (1979) have noted that as the client becomes more fluent with this kind of therapy, so he gets less opportunity to 'practice' his fluent stuttering. Williams goes on to say that this may lead to an increased desire to keep fluent and thus avoid stuttering. The use of voluntary stuttering at such times could counteract this tendency.

Van Riper's therapy approach has been criticised by some as being too abstract. To the extent that it deals with events which are less directly observable this may be so. There is a danger of the therapy becoming vague and mysterious if the therapist is not familiar with the rationale or the techniques. However, the procedures have been fully and clearly described (Van Riper 1973) and with this outline the programme becomes anything but abstract. The operant procedures used by many of the speak-more-fluently school give their work a more concrete appearance. There is, however, no reason why operant procedures cannot be successfully incorporated into some of Van Riper's therapy. Indeed, Ryan himself developed his traditional programme based on Van Riper's work (Ryan 1974).

In summary, it would seem that, as with the programmes of Ryan (1974) and Howie, Tanner and Andrews (1981), the therapy is successful in its own terms with many clients. However, there is a need for more objective research.

'Either/Or' or 'And/Or' — Can the Models be Combined?

The City Literary Institute in London runs four-week intensive courses for adults who stutter. Clients attend for three weeks *en bloc* and return for their final week one month later. Courses in recent years have focused on the teaching of slowed speech in a programme similar to that described earlier (Howie, Tanner and Andrews 1981). It was apparent that although most clients did well in the short term some were unable to maintain their progress. It was also apparent that when people did relapse the nature of their stuttering was often unchanged from its pre-therapy form. In addition, despite much discussion work on the course, many felt just as negative about their stuttering. Indeed, some felt worse in that they felt guilty for not controlling their stuttering more effectively. It was largely for these reasons, that in 1981 we decided to experiment with different courses. Although the research programme is incomplete, results to date are encouraging.

Clients now follow one of two programmes. The first three days of the course are seen as largely diagnostic and back-up other assessment procedures, including an initial interview, the S24 and the 'stutterer's self-rating of reactions to speech situations (Johnson, Darley and Spriestersbach 1963; (see Chapter 2). All clients spend the first three days identifying the overt and covert aspects of their stutter, as described earlier. They also follow various trial therapy procedures. For example, can they slow their speech down?, can they vary their stutter in any way?, how do they respond to voluntary stuttering? Clients are then placed in one of two groups. One group follow a Van Riper-type programme (Group I) and the other a fluency technique programme (Group II). The following criteria are used in dividing the group.

Attitude Towards Stutter. Clients who have considerable negative feeling associated with their stutter and who may have developed complex avoidance behaviours and postponing devices are more likely to join

Group I. Clients who show little avoidance with a more open attitude towards their stutters and who show more open stuttering behaviour will be likely to join Group II.

Previous Therapy. If a client has derived little benefit after considerable exposure to one kind of therapy it may indicate the need to try something else. Here we bear in mind that the same therapy undergone intensively can be successful where it failed on a once-weekly basis.

Nature of the Stutter. It is difficult to be specific but it appears that the client with an infrequent but moderate or severe stutter may do better with block modification, both because he does not need or want to change the majority of his speech and because he is likely to have increased anticipation and possibly fear and avoidance of his stutter.

Clients' Wishes. Some clients come with their therapy plan firmly in mind and will not contemplate an alternative. There may not be time to try and change these feelings but usually people are happy to join the recommended course.

Trial Therapy. As yet we are unsure what various responses indicate. An inability to use voluntary stuttering, i.e. if it becomes involuntary, may imply the need for some desensitisation. Stuttering modification therapy may be indicated if the clients' severity of stuttering is lessened by this approach during trial therapy. Slowed speech may be indicated if the client is quite easily able to achieve fluent speech using the technique, still retains some prosodic features and feels at ease with it.

Procedures

Group I follow a Van Riper type programme as described. Each client has an individual programme within this.

Group II move on to the establishment stage of a slowed-speech programme and then progress on to transfer activities. These courses incorporate desensitisation techniques and sessions planning avoidance-reduction hierarchies. Having experimented with a variety of sequencing, our feeling now is that this group too should have a period of desensitisation therapy *preceding* the teaching of a technique. Techniques such as voluntary stuttering can then be carried on throughout the programme where necessary. Goals of zero per cent SS are rarely set and the course aims to help people speak-more-fluently but to be able to tolerate and not avoid stuttering when it occurs. We do not feel that these two aims are incompatible but it is important that clients understand the rationale of the programme and know how they are to assess success in a given situation. For example, a client in this group may aim to speak fluently by controlling his stutter in situation A, but in situation B may measure success, not by whether he spoke using slowed speech, but by whether he entered the situation and spoke at all.

We have many questions at this stage. For example, how well is block modification suited to relatively short courses? We have learnt that desensitisation cannot be rushed and some clients do not enter the modification phase until the final week. How can we combine aspects of both therapies? What is the best sequence for combined therapy to follow: technique learning and then desensitisation with block modification if necessary, or desensitisation followed by slowed speech? Probably some clients do well with either therapy. The important issue now is, how can we most accurately predict the optimum therapy programme for the remainder. (For further discussion of combined therapeutic strategies see Guitar and Peters 1980.)

Conclusion

This chapter contains a sample of current techniques. No attempt will be made either to present an overall comparison of the broad approaches, or say which is thought 'better', 'more correct' or 'truer'; 'comparing therapies with differing standards for what constitutes improvement is like comparing apples and oranges — there is just no real comparability so that the effort becomes misleading and meaningless' (Sheehan 1980, p. 393).

Both approaches have achieved some success. Whilst not in favour of the use of the stutter-more-fluently approaches to the exclusion of the many good and valuable ideas that have followed them, a plea is made that they should not be washed away under the tidal wave of fluency techniques. What is now needed is a comprehensive investigation of *individuals* who have therapy for their stuttering. It is probable that some do well regardless of the type of therapy they have, while others may only respond with particular kinds of help. Journals favour group-based data and there is a need for more data to be published, but stuttering therapy now also needs to research those individuals comprising the groups. 'Client variables' including feelings about stuttering, the way the self is seen in relation to others, ideas of what being a fluent speaker is like and perception of client role in therapy, are hypothesised as being important. 'Clinician variables' are doubtless important as well. For example a therapist may be happier working within some therapeutic models than others. The list of factors is endless but in-depth case reports of both successes and failures in therapy are necessary to improve diagnosis and treatment.

It is postulated that the two opposing camps can be brought together, and further, that some clients do best with a combined approach. Gregory (1979) makes this prediction and is supported by our experience at the City Lit. and by Guitar and Peters (1980). Stuttering is a complex phenomenon — it is one name given to many different problems. Therapists who work with stutterers have a duty to be familiar with a variety of therapeutic strategies. They should be prepared to change their approach with any client if indicated. Our work on intensive courses has shown we are in a better position to prescribe an approach for each individual *after* four weeks of therapy. Although we can now select programmes more accurately, therapy is still diagnostic. Therapists need some general beliefs about stuttering and are usually happier working with stutterers if they have a rationale for whatever technique they use, based on their understanding of the problem, 'Before a clinician can begin to do stuttering therapy meaningfully he must assess his own belief about the nature of stuttering.' (Williams 1962, p. 441). If they can also see their clients as individuals with their own, unique problem; if they can take some pressure off themselves by allowing themselves not to have to know all the answers; if they can become experimenters in therapy with their clients, stuttering therapy can become an exciting challenge rather than a repetitive bore or an anxiety-provoking confusion.

George Kelly's vision of the therapeutic relationship may be an appropriate note on which to end:

'under the circumstances there is nothing for them to do except for both to inquire and both risk occasional mistakes . . . they formulate their hypotheses jointly. They even experiment jointly and upon each other . . . it is, as far as they are able to make it so, a partnership.' (Kelly 1958, p. 229).

References

Adams, M.R. (1974) 'A Physiologic and Aerodynamic Interpretation of Fluent and Stuttered Speech', *Journal of Fluency Disorders, 1*, 35-47

Andrews, G. and Cutler, J. (1974) 'Stuttering Therapy: the Relationship Between Changes in Symptom Level and Attitudes', *Journal of Speech and Hearing Disorders, 39*, 312-19

Andrews, G. and Harris, M. (1964) *'The Syndrome of Stuttering'*, Spastics Society Medical Education and Information Unit, London

Andrews,G. and Ingham, R. (1971) 'Stuttering: Considerations in the Evaluation of Treatment', *British Journal of Disorders of Communication, 6*, 129-38

—— (1972), An Approach to the Evaluation of Stuttering Therapy', *Journal of Speech and Hearing Research, 15*, 296-302

Bellack, A., Rozensky, R. and Schwarts, J. (1973), 'Self Monitoring as an Adjunct to a Behavioural Weight Reduction Program', Paper presented at the American Psychology Association Convention

Bloodstein, O. (1975) 'Stuttering as Tension and Fragmentation' in J. Eisenson (ed.) *Stuttering: A Second Symposium*, Harper and Row, New York, pp. 1-95

Boberg, E. (1980) 'Intensive Adult Therapy Program', *Seminars in Speech, Language and Hearing, 1*, 365-73

Brady, J.P. (1968) 'A Behavioural Approach to the Treatment of Stuttering', *American Journal of Psychiatry, 125*, 843-8

Cherry, E.C. and Sayers, B.M. (1956) 'Experiments upon the Total Inhibition of Stammering by External Control and some Clinical Results', *Journal of Psychosomatic Research, 1*, 233-46

Cooper, E.B. (1979) 'Intervention Procedures for the Young Stutterer' in H.H. Gregory (ed.) *Controversies About Stuttering Therapy*, University Park Press, Baltimore, pp. 63-96

Costello, J.M. (1977) 'Programmed Instruction', *Journal of Speech and Hearing Disorders, 42*, 3-28

Erickson, R.L. (1969) 'Assessing Communication Attitudes among Stutterers', *Journal of Speech and Hearing Research, 12*, 711-24

Florance, C.L. and Shames, G.H. (1980) 'Stuttering Treatment: Issues in Transfer and Maintenance', *Seminars in Speech, Language and Hearing, 1*, 375-87

Fraser, M. (ed.) (1970) *Conditioning in Stuttering Therapy: Applications and Limitations*, Speech Foundation of America, Memphis, Tenessee

—— (ed.) (1974) *Therapy for Stutterers*, Speech Foundation of America, Memphis, Tennessee

—— (1979) *Self Therapy for the Stutterer*, Speech Foundation of America, Memphis, Tennessee

Goldiamond, I. (1965) 'Stuttering and Fluency as Manipulatable Operant Response Classes' in L. Krasnar and L.P. Ullman (eds.) *Research and Behaviour Modification*, Holt, Rinehart and Winston, New York, pp. 105-56

Gregory, H.H. (ed.) (1979) *Controversies About Stuttering Therapy*, University Park Press, Baltimore

Guitar, B. and Peters, T.J. (1980) *Stuttering: An Integration of Contemporary Therapies*, Speech Foundation of America, Memphis, Tennessee

Helps, R. and Dalton, P. (1979) 'The Effectiveness of an Intensive Group Speech Therapy Programme for Adult Stammerers', *British Journal of Disorders of Communication, 14*, 17-30

Howie, P.M., Tanner, S. and Andrews, G. (1981) 'Short- and Long-Term Outcome in an Intensive Treatment Program for Adult Stutterers', *Journal of Speech and Hearing Disorders, 46*, 104-109

Ingham, R.J. and Andrews, G. (1972) 'Stuttering: A Comparative Evaluation of the Short-Term Effectiveness of Four Treatment Techniques', *Journal of Communication Disorders, 5*, 91-117

Johnson, W., Darley, F.L. and Spriestersbach, D.C. (1963) *Diagnostic Methods in Speech Pathology*, Harper and Row, New York

Kelly, G.A. (1958) 'Personal Construct Theory and the Psychotherapeutic Interview' in B. Maher (ed.) *Clinical Psychology and Personality: The Selected Papers of George Kelly*, Robert E. Knieger, New York, pp. 224-64

Knepflar, K.S. (1972) 'Voluntary Normal Disfluency: a Speech Therapy Technique for Stutterers' in G.R. Moses (ed.) *Readings in Speech Disfluency*, MSS Information Corporation, New York

Martin, R. and Haroldson, S. (1969) 'The Effects of Two Treatment Procedures on Stuttering', *Journal of Communication Disorders, 2*, 115-25

Mowrer, D. (1977) *Methods of Modifying Speech Behaviours*, Charles E. Merrill, Columbus, Ohio

Perkins, W.H. (1973a) 'Replacement of Stuttering with Normal Speech I. Rationale', *Journal of Speech and Hearing Disorders, 38*, 283-94

—— (1973b) 'Replacement of Stuttering with Normal Speech. II. Clinical Procedures', *Journal of Speech and Hearing Disorders, 38*, 295-303

—— (1979) 'From Psychoanalysis to Discoordination' in H.H. Gregory (ed.) *Controversies about Stuttering Therapy*, University Park Press, Baltimore, pp. 97-127

Perkins, W.H., Rudas, J., Johnson, L., Michael, W.B. and Curlee, R.F. (1974) 'Replacement of Stuttering with Normal Speech: III. Clinical Effectiveness', *Journal of Speech and Hearing Disorders, 39*, 416-428

Perkins, W.H., Rudas, J., Johnson, L. and Bell, J. (1976) 'Stuttering: Discoordination of Phonation with Articulation and Respiration', *Journal of Speech and Hearing Research, 19*, 509-22

Rozensky, R.H. (1973) 'The Manipulation of Temporal Placement of Self-Monitoring: Case Study of Smoking Reduction'. Unpublished paper

Ryan, B.P. (1974) *Programmed Therapy for Stuttering in Children and Adults*, Charles C. Thomas, Springfield, Illinois

—— (1979) 'Stuttering Therapy in a Framework of Operant Conditioning and Programmed Learning' in H.H. Gregory (ed.) *Controversies about Stuttering Therapy*, University Park Press, Baltimore, pp. 129-73

Schwartz, M.F. (1974) 'The Core of the Stuttering Block', *Journal of Speech and Hearing Disorders, 11*, 277-98

—— (1976) *Stuttering Solved*, J.B. Lippincott, Philadelphia

Shames, G.H. and Egolf, D. (1976) *Operant Conditioning and the Management of Stuttering*, Prentice-Hall, Englewood Cliffs, N.J.

Sheehan, J.G. (ed.) (1970) *Stuttering: Research and Therapy*, Harper and Row, New York

—— (1979) 'Current Issues on Stuttering and Recovery' in H.H. Gregory (ed.) *Controversies About Stuttering Therapy*, University Park Press, Baltimore, pp. 175-207

—— (1980) 'Problems in the Evaluation of Progress and Outcome' *Seminars in Speech, Language and Hearing, 1*, 389-401

Stunden, A.A. (1965) 'The Effects of Time Pressure as a Variable in the Verbal Behaviour of Stutterers', *Dissertation Abstracts 26*, 1784-5

Travis, L.E. (1936) 'A Point of View in Speech Correction', *Proceedings American Speech Correction Association, 6*, 1

Van Riper, C. (1939) *Speech Correction: Principles and Methods*, Prentice-Hall, Englewood Cliffs, N.J.

—— (1958) 'Experiments in Stuttering Therapy' in J. Eisenson (ed.) *Stuttering:*

A Symposium, Harper and Row, New York, pp. 275-390
——— (1971) *The Nature of Stuttering*, Prentice-Hall, Englewood Cliffs, N.J.
——— (1973) *The Treatment of Stuttering*, Prentice-Hall, Englewood Cliffs, N.J.
Webster, R.L. (1974) 'A Behavioural Analysis of Stuttering: Treatment and
  Theory' in K. Calhoun *et al.* (eds.) *Innovative Treatment Methods in Psycho-
  pathology*, John Wiley and Sons, New York
——— (1975) *The Precision Fluency Shaping Program: Speech Reconstruction for
  Stutterers*, Communication Development Corporation, Ronake, V.A.
——— (1979) 'Empirical Considerations Regarding Stuttering Therapy' in H.H.
  Gregory (ed.) *Controversies About Stuttering Therapy*, University Park
  Press, Baltimore, pp. 209-39
Williams, D.E. (1979) 'A Perspective on Approaches to Stuttering Therapy' in
  H.H. Gregory (ed.) Controversies About Stuttering Therapy, University Park
  Press, Baltimore, p. 241-68
Williams, J.E. (1962) 'Acceptance by Others and its Relationship to Acceptance
  of Self and Others', *Journal of Abnormal and Social Psychology*, *65*, 438-42
Wingate, M. (1976) *Stuttering: Theory and Treatment*, John Wiley and Sons, New
  York

5 PSYCHOLOGICAL APPROACHES TO THE TREATMENT OF STUTTERING

Peggy Dalton

At no other time in the history of stuttering therapy has it been more difficult than it is today to assign researchers and clinicians to any one school of thought, theory or practice. Up until the early 1960s, for example, we had the psychoanalytically oriented group, with their view that stuttering resulted from fixation at one or another of the stages of development outlined by Freud. For Coriat, writing in the 1920s through to the late 1940s, stuttering was without doubt an 'oral' fixation. Along similar lines, Stein (1953) discussed the problem in terms of a compulsion neurosis, with syllable repetitions representing regression to babbling, and prolongations or blocks the expression of repressed aggression. Glauber (1958) focused on the conflict between the Id and the Super-ego in his treatment, and so on. Perkins (1979), now best known for his dis-co-ordination hypothesis and his shaping procedures aimed at facilitating speech coordinations, describes himself as at one time 'aligned with the "toilet trainers" ' (p. 97). Attracted by the psychoanalytic teachings of Travis and some impressive clinical results, he and his colleagues saw psychotherapy as the obvious way to relieve the speech difficulty of one clearly suffering from an underlying neurosis.

At the same time, working along what has come to be known as 'traditional' lines, clinicians such as Johnson and Van Riper were, in Perkins' words, turning the mainstream of stuttering therapy 'into the channel of learning-to-live-with-it-successfully' (p. 97). The two opposing camps viewed each other with disapproval: the first seeing the traditionalists as too preoccupied with the symptoms of stuttering, the second rejecting the notion that people who stutter are any more neurotic than people who do not.

Then behaviourism, with its emphases on measurability, programming and data-collection, began to be applied to stuttering. Demands were made for evidence that what the psychotherapists were doing in treatment actually caused the changes in speech, when they did occur. If other sorts of behaviour could be changed by conditioning new responses with the use of carefully chosen stimuli in appropriately designed steps, why not speech? Why go through the long process of analysing early emotional conflicts which were not proveably connected with disfluency when current speech behaviour could be manipulated in the here and now? Equally, why should a stutterer seek to learn to live with his problem when 100 per cent fluency was obtainable by these new methods?

The purely psychoanalytic approach, as it stood then, could not last under such fire. But though Perkins himself turned from psychotherapy to behaviour modification during the 1960s, he admits to a suspicion that some of the psychoanalytic conceptions of stuttering are probably valid, at least for some stutterers. He has chosen to use the behavioural tools which enable even the most severe stutterers to achieve normal-sounding speech but, at the same time, he cannot align himself with those working on fluency programmes to the exclusion of concern for the stutterer's attitudes.

It will be seen from Cheasman's outline of Van Riper's more recent work (Chapter 4), that he too has developed extensively from his earlier approach. While still including analysis of the overt and covert aspects of stuttering in his treatment and seeking to help the speaker accept his disfluency initially, he makes use of modern technology (e.g. DAF), aims for changes in speech pattern in carefully planned steps and, while setting no such target as 100 per cent fluency, has clearly gone far beyond the notion that a stutterer can only learn to live with his difficulty.

So, there is no longer a psychoanalytic school, no longer pure 'traditionalism'. Have we, then, a definable group of workers who may be called 'behaviourists' in the old sense of concentrating entirely on the speech behaviour of the person with no reference to his attitudes or fears? The answer is a tentative 'yes'. Perhaps the most extreme example is found in Webster, with his highly structured Precision Fluency Shaping Program (1979). He sees no necessity for any direct work on self-concept or attitudinal changes. Pointing out the 'formidable technical problems in measuring attitudes and in determining their relationship to overt actions', he states that it is 'incumbent upon those who stress the importance of attitude change procedures to demonstrate the relationship of such procedures to the efficacy of therapeutic practice' (p. 221). He does not believe that this has been done so far and further maintains that:

'if stuttering therapy is sharp enough in its focus on speech details, properly comprehensive in its choice of physical responses to be changed and suitably administered, then the issue of attitude change as an active component in therapy may be largely tangential to the main course of treatment.' (p. 227)

Ryan (1979) and Ingham (1981), while acknowledging that psychological change does take place with changes in speech behaviour, concur with Webster in their doubts about attitude measures revealing independent factors related to behaviour change, and neither includes this aspect of the problem of stuttering in their programmes.

These workers, however, and those who adhere strictly to their programmes, are the exceptions. For the most part, behaviour modifiers in stuttering therapy have, like those in other areas of behaviour modification, moved on to include the modification of attitudes in their treatment plans. Shames and Egolf (1976) for example, in discussing operant conditionig, refer to procedures used to shape the thematic content of the client's verbalisations and thus to modify the content of the stutterer's thinking through operant principles. Gray and England (1972) have applied Wolpe's (1969) systematic desensitisation-counter-conditioning approach, in a direct attempt to reduce the affective reaction of negative emotion associated with certain speech cues.

In fact, most workers of whatever persuasion acknowledge the importance of the psychological aspects of stuttering. None would deny that, in older children and adults at least anxieties about speech situations, negative attitudes and avoidance strategies in relation to communication can play a large part in the complexity of the problem. Some focus more strongly in their treatment on these aspects than others. Some go beyond the *speaker* and are more concerned with the person as a whole. In the rest of this chapter we shall mainly consider the work of two, who perhaps exemplify a 'psychological' approach most clearly: Sheehan and Fransella. Then we shall discuss later developments of Fransella's personal construct theory approach to treatment as it is practised in Britain and elsewhere today.

Sheehan's Avoidance-Reduction Therapy

In his work and writings over more than three decades, Sheehan has developed a very powerful and clearly-defined approach to therapy for stuttering. In his exposition of his Role Therapy (1970), he can be seen to be the most extreme of the stutter-more-fluently group, referred to by Cheasman (Chapter 4), as well as the most critical of what he describes elsewhere as the 'fluency-stretching, avoidance-cultivation camp' (1980, p. 397). The main beliefs expressed in his clinical philosophy are that stuttering is a false-role disorder, whereby the person will remain a stutterer so long as he continues to pretend not to be one; that he has a choice about *how* he stutters, not as to *whether* he stutters; and that what he calls his stuttering consists mostly of the tricks and crutches he uses to conceal it. He emphasises that stuttering is something the person does, not something that happens to him and that it is within the person's own hands to learn a new set of attitudes, feelings and habits, which will enable him to become a more honest, relaxed speaker and develop 'solid fluency'.

His Basic Therapy Procedures (1970) have been evolved primarily for the adult, but he sees them as applicable, with modifications, to any stutterer who needs to be worked with directly. (For an account of his Avoidance-Reduction Therapy for Children see Sheehan 1975.) These procedures consist of a series of steps which combine the aims of acceptance of his problem by the stutterer himself, acknowledgement to others of the fact of his stuttering and, only then, of more relaxed and effective communication. His concern with exploring stuttering behaviour relates strongly to Van Riper's identification stage, discussed in Chapter 4. The attention to eye-contact, reduction of struggle and the use of appropriate pausing and phrasing is reflected in the work of many clinicians.

The most out-standing feature of Sheehan's programme, however, and the area in which he makes more demands on his clients than any other, is contained in those steps involving acknowledgement to others. The person is asked to discuss his stuttering freely with friends and strangers alike, make his stuttering a 'public event', stutter voluntarily on non-feared words. All this as an antidote to the old habits of concealment and the use of crutches. When he refers to monitoring, it is of how much the person avoids or manages not to avoid. Counting successes and failures does not relate to fluency or disfluency, but to stuttering openly as against retreating in fear. Sheehan admits that following his procedures will require a great deal of courage. He sees the group context here as a useful one, offering the support of others undergoing the same threatening adventure. It is certain, too, that the therapist needs courage and the conviction that what she is asking the client to face will not result in trauma.

While appreciating the undoubted harm that the continual practice of avoidance mechanisms will do to the self-esteem of most stutterers, the lengths to which the client is asked to go in order to overcome his fears seems completely to ignore differences in personality amongst those who stutter. To one person, the 'Gallup-type poll' approach to strangers to find out their attitudes towards stuttering, and the open display of feared behaviour might be exactly what is needed to free them from years of shame and frustration. By another, such comprehensive involvement of others might be seen as attention-seeking, socially inappropriate and against all the notions they have of shared interaction between people. Throughout his writings, Sheehan shows a deep understanding of the stutterer's situation. And yet there is a sense from him, as from many workers, that there is 'one way' of dealing with the problem for all who stutter. 'One of the beauties of avoidance-reduction therapy is that, if the person really adheres to the principles of the therapy, he cannot fail.' (1975, p. 146). He offers no alternative to those who are unable to do so.

It would be false to suggest, however, that Sheehan's only concern is with the elimination of avoidance. He acknowledges that, even when such fears of failure are overcome, there is need for further steps in therapy. In an otherwise excellent brief overview of contemporary therapies, Guitar and Peters (1980) state that all pay 'minimal attention to general communication skills' (p. 20). In saying this they do an injustice to many workers, including Sheehan. (See also the discussion in Chapter 3 and Chapter 6). Not all clinicians see their's and their client's task as completed when they are fluent or sound normal to the listener. They recognise that many people who have been disfluent for most of their lives will need to work actively to develop conversational and wider social skills in situations which they have formerly avoided or dealt with in a limited way. Sheehan sees such development as an important aspect of psychological change and cites examples similar to those quoted by Guitar and Peters, and found throughout the literature of speakers now able to say what they want to say, but lacking the experience to engage in normal social interchange.

Sheehan points out that it is not just social ineptness which might threaten the development of this new role.

'With the attainment of relative fluency and ease of communication in the speaker role, the stutterer gains strength. But in the exercise of that new-found strength he discovers and exposes other weaknesses . . . He has attained parity with normal speakers, but at the price of new competition with them' (1975, p. 174).

It is particularly when the person who stutters has seen his speech difficulty as the main reason for lack of attainment in all spheres that he is in danger of retreat to the defensive position, where the concepts of what might be possible were he fluent can again no longer be challenged.

The Stutterer as Speaker or Person?

This reference to the threat of the wider changes involved in changing speech behaviour and attitudes towards speaking brings us to one of the most important factors in therapy, which does not seem to be taken sufficiently into account by practitioners of either of the two broad approaches. In his paper, 'Facilitating Maintenance of Behaviour Change', Owen (1981), emphasises the need for placing any attempt at specific change in the context of much more wide-reaching personal adjustment.

'A specific behavioural adjustment takes place in a social context and within an individual life-style. We do not deal with addicts, alcoholics or stutterers; we deal with people whose lives are multifaceted and complex and whose specific behavioural disorder is part of an over-all pattern of behaviour, thought-processes, interpersonal relationships and environmental contingencies.' (p. 59).

Although, as quoted in Chapter 4 (p. 94) Travis long ago asserted that the 'primary concern of speech correction is the person', he expresses some limitation to his view when he goes on to say that he is not concerned with 'speech defects, but with speech defectives'. Van Riper, too, while warning the speech correctionist against thinking that he is dealing with 'stuttering' rather than with 'stutterers', is viewing the person in this one respect only – his role as a speaker.

Florance and Shames (1980), quite clearly recognise the need for attention to other than speech behaviour and one purpose in their introduction of unmonitored speech into their programme (to be discussed more fully in Chapter 7) is to help bring about a change in self-concept. They aim to develop self-regulation and the enhancement of self-esteem in their clients. Like Sheehan, they acknowledge the risks involved in change and seem to be taking a much wider view of the people they work with when they speak of unmasking 'the real person who may have been hiding from society' (p. 385). And yet, when they outline the results of their treatment, changes in self-concept are considered only in terms of speech. Clients are listed (p. 384) as:

    A. Still a stutterer
    B. No longer a stutterer — does not monitor
    C. No longer a stutterer with occasional monitoring
    D. Perceived as a stutterer who speaks fluently
    E. Perceived as a mild stutterer who exhibited mild stuttering
    F. Perceived as a non-stutterer, mild stuttering

There is some confusion as to whether the heading 'Present *Self*-Concepts', under which these are listed, is an appropriate one. The Table seems to combine both self-perception and the perception of listeners, which Florance and Shames use as a measurement of the effectiveness of their therapy. However, they do state that of 37 clients in the follow-up stage of therapy, 27 of them no longer stutter, no longer monitor and no longer see themselves as stutterers.

    Although, as we see, the emphasis in this and other studies is on the person as a speaker, this is not, of course, to suggest that these particular clinicians and the majority of therapists working with people who stutter ignore other aspects of their lives. Nor is the fact disregarded that verbal communication is involved in much that people undertake. What *is* suggested is that both changes in speech behaviour and changes in the client's concept of himself as a speaker should be related, from the beginning, to possible changes in the person's whole view of himself, other people and the world around him. Change in one area as crucial as communication will ultimately depend on a person's ability to make it compatible with his way of life as a whole. It would be of value to understand how, for example, those in the Shames and Florance study who did not stutter but still perceived themselves as stutterers differed in other respects in their views of themselves and their lives from those who neither stuttered nor saw themselves as stutterers.

The Personal Construct Approach to Stuttering

In the late 1960s and early 1970s, Fransella first developed her theory of stuttering, based on Kelly's psychology of personal constructs (Kelly 1955). Before discussing Fransella's work and comparing it with Sheehan's, it is necessary to outline briefly some of the clinical implications of Kelly's psychology. He sees a person as attempting to make sense of himself and his world through his system of personal constructs, which he has developed throughout his life from his experience of things and his interpretation of their meaning. The bipolar nature of constructs is explained in Chapter 2 and some examples given (p. 39).

Kelly is at pains to point out that construing is not the same as thinking. We construe as we see, touch, hear, smell. Our emotions are inseparably involved with thought processes in this activity and our behaviour part of the whole attempt to find some meaning in what is going on around and within us. Words such as 'strong-willed' or pleasant' are not in themselves the constructs. They are simply one communicable form through which a person may try to convey his or her understanding of something to another. Many constructs cannot be verbalised. They may have been formed before a child developed language. One pole of a construct may be more accessible than another: it may be relatively easy to elaborate one's idea of what it is like to be 'vulnerable', but hard even to put a name to its opposite or imagine how it would be if one were not vulnerable.

It is through this increasingly complex system of constructs that a person attempts to anticipate the future 'so that future reality may be better represented' (p. 49). In the corollaries to his fundamental postulate ('A person's processes are psychologically channelised by the ways in which he anticipates events.' p. 46), Kelly puts forward a series of assumptions about the nature of the personal construct system, all of which are important to the understanding of his theory. Particularly relevant here is the experience corollary, which emphasises the continuous development of the person, who changes as he or she 'successively construes the replication of events' (p. 72). Though looked at in terms of an organised structure, the personality is not static. Existing constructs may be modified, new constructs created, old ones discarded as no longer useful.

It is this capacity for change which Kelly presents as the basis of his philosophical position, Constructive Alternativism:

'We assume that all our present interpretations of the universe are subject to revision or replacement . . . We take the stand that there are always some alternative constructions available to choose among in dealing with the world. No one needs to paint himself into a corner; no one needs to be completely hemmed in by circumstances; no one needs to be the victim of his biography.' (p. 15)

In volume two of his major work (1955), Kelly focuses on psychotherapy. This view of our having the ability to shape our own destiny pervades his writing on the process of *reconstruction*. A person comes to a therapist for help, he maintains, not because he is 'sick', but because he is construing certain aspects of his life in an ineffective way. The therapist's task is to explore, with the client, the ways in which he sees himself and his situation and to discover where changes are needed and how best they might be accomplished. It will be seen from the discussion in Chapter 2 of the techniques for exploration, grids and self-characterisations, that the focus of attention is on the way in which the person is functioning as a whole. Through them, the therapist is enabled to put herself into her client's shoes, see things through his eyes and thus approach his problem in the context of an individual life-style, as suggested by Owen above. It is on these data that hypotheses are based and experiments for change set up. The therapist helps the client to plan these experiments, the client carries them out and together they consider the results, modify plans perhaps, and so move forward until the client is able to continue alone.

It is hoped that this necessarily brief reference to one or two aspects of Kelly's approach to psychotherapy will serve as a background to the following discussion of Fransella's work with people who stutter. (For more recent accounts of the application of these ideas to a wide variety of psychological difficulties see Bannister 1975; Bannister and Fransella 1980; Landfied and Leitner 1980; Epting 1981.) Further reference will be made to Kelly's ideas on the therapeutic relationship in our final chapter.

The Work of Fay Fransella

Superficially, Fransella's theory in relation to the treatment of stuttering would appear to be similar to Sheehan's, in that the stutterer's *role* as a speaker is the major focus of concern. The aim of her therapy, as in the later stages of Sheehan's, is to help the stutterer build new concepts of himself as a fluent speaker. While he tells the stutterer 'you have to accept your role as a more normal speaker' (1970, p. 194) and recognises how difficult this adjustment can be, Fransella refers to 'increasing the meaningfulness of being fluent' and goes further in her preface to *Personal Change and Reconstruction* (1972) in expressing the belief that 'It is no easier for the stutterer to act the fluent speaker than it would be for you or me to adopt the psychological posture of a person of the opposite sex' (p. v). Sheehan's therapy is action-orientated, demanding that the client go out into the world and experiment with change in order to achieve it. Fransella's approach, too, involves the client in active participation. In both cases, the emphasis of this activity is on changing perception as well as behaviour in order to free the person from the constrictions of his old role as a stutterer.

But there the resemblance ends. With his basic hypothesis that stuttering develops through the speaker's attempts to conceal his original disfluency, the major part of Sheehan's therapy is concerned with the acknowledgement, the exploration and the open revelation of disfluency. To Fransella, the focus must be on *fluency*, on 'helping the stutterer increase the implications of construing himself as a non-stutterer'. Her treatment is aimed at 'changing his personal philosophy about himself as a speaker, rather than treating his speech, since the way in which we see the world determines our behaviour towards it' (1970, p. 24).

Adopting Kelly's proposal that a person chooses for himself 'that alternative in a dichotomized construct through which he anticipates the greater possibility for extension and definition of his system' (1955, p. 64), she takes the speaker's 'stutterer . . . non-stutterer' construct and sees him as having a highly elaborated network of ideas about himself as a stutterer, being able to predict how he himself will behave in a situation, how other people will react to him, and so on, but very little knowledge of how things would be if he were fluent. The 'choice', therefore, is not based on preference in the usual sense but on familiarity as against the unknown, which is threatening, however desirable it may seem.

This idea may appear puzzling from the outside, when most people who stutter can also be fluent. But any experienced therapist will recognise that it is indeed his stuttering that the client registers, remembers and construes, not his fluent moments or periods. He can list 'easy' situations where he has little or no trouble and people who are easy to talk to, as against 'difficult' situations and people. But it is the latter which he can describe in detail. The feelings involved are vividly experienced; the physical manifestations of tension or sweating or shaking – the whole sense of being out of control. Few people who stutter, however, can describe what it feels like to be in control. Fluency is, on the whole, construed as the absence of stuttering. There may sometimes be a feeling of elation at the realisation that things are going well. But then come doubts as to whether the person can keep it up, which are followed by a return to familiar ground.

In her chapter 'A Personal Construct Theory of Stuttering' (1972), Fransella discusses how this role as a stutterer comes to be so highly elaborated. With friends, people who know more about him than just the way he speaks, with children perhaps, he can just 'be himself', with little attention to his speech behaviour. In other situations, however, where, it is harder to predict the outcome of the exchange, his attention is on himself and his difficulty. He gives himself little opportunity to construe others and only focuses on his own performance, the content of the conversation being secondary. The social event is thus narrowed down to this one issue of his ability to cope with his side of the verbal communication. And, if he has stuttered many times before in such a situation he will stutter again, because it is the only way he knows to make the outcome predictable. Thus 'a person stutters because he knows how to do it', he has construed what he does when he stutters and the reactions of others to him. He lacks the skill of fluency because he has not construed it; 'no one has told him the rules of the game' (p. 69).

Her therapy, therefore, is concerned with the person's learning those rules. He is asked to focus on situations in which he is fluent and construe himself in relation to his environment in that role; to try to put into words everything that happened — what he felt like, who else was present, what their reactions were, how he felt about them. Thus he is actively construing events which he would generally let pass and in terms wider than his own performance.

It should be pointed out that Fransella's work at this time took the form of a research project, an attempt to investigate the hypothesis that 'a stutterer's disfluencies would decrease as the meaningfulness of being a fluent speaker increased' (1972, p. 74). This imposed certain constraints on what she could do in the sessions. She could not, for example, take any active steps to increase fluency through attention to speech production. She steered clear of discussing issues not related to her primary aim. Although, as she states, in other circumstances, she would have explored, for instance, the meaning of a dream, with a client if he related it, or a reference to some difficulty with his father. In this early work, therefore, assessment procedures used were also quite specific to her purpose.

They consisted, firstly, of 'Stutterer' (S) and 'Nonstutterer' (NS) implications grids. Hayhow (Chapter 2) has described a rated grid in some detail. Here, it may be recalled, the client is asked to rate certain important people (elements), including relevant selves, on, for instance, a scale of 1-9, in relation to constructs elicited by comparing and contrasting the elements with one another in triads. For the implications grids, modified from Hinkle's original (1965) format, constructs were elicited using triads of two photographs of unknown people of the same sex as the client, plus a card on which was written either 'me as others see me

when I am stuttering' (S-grid) or 'me as others see me when I am not
stuttering' (NS-grid). The elicited constructs were then laddered (a process to be exemplified in a later section) and two additional constructs
supplied: 'like me in character . . . not like me in character' and 'stutterers . . . non-stutterers'. Finally the client was asked to focus on one
pole of each construct in turn and, scanning the rest, say which of the
poles of the other constructs was implied by the one concerned. A
method of analysis was worked out to show the relationships between
the poles of the constructs used (details of which are given in Fransella
(1972) Appendix 1) and the total number of implications taken as the
operational definition of *meaningfulness* when the two grids were compared on each test occasion.

A 'situations' repertory grid, using supplied elements such as 'talking
to a small group of strangers' and supplied constructs, such as 'situation
in which it is most likely to matter if I make a mistake' was also used,
together with self-characterisations (see Chapter 2). Additionally,
measures of disfluency and rate of utterance were taken from a series of
recordings of reading and spontaneous speech. Chapters 5 and 8 in
Personal Change and Reconstruction give a full account of these
measures and how they were presented.

Fransella's sample consisted of 16 adults, taken as they were referred
to a London hospital. As a group, with a mean total disfluency score of
42.06 per cent at first testing of spontaneous speech and a mean
speaking rate of 82.40 wpm, they can be considered 'severe' by any
standards. Taking 50 per cent reduction in disfluencies as an indication
of significant improvement, 81 per cent of the 16 improved significantly by the end of treatment. Of the 9 for whom follow-up data were
available (the interval ranging from nine months to three years), one
had become more disfluent, two maintained their improvement, the
others continued to improve, one to 100 per cent.

More rigorous measures and conditions of measurement of improvement which are currently favoured would raise a number of questions
about Fransella's methods for collecting these follow-up data (largely
by self-report). But she was not in the business, in 1972, of refining
such procedures. Of more interest is her discussion (pp. 133-4) of the
relationship between speech disfluency changes and changes on the
implications grid measures. Her basic hypothesis was that reductions in
speech disfluency would be related to increase in the meanfulness of
being a non-stutterer. Therefore, if the total number of implications
related to being a non-stutterer parallelled a decrease in disfluency, her
hypothesis has been supported, and this proved to be the case. She

also notes that there was a significant correlation between the number of NS implications on the first test session and the per cent reduction of disfluencies. Thus, 'the more the "non-stutterer" construing system was elaborated before the start of treatment, the greater was the chance of a reduction in speech errors'. This would suggest that the measures might have considerable predictive value when treatment of this kind is contemplated for a client.

In Chapter 9 (1972) Fransella presents that rarity in literature on stuttering, a full and detailed description of her work with 'Luke', one particular person involved in her research project. Based as it is on long extracts of tape-recorded sessions, interspersed with her comments on what she saw as happening in personal construct terms, it is to be recommended on many counts for the opportunity it gives us to study in depth the psychotherapeutic process as it developed. No attempt will be made to summarise the changes brought about in Luke, as it is hoped that readers will read the chapter for themselves. We can, however, extract some of the more striking aspects of her approach.

From her knowledge of his construct system, gained from the implications grids and self-characterisations and her attention to the recurring themes in his discussion of himself and the events in his life, she places her attempts at change firmly within the frame-work of this man's personal philosophy. He is, for example, deeply concerned with being considered 'worthy of respect'. In fact, he scarcely construes other people except in this way. Over many sessions this superordinate core construct (i.e. one which governs much of what he does) is gradually revised until he is able to say that he does not need respect from everyone he encounters. He comes to see how the sympathy he gains through stuttering might have become an acceptable alternative to this respect he seeks, in a situation where he cannot be sure of being 'master'.

Luke has great difficulty in construing himself as a fluent person, partly because he construes fluent people naively as able to deal with *any* situation and contrasts himself with 'the majority' in his inability to cope, for example, with refusals of help or downright rudeness. Only after some discussion of the difficulty for anyone in dealing with aggression in others does he begin to see that there are problems of interpersonal interaction quite independent of the question of stuttering. When he does begin to imagine what it will be like for him when he is fluent, it is in very over-simplified terms: 'Whenever I have something to say I'll feel completely confident' (p. 191). When challenged that as a normal human being he could not be confident all the time he can only say that he would not feel his present 'lack of confidence'. Later, however, he extends his ideas and predicts that he might become a 'chatterbox'. He sees himself as indicating some 'force of character' in his new role, able to be the kind of person who is in a position of authority — very important to him, with his concern for respect and 'status' (p. 192).

It is at this stage in therapy that Luke experiences the 'threat of fluency' referred to by a number of writers and yet never fully explained. Florance and Shames (1980) describe the stutterer as being 'overwhelmed by his expectations and ambiguities about the future' and speak of him as beginning to 'sabotage his therapy' (p. 385). Fransella sees Luke's situation in terms of Kelly's definition of threat: 'the awareness of an imminent comprehensive change in one's core structure' (Kelly 1955, p. 489). Having construed himself as a stutterer, the increase in fluency and the beginnings of his construing himself as fluent prove too much for him. He is forced to compare himself more directly with other fluent speakers and question whether he would really know how to deal with things in the way they do. He has not yet established sufficient implications of being without his speech problem to be able to face the prospect without many doubts. He therefore retreats into the 'self he knows' (p. 193).

Seen in these terms, Luke's temporary set-back of becoming more disfluent makes sense. Fransella discusses it with him and he is able to express his feeling that there is something in the 'fluent world' that he is afraid of. He is aware of the change that is taking place in him and he 'is in a personal no-man's land: he has had too much fluency to be a dedicated stutterer and not enough to be a really assured speaker' (p. 202). He reveals his very real fear that fluency will lead to uncontrolled behaviour on his part, insulting people, leading to his being disliked. He is aware of the controlling effects of stuttering and yet not ready to understand the social rules of communication which limit the verbal interactions of others. Later, he is faced with the implications of fluency in relation to his job — that other constructions would be put to the test, such as his abilities to rise in his career, and that these might prove to be invalid. He is afraid that, as he becomes more and more fluent he will become more and more 'clever' and not be happy about people's reactions to his being 'so clever and so articulate'.

We have dwelt on this aspect of the reconstruction process with Luke because it seems that here we have one of the most important features of the work needed to help a person to change in this way — attention to possible threat to his core-role construing, his essential sense of self, so evident in this case. Without such knowledge of the important issues governing a person's view of himself we cannot hope that he will simply change his behaviour. The implications of being fluent will be different for each stutterer and will not always, of course, be so alarming. But in many cases they may be seen to be equally disturbing. And unless we take account of them, bring them into the light and work through them with the client, both our efforts will be doomed to failure.

Some Recent Developments in the Personal Construct Approach to Stuttering

Despite the fact that the constraints of Fransella's research project dictated that she focus only on this change from stutterer to nonstutterer, it will be clear from these few references to sessions with Luke that this form of treatment does indeed, as she claims, go far beyond the reduction of a speech defect. A number of therapists in Britain and elsewhere have been applying the personal construct approach to stuttering since the publication of Fransella's work and the establishment of training courses in this form of psychotherapy. We have found that it enables us to relate the speech difficulty and the person's concepts of himself as a speaker, to his development as a whole. In the process of reconstruction we can draw on other roles available to him and, above all, we attempt to place the attainment of fluency in the context of what Perkins (1981) has called 'the major life goals' (p. 259) of people who stutter, in terms of personal relationships, advancement in a career or in the pursuit of some interest which might enhance an otherwise restricted life. In most cases, speech modification procedures are involved in the treatment programme, themselves speeding the process, as Fransella suggested they might. But discussion of such a combined approach and its potential for more effective maintenance will be reserved for Chapter 7.

Exploring the Person: Repertory Grids and Self Characterisations as Therapeutic Tools

A description has been given in Chapter 2 of one form of repertory grid and its contribution to assessment discussed. In this section we hope to show how such procedures may help us in our understanding of the person we are working with and indeed itself be the initiator of change.

As has been shown, in setting up a grid the client is asked first to think of significant people in his life: his parents, wife or girl-friend, a close male friend, someone he admires, feels uneasy with and so on. This very first step in the process can be revealing in itself. If a client has great difficulty in producing these elements, has no friends, cannot think of anyone he admires, feels uneasy with everyone, we already know something important about him. If at the next stage of eliciting constructs a person can only produce ideas related to himself, for instance 'is critical of my speech . . . doesn't seem to notice my speech', or 'understands my problems . . . doesn't care about me', he is in a very different position from one who construes people in terms of their own attributes as he sees them: 'organised . . . disorganised', 'has drive . . . lethargic'. The latter are, of course, important attributes to the client and may not be of significance to the people he is describing, but he is construing them in other terms than the effect they have on him.

Hinkle (1965) first introduced the 'laddering' procedure, described by Bannister and Fransella (1980) as enabling the person to 'indicate the hierarchical integration of their personal construct system' (p. 68). This has been found to provide a very direct method both for clarifying what the person means by his verbal descriptions and tapping the major themes of his construing. The following is an example of this process with a particular client:

Therapist When we were looking at some of your people you said that two of them were 'understanding and gentle' and that the third was 'an aggressive personality' Which would you prefer to be?
Client Understanding and gentle, of course.
Therapist Why?
Client Because you are more attractive to other people.
Therapist Whereas, if you are an aggressive personality . . . ?
Client You are alienating to them.
Therapist Why is it important for you to be more attractive to other people?
Client Well, then people are more comfortable in relation to you.
Therapist And if you are alienating . . . ?
Client Relationships are difficult — people are uncomfortable with you.
Therapist What's the advantage of people's being comfortable in relation to you?
Client You can get closer to them — talk about things — share private things.
Therapist Whereas if they aren't comfortable . . . ?
Client Relationships are just superficial.

Therapist Why is it important to you to get closer to people, share private things?
Client Then you're not alone, not isolated.
Therapist Which you are if relationships are superficial?
Client Yes – you are – you're isolated.

In this way, it can be seen how a more super-ordinate construct may be arrived at by tracing the meaning to a particular client of the construct 'understanding, gentle . . . aggressive personality' to that of being 'not isolated', as against 'isolated'. The theme of this person's sense of isolation was a recurring one in therapy and much of our work concerned experiments in sharing private feelings with others, being less alienating in behaviour towards them.

The rating stage of the kind of repertory grid where the client is asked to place the elements on a scale, say, 1-7 or 1-9, can also tell us something about the person. He may, for example, place everyone except himself on the preferred end of his constructs, thus presenting a picture of a world of 'good' people, with himself as the exception. Perhaps he rates cautiously on either side of the mid-point or in extremes, with people seen as either very 'successful', 'sensitive', 'generous' or extreme 'failures', highly 'insensitive', 'mean'. Where the person uses the midpoint a great deal, either for himself or a particular element, it may mean that he has difficulty construing that person or himself. This is only one possible interpretation, however, and it is for the client to say what such rating meant. Ideally, this process should be undertaken together. The client, if the therapist is present with him, may express feelings of guilt, for instance, at rating his mother low on sympathy or surprise that an element he chose as someone he dislikes is turning out as rating positively on constructs he has never thought of applying to him or her, having focused formerly only on aspects which irritate or disturb him. The last is an example of what may in itself be the beginnings of a process of reconstruction: looking at someone in a new light.

Hayhow (Chapter 2) has described the statistical analyses of repertory grid data, arrived at through these processes. How we can learn something of the structure of a person's construing; how constructs cluster together to form networks of personal meaning; how we may abstract a profile of a particular element. We can, for example, look at the relationship between the 'self now' and the 'ideal self'. The focus in this section, however, is on the potential for establishing a basis of understanding during the assessment process itself. Instead of being asked to answer 'yes' or 'no' to specific questions pre-set by the therapist, the client is enabled to present his own important issues and priorities for consideration. The therapist begins to learn the 'langguage' of his construing, what matters to him when he reflects on his life, his relationships and his view of himself.

In the same way, self characterisations are so designed as to bring out the important themes for a particular person. As he is asked to write a character-sketch of himself, with no pointers as to what he should focus on, he is free to dwell on those aspects of himself which are of real concern for him. One young man whom this author worked with wrote extensively of his academic achievement and the goals for his career with no reference, for example, to relationships with others. Another described himself only in terms of the pain his stutter caused him and how it dominated his life. A woman listed her 'faults' and 'assets'; another wrote largely of her role as a wife and mother. Self characterisations, then, as has often been said, are not tests or a method of collecting factual data for a case history, but another means through which one person may communicate with another. For someone particularly with a severe stutter, writing may be the primary channel of communication at this deeper level and furnish the person with his first opportunity to tell someone how he feels and how he sees things. Sometimes, having written in this way, a client may begin to talk about things he has never discussed before.

There are many variations on the use of self characterisation both in the exploratory phase and later on in therapy (see Fransella 1981). It is always important, for example, to discover the client's expectations of the outcome of treatment, so he may be asked to depict in writing the changes he envisages when it is over. The content may reveal expectations of a radical change from someone severely hampered by his speech problem to one who can forge ahead and conquer the world without it. Or a client may, more realistically, forsee an easing of stress in many situations, but no essential solution to the whole of life's difficulties. The therapist's major task in the first instance will be to help the person to set up for himself possibilities which are more truly within his reach. Changes in expectations during the course of treatment may also be shown in this way, when a client repeats the task after a period of work. Reference will be made in a later section to the use of such writing in the elaboration of a new role.

Not all, of course, will find the writing of these character-sketches either easy or productive. For some, writing is as difficult a task as speaking. A person may initially be anxious on many counts about committing himself to paper and so the procedure may be waived, at least for the time being. In our experience, however, once a client is assured that his hand-writing, spelling and grammar are not what we are concerned with, that what he says is entirely of his own choosing and that the content is to be treated with as much confidentiality as anything else produced in the therapy room, most people will find it a useful means of discovering where they stand in relation to their difficulties. As with setting up a grid, the processes of writing and then reflecting on the self characterisation with a therapist can help the client to elaborate his personal theories about himself and his life and, often, even at this early stage, lead to questioning of some long-held and restricting beliefs and thus to the beginnings of reconstruction itself.

How, though, may all this information help the therapist with the client to plan what moves to make in the initiation of change? Of what relevance is it to understand how someone feels in terms of achievement or what sort of relationships he wants to develop when he has come for improvement in his speech? We believe that in trying to help someone to change so significant an aspect of behaviour as the way in which he communicates, the therapist must plan according to the implications that change might have for him as a person. Where, on the one hand it is found that he already has a reasonable level of self-esteem, can elaborate his construction of himself in a range of roles and that fluency would, in his eyes, take him forward in the direction in which he is already going, then change should not only be possible, but lasting. On the other hand, if his core constructs are shown to be largely in terms of himself as a handicapped speaker, with no account taken of his functioning on other dimensions, then the process of reconstruction will need to be a slow one – a careful turning of his attention to the possibilities which lie in the aspects of himself which he is ignoring and to the construing of the people in his life in other, wider terms than how they might be reacting to him.

Two differing examples may serve to illustrate this point.* 'Eric' was a 25-year-old man involved in scientific research. At the first interview he said that although he had 'lived with' his stuttering for some years reasonably well, he now found himself unable to advance the next step in his career, which entailed teaching. He presented with moderately severe repetitive stuttering, alternating with fluent, normal-

---

*The clients concerned have agreed to some points from their initial assessments being discussed. Their real names and details which might identify them have been omitted.

sounding spells. A programme of slowed speech work ran parallel with the procedures about to be described.

As can be seen from the plotting of his grid shown in Figure 2.1 on p. 41, he construed the people he chose to include in varied terms: 'witty . . . vs boring', 'has organising ability . . . disorganised', 'has self doubt . . . not self-doubting'. Laddering revealed the recurring theme of wishing to lead a balanced life: to enjoy work but not be dominated by it, to be independent and enjoy his own company, yet seek 'fulfilling relationships' with others. He was interested to find that 'witty . . . boring' turned out to be the principal construct of the first component as shown in the grid analysis, but it was not surprising when we looked back at our laddering of that particular dimension. On the witty side the steps were: he preferred to be witty because that implied that a person was 'quick-minded', had 'fluency of expression' was 'articulate and well-read'. This was important because such a person 'can react in positive, enjoyable and fruitful ways with others', which led to 'the ability to make the most of situations' and 'live life to the full'.

He rated four selves among the elements: 'me now as a person', 'me as I'd like to be', 'me as a stutterer' and 'me fluent'. 'Me now as a person' was clearly distinguished from 'me as a stutterer', the first being mostly on the preferred side of the constructs, the second on the non-preferred side in relation to such dimensions as 'witty . . . boring', 'confident . . . lacking in confidence', 'not self-doubting . . . has self-doubt'. 'Me as I'd like to be' was fairly highly correlated with 'me now as a person', highly correlated with 'me fluent' and showed a high negative relationshipwith 'me as a stutterer'

His self-characterisation described Eric as a 'pleasant personable young man with no violent extremes of character in any direction'. This theme of one 'average' characteristic balancing with another appears throughout. Socially, he is seen as capable of mixing well, but sometimes rather withdrawn and quiet. He is 'averagely kind and even-tempered' but occasionally becomes argumentative and somewhat sarcastic. He is a conscientious worker, but not particularly original, appreciative of music and literature, but not himself very creative.

When we discussed the full findings, of which this is only a small sample, we looked, for instance, at the 'witty . . . boring' construct related to his teaching ambitions and the problems he had experienced with the few attempts he had made so far. He said that he felt he had stuttered severely because he feared above all things that he might bore the students. To him, a teacher needed to be amusing as well as knowledgeable. He felt himself to be knowledgeable but it was difficult to be amusing when your speech was hampered by disfluency.

One hypothesis which was made from this material was that, if this man was to overcome his apprehension about teaching, he needed to elaborate his view of what effective teaching comprised beyond this particular attribute. First, he was asked to build up a picture in detail of how he saw himself as conducting a lecture effectively. Not only how he would speak, but how he would interact with the students, what he saw as the most appropriate way of handling materials. The person behind the speaker was to be 'calm' and 'authoritative' without being 'dictatorial', attributes he already knew he had in other situations. He was to be attentive to the non-verbal signals from students as to whether they had understood, unflustered by the sort of 'clever character' who always tries to catch the lecturer out (something he had been thrown by earlier) and so on. Through setting up enactments involving mini-lectures to the therapist, who produced varying reactions and challenges, this 'teacher' role was elaborated behaviourally and in discussion and later tried out and validated in the real situation.

One of the key changes he had to make was in terms of the speed with which he did everything. He not only needed to speak more slowly in order to present himself as he wished, but also to pause more, give himself time to sort out his materials, respond to questions in a 'thoughtful' way, instead of feeling compelled to blurt out some answer immediately. In fact, he adopted a role which he saw as based partly on attributes which he had found attractive in people who had taught him in the past and partly on aspects of himself which he had access to in other circumstances.

Interestingly, when he came to do another grid towards the end of treatment, the construct 'witty . . . boring' was no longer used, although many of his original ones were still kept in as meaningful. Although therapy centred on this particular role elaboration, attention was also paid to certain social situations where he felt ill-at-ease and as he learned to take the focus off his own performance and relate to an event as a whole his disfluency decreased here too.

In contrast to this relatively straight-forward example, there was 'Robert'. He was a young man who had stuttered severely since the age of three. He achieved a high level of fluency on an intensive course during his last year at school. From that time on, he fluctuated between periods of fluency (during which, however, he was avoiding using the telephone and a number of other situations) and 'bad times', when he reported circumstances as overwhelming him and he found himself almost back to square one.

After a gap of three years at university he returned for individual therapy, recognising that although 'the technique' and other aspects of his course had brought about a striking change in his speech at times, his concept of himself as unable to cope remained unaltered. Any distinction between 'me now as a person' and 'me as a stutterer' was at this time unthinkable. Both emerged from his initial grid as 'getting overwhelmed by situations', being 'boring', 'inarticulate', having to 'put up a front', 'being controlled by others'.

Two major constructs seemed to stand out as the possible causes of his remaining in this unhappy position. First, he divided people between those who had 'suffered and emerged' and those who had 'not suffered'. Suffering implied being sensitive, sympathetic to the hurt in others and,, it transpired, 'responders' rather than 'expressors'. People who had not suffered were 'truly masters of their situation', could 'make people do what they want', but lacked the essential sensitivity and all it involved. 'Me fluent' stood firmly amongst this second group.

The other important dimension along which he construed the people in his life was 'roots for me obviously' as against 'will help me backstage'. They also were 'on my side from the word go' or 'put people on trial'. One way or another he saw himself as dependent on whether people helped him or not and felt deeply inadequate as a result.

His self-characterisation revealed, among other things, a major theme to do with fear of change, 'I think his life is dominated by a desire for equilibrium at all costs . . . any mention of moving or breaking the *status quo* is likely to throw him into a terrible panic . . . But the day when he will have to change will eventually arrive and this is too disturbing to contemplate at the moment.' He also wrote of his desperate need for sympathy, encouragement and love from other people, his eagerness to please them and not let them see his deep sense of inadequacy.

It was clear from all this that a great deal of work would need to be done and done slowly, in very small steps. His fear of *any* change had to be approached through experiments with minor changes at first, with little impingement on core structures — handling situations in a *slightly* different way. He needed, gradually, to see that it was possible to remain sensitive and responsive without accompanying suffering. It was necessary for him to realise that people construed him in other ways than as someone in need of help and that he could, in fact, help himself. He gradually learned through his own experience, that he could cope with responsibility and had considerable knowledge and skill to offer in relation to his job; facts which others had assumed all along. He no longer had to 'put up a front' socially, since people enjoyed his company, weren't looking for his inadequacies. All this took a long time and the work is not yet finished. He is, however, continuing to develop on his own, with occasional references back to 'report progress'. Stuttering is no longer an important issue. It occurs mildly on occasions but no longer bothers him.

Not all clients can change. Though Robert's life was initially largely governed by the fact that he was a stutterer and he expressed his fear of change, there were other resources to tap; he could find the courage to experiment and he *could* acknowledge the success of his endeavours, however cautiously at first. For another young man, who had had years of therapy of every kind, from intensive to long-term, individual to group, personal construct psychology turned out to be just another try at something new. He regarded therapy as a matter of 'the patient submitting himself to whatever treatment the therapist thinks best', and although he expressed interest in a process which was to be more in the nature of a partnership, he could not follow it through.

He had some very powerful constructs about personal development: enthusiasm, excitement, belonged to childhood. Adults had to keep all emotions, every aspect of behaviour under firm control. People were 'set' by the age of 20, if not before. He experienced extreme anxiety when faced with anything he could not predict and pin down and had organised a life that was ordered and restricted and therefore just manageable. Change of any kind threatened chaos. Although continuing to seek help, he expressed this in terms of a duty. He had no real hope. An approach, therefore, with its emphasis on active participation and change was no use to him.

The Reconstruction Process: Some Examples from Individual Therapy

Some single-case studies are in preparation, showing the therapeutic process in detail with a number of clients. In this section we can only hope to give a few examples to illustrate some of the potential of the personal construct stance towards change.

Reconstruing Situations. As has been indicated throughout this chapter, many people who stutter predict certain events in terms which seem to leave them no option as to how to behave in relation to them. They are stressful, are approached with extreme apprehension and the only possibility seems to lie in going into the same routine of stuttering their way through, if they go through them at all. As we have said, the focus is entirely on the person's speech performance.

One line of work which is useful for many clients, therefore, as suggested by Fransella, is to widen the person's view of these events and extend the focus of attention beyond himself. For instance, one client described as 'ridiculous' the state of panic which overtook him when going into a particular stock-room to ask for something as simple as a box of nails. Taking him through the event moment by moment revealed that he had a vidid impression of himself walking down the corridor, every muscle tensed, rehearsing the request, then seizing the door-handle, hurling himself through the doorway and standing paralysed as a face looked up at him and asked eagerly 'Can I help you?' He had only the haziest idea of what the room was like, could not say for sure what other people were generally there. And as for the face – it belonged to a female, certainly, but that was all he could say. On reflection, he decided that it was the immediacy and inevitability of that question of hers which he dreaded, since it seemed to demand an immediate response. This he knew he could not make, just as he had known he cold not answer when 'pounced on' at school.

Even in the process of describing what went on, it was clear to him that there must be some other way of handling it. It had proved useless for him to tell himself 'use your technique'. He had to reconstrue the event in much broader terms and on many different levels. The first change suggested was a very simple one: he was to walk down the corridor as if he were strolling in the park, open the door quite slowly, pause while he closed it behind him and simply smile at the girl in response to her question before he answered. We rehearsed this together. When he tried this at work, his heart still thumped, he still stuttered when he spoke, but felt more in control because he had changed something. The next step was to stay in the stock-room, look around to take in what it was like, observe the girl if he could and see whether he was able to describe her. This too he managed and his staying in the room led to a conversation with her. Next time he was able to greet her as someone he 'knew', relax with her, find out something about her, tell her something about himself, and he was fluent, as he usually was with friends. He later used this approach as a model for dealing with other situations.

'Reconstruction' may seem a ponderous term for what was occurring here. And anyone looking for a sharp distinction between behaviour modification and change of attitude, or wondering what all this has to do with Kelly's theory may well be somewhat confused. We have said, however, that Kelly does not split a person's processes into behaviour, thinking, feeling and the rest. In changing this event from one narrowed down to an automatic response to a threatening stimulus, this man brought into play his capacity for choice about the way he moved, touched, perceived visually and aurally. He was able, gradually, to relate to another as the 'friendly', 'easy-going' person he knew himself to be, not just to stutter. He allowed her to become a person, not simply a threat. Instead of being overwhelmed by the one emotion of fear, there was space in him for whatever shifts of feeling usually occur when two people communicate with each other. Thus the change in experience for him can be seen to be a total thing, involving the whole of him. That is reconstruing.

Construing others: the establishment of role relationships. In the previous example, we touched on an aspect of change which may apply to many people in many kinds of difficulty. When a person is turned in on himself and approaches life through his 'problem', he often fails to establish relationships because he simply cannot raise his head and find out what others are like. In his 'sociality corollary', Kelly (1955) looks at relationships from a particular stand-point: 'to the extent that one person construes the construction processes of another, he may play a role in a social process involving the other person' (p. 95). Relating to others, then, involves construing how they construe things. Learning from listening, looking, sensing how they view their worlds. This is how we come to 'know' people. If we are solely concerned with our own processes, we cannot know others or form relationships.

There are many people who have difficulty relating in this way. Many who stutter do not have this problem. Some, however, do. And part of therapy may be aimed at helping them to construe others more fully, instead of making assumptions about what they are thinking, feeling and so on. These assumptions may be restricted to what is believed to be the other's reaction towards the person concerned and if these are seen to be only as judging or criticising or rejecting, then there is no possibility of a real meeting. It is rare for anyone to construe *all* people in this way, but it is not uncommon for most of us at some time to restrict our view of certain figures in our lives to these self-related constructs. Some stutterers have particular difficulty in widening their range of perception of people. Those, for example, 'in authority'. If the stutterer feels deeply inadequate, then an even more super-ordinate construct such as 'superior' may subsume those in authority, from the boss to the ticket collector, anyone who is a success, anyone who can express themselves well, with the person himself largely isolated on the 'inferior' pole.

The last is an extreme example but may have a familiar ring to some readers. In most cases, where someone feels unable to cope in communication with another, he has come to construe him only as threatening because he represents some past experience which was painfully vivid and he has not been able to free himself from the old attitude of fear or helplessness. He behaves, to some extent, as he originally behaved and until he can step back and view the other person through the wider range of constructs which he applies elsewhere, he will continue to replicate the same pattern.

One particular client found the experiment of deliberately setting out to construe the construction processes of others especially rewarding. She recognised that she was ill at ease with many people, mainly because she was wondering all the time what they were thinking about her. So she set about listening attentively to what they were saying, observing their non-verbal behaviour. She found that they became more real to her, felt that she understood them better and, as an unlooked-for by-product, they seemed to warm towards her, responding to the attention she was paying them. One of her most worrying constructs about herself was that she was 'unapproachable'. Now she could begin to feel that people might want to come closer to her. This did not solve all her problems and was only one part of the work she needed to do, but it proved to be a major step in her development.

Elaboration of the Self. We have touched on the usefulness of elaborating other roles than that of speaker or, more narrowly, stutterer. 'Roger' became very interested in this notion and asked to rate a grid including as elements 'self as writer', 'self as father', 'self at work', 'self as friend', as well as 'self naturally fluent', 'self as stutterer' and 'self controlling speech'. This last element evolved through writing beyond the issue of speech control into The Sea-Captain — a kind of ideal self towards which he wanted to work:

> He steers a course through natural obstacles; knows the elements like the back of his hand — a combination of knowledge and intuition; is in command of what goes on; can give orders to other people, but can also listen and be friendly; is respected; is self-sufficient and doesn't mind what others think of him; ambitious, but has his own goals; goes beyond everyday experiences and comes back wiser from them; cares for other people; has a sense of humour.

Others have worked in a less complex way on filling out their definitions of themselves in various life roles, which seems to help some to place the stutterer in a more peripheral position and allow other aspects of themselves to assume more significance in their dealings with the world.

The Range of Personal Construct Psychology in its Application to Therapy for Stutterers

Therapists who have only come across Kelly in psychology textbooks have expressed concern that this approach can only have relevance to the adult 'intellectual' client. Largely, perhaps, because of the complexity of his theory and Kelly's unfamiliar use of language, the impression is that the client himself has to struggle with Constructive Alternativism, to cogitate on what he simply thought was his firm belief in independence in terms of super-ordinacy or permeability or whatever. But just as clinicians using operant procedures would not, generally speaking, go into the finer points of positive vs negative reinforcement, so the personal construct therapist will use as guidelines the professional constructs defined by Kelly and modify her presentation of techniques to suit the interests and needs of the client. Exploration of the kind suggested can proceed and reconstruction be embarked upon without a mention of a construct or an element or a single reference to psychological processes or core roles.

In various therapeutic fields the personal construct approach is being used to help children in difficulty (see, for example, Ravenette 1977, 1980). A number of speech therapists are now bringing the ideas and exploratory procedures developed by Ravenette, Salmon (1970, 1976) and others into their therapy to enhance their understanding of the young people they are working with. It has been found, too, that some parents are willing and interested to be involved in this aspect of their child's treatment and can gain through it a fuller understanding of the child as a whole and the nature of his problem. Communication between parent and therapist can take many forms other than the giving and receiving of information and advice. Some case studies are currently in preparation which describe in detail a treatment programme combining personal construct and speech modification procedures with children.

Another doubt expressed by many therapists, inexperienced in this approach to work with either children or adults, is that we are dabbling in areas which do not come within the province of a speech clinician. It is our belief, however, that the *person* is our province. If we are to help him or her, child or adult, the more we understand of the way in which an individual's world is construed, the more likely we are to be able to suit the therapy we offer to particular needs. Conversely, we are less likely to impose our own beliefs and models of improvement. When we facilitate the expression of personal feelings and ideas we are doing so because the client has indicated to us that he wishes to share them with us. If he chooses to confine the dialogue to speech issues, there is no question of probing into his privacy. In many cases, however, it is the client's choice to relate his anxieties about stuttering to the effects it has on much of his life. The question of whether a particular therapist is prepared to work with clients in areas other than speech is also a matter of choice — hers. This point will be discussed further in Chapter 9.

Change of Attitude or Psychotherapy?

In his book *Controversies About Stuttering Therapy*, Gregory (1979) presents a number of issues to the contributors for consideration. Two of them are worded as follows: 'Attitude Change: what is it and is it needed?' and 'Psychotherapy for stutterers: what is it and is it needed?' (p. 1.). This wording seems to imply that there is a sharp distinction between the two. Most of the authors respond with the same implication. Attitude change is regarded either as something the clinician allows to occur naturally or something which is worked for deliberately. Psychotherapy, on the other hand, is set apart by the majority of the contributors as an unnecessary aspect of treatment for stuttering and not the province of the speech therapist. Williams (1979) in his response to Gregory's question, does point out that the psychotherapists' major goal 'is to help resolve human interpersonal and intrapersonal difficulties' (p. 260) and sees this goal as not too different from that of the speech clinician. However, he still regards problems other than those directly related to speech as needing referral to psychotherapy and mentions occasions when he has worked with clients at the same time as they have been receiving psychiatric assistance.

It is Sheehan (1979) who links 'attitude work' and supportive therapeutic functions with psychotherapy, and warns that we should not 'pass the buck too readily to those in allied fields' (p. 193). He suggests for the future that some speech clinicians might become specialists in treating people who stutter, with added psychological training relevant to that role (a point which will be taken up in Chapter 9). He clearly does not see those in need of psychotherapeutic help as 'neurotic' or 'psychologically sick'. Nor, it may be added, do many others practising psychotherapy developed more recently than traditional psycho-analysis, such as that of Rogers (1951) and Ellis (1962). Kelly saw people in need of help as construing certain aspects of their lives in an ineffective way, leading to distress or causing an obstacle to development. Looked at in this way, psychotherapy takes on a very different meaning. And how it differs from 'change of attitude' it is hard to see.

References

Bannister, D. (1975) 'Personal Construct Theory Psychotherapy' in D. Bannister (ed.), *Issues and Approaches in the Psychological Therapies*, J. Wiley, New York, pp. 127-46

Bannister, D. and Fransella, F. (1980) *Inquiring Man* (2nd Edn), Penguin, Harmondsworth

Ellis, A. (1962) *Reason and Emotion in Psychotherapy*, Lyle Stuart, New York

Epting, F.R. (1981) 'An Appraisal of Personal Construct Psythotherapy' in H. Bonarius, R. Holland and S. Rosenberg (eds.) *Personal Construct Psychology: Recent Advances in Theory and Practice*, Macmillan, London pp. 189-210

Florance, C.L. and Shames, G.H. (1980) 'Stuttering Treatment: Issues in Transfer and Maintenance', *Seminars in Speech, Language and Hearing, 1*, 375-88

Fransella, F. (1970) 'Stuttering: Not a Symptom But a Way of Life', *British Journal of Disorders of Communication, 5*, 20-9

—— (1972) *Personal Change and Reconstruction*, Academic Press, New York

—— (1981) 'Nature Babbling to Herself' in H. Bonarius, R. Holland and S. Rosenberg (eds.), *Personal Construct Psychology: Recent Advances in Theory and Practice*, Macmillan, London, pp. 219-30

Glauber, I.P. (1958) 'The Psychoanalysis of Stuttering' in J. Eisenson (ed.), *Stuttering: a Symposium*, Harper and Row, New York, pp. 71-119

Gray, B. and England, G. (1972) 'Some Effects of Anxiety Deconditioning upon Stuttering Frequency', *Journal of Speech and Hearing Research 15*, 114-22

Gregory, H.H. (1979) *Controversies About Stuttering Therapy*, University Park Press, Baltimore

Guitar, B. and Peters T.J. (1980) *Stuttering: An Integration of Contemporary Therapies*, Speech Foundation of America, Memphis, Tennessee

Hinkle, D.E. (1965) 'The Change of Personal Constructs from the Viewpoint of a Theory of Implications', unpublished PhD thesis, Ohio State University

Ingham, R. (1981) 'Evaluation and Maintenance in Stuttering Treatment' in E. Boberg (ed.) *Maintenance of Fluency*, Elsevier, Amsterdam, pp. 179-218

Kelly, G.A. (1955) *The Psychology of Personal Constructs*, Norton, New York

Landfield, A.W. and Leitner, L.M. (1980) *Personal Construct Psychology, Psychotherapy and Personality*, J. Wiley, New York

Owen, N. (1981) 'Facilitating Maintenance of Behaviour Change' in E. Boberg (ed.) *Maintenance of Fluency*, Elsevier, Amsterdam, pp. 31-70

Perkins, W.H. (1979) 'From Psychoanalysis to Discoordination' in H.H. Gregory (ed.) *Controversies About Stuttering Therapy*, University Park Press, Baltimore, pp. 97-127

—— (1981) 'Measurement and Maintenance of Fluency' in E. Boberg (ed.), *Maintenance of Fluency*, Elsevier, Amsterdam, pp. 147-78

Ravenette, A.T. (1977) 'Personal Construct Theory: An Approach to the Psychological Investigation of Children and Young People' in D. Bannister (ed.) *New Perspectives in Personal Construct Theory*, Academic Press, New York, pp. 251-80

—— (1980) 'The Exploration of Consciousness: Personal Construct Intervention with Children' in A.W. Landfield and L.M. Leitner (eds.), *Personal Construct Psychology, Psychotherapy and Personality*, J. Wiley, New York, pp. 36-51

Rogers, C. (1951) *Client-Centred Therapy*, Houghton-Mifflin, Boston

Ryan, B.P. (1979) 'Stuttering Therapy in a Framework of Operant Conditioning and Programmed Learning' in H.H. Gregory (ed.), *Controversies About Stuttering Therapy* University Park Press, Baltimore, pp. 129-73

Salmon, P. (1970) 'A Psychology of Personal Growth' in D. Bannister (ed.), *Perspectives in Personal Construct Theory*, Academic Press, New York, pp. 197-221

—— (1976) 'Grid Measures with Child Subjects' in P. Slater (ed.), *Explorations of Intrapersonal Space*, J. Wiley, New York, pp. 15-46

Shames, G.H. and Egolf, D. (1976) *Operant Conditioning and the Management of Stuttering*, Prentice-Hall, Englewood Cliffs, N.J.

Sheehan, J.G. (1970) *Stuttering Research and Therapy*, Harper and Row, New York

—— (1975) 'ConflictTheory and Avoidance-Reduction Therapy' in J. Eisenson (ed.), *Stuttering: a Second Symposium*, Harper and Row, New York

—— (1979) 'Current Issues on Stuttering and Recovery' in H.H. Gregory (ed.) *Controversies About Stuttering Therapy*, University Park Press, Baltimore, pp. 175-207

—— (1980) 'Problems in the Evaluation of Progress and Outcome', *Seminars in Speech, Language and Hearing, 1*, 389-401

Stein, L. (1953) 'Stammering as a Psychosomatic Disorder', *Folia Phoniatrica, 5*, 12-46

Webster, R.L. (1979) 'Empirical Considerations Regarding Stuttering Therapy' in H.H. Gregory (ed.), *Controversies About Stuttering Therapy*, University Park Press, Baltimore, pp. 209-39

Williams, D.E. (1979) 'A Perspective on Approaches to Stuttering Therapy' in H.H. Gregory (ed), *Controversies About Stuttering Therapy*, University Park Press, Baltimore, pp. 241-68

Wolpe, J. (1969) 'Behaviour Therapy of Stuttering: Deconditioning the Emotional Factor' in B. Gray and G. England (eds.) *Stuttering and the Conditioning Therapies*, Monterey Institute for Speech and Hearing, Monterey, California

6 GROUP THERAPY WITH ADULTS

Celia Levy

Introduction

Group therapy has become an accepted and often preferred form of treatment for adults who stutter. Although the literature on stuttering is full of references to group work, few writers have elaborated on the processes involved in group therapy. Many speech therapists have few resources in either their training or the literature if they want to become skilled group therapists. This has often resulted in stuttering groups becoming an economical extension of individual therapy without the special properties of the group being fully mobilised.

Speech therapists are generally trained in the skills of facilitating fluency, with this being their major contribution to those who stutter. Yet, once operating in the field, where they are confronted with instant successes and almost as many instant relapses, many therapists become aware that stuttering is often more than just a speech problem. Therapy then involves helping the stutterer change both his speech and his perspective of himself and others.

Therapy with adults who stutter draws upon a multitude of techniques from a number of disciplines. The group situation is a very special enterprise in which the *person* who stutters participates, and not merely his stuttered speech. In the hands of a skilled therapist it provides a powerful means of facilitating both speech and psychological change.

Functions of Group Therapy

Therapists who work with adults who stutter are called upon to direct their efforts towards both the speech and the well-being of their client. Different techniques adapt more readily to the group or individual situation, and will be evaluated with this in mind in a later section. In an ideal world, the adult who stutters would be offered both individual and group therapy, each being directed at different aspects of the presenting problem. However, such facilities are rarely available, and there are many reasons why group therapy may be an appropriate choice for treatment.

Both Sheehan (1970) and Fransella (1972) emphasise that stuttering in adults usually occurs in communicative situations where other adults are present. 'Since stuttering is an interpersonal, self-presentation disorder and occurs in a social context, group therapy is a natural choice for adults'. (Sheehan 1970, p. 297).

Groups can often achieve more, more quickly than is possible in inividual therapy. Feelings of isolation are speedily reduced when the person meets others with similar problems. It is important to emphasise that the commonality thus achieved may have little to do with discovering that others stutter in the same way, but rather that others have similar feelings about it.

On this theme, Barbara (1965) points out that the group creates a situation 'in which the stutterer is brought face to face with himself and experiences himself as he really is and how he may appear to other members of the group' (p. 171). While this can be threatening to the individual who does not like the feedback he receives from the group, it can also promote feelings of understanding, of being understood, and of support through identification with other members.

Once group members start to relate to each other more meaningfully, they begin to view other members as people, rather than as stutterers. This may cause an individual to reappraise his view of himself, and to feel more like a human being and less like 'just a stutterer'.

Members learn to give honest, but sensitive feedback to each other. This can speed up the process of change by virtue of the fact that it is given directly after a new behaviour is tested by a group member. Collecting evidence that the new behaviour is a success outside therapy is often complicated by the ambiguity of the messages received. In the group, members can be given responsibility for providing each other with accurate feedback. Learning to evaluate the outcome of another's experiment can prove invaluable in the process of learning to evaluate one's own behaviour. In this way, the group can facilitate the process of each member becoming his own therapist (Van Riper 1973). The group situation is also helpful to the individual who is finding change difficult. The realisation that others also have problems, albeit not the same ones, can encourage more self-acceptance (Barbara 1965).

The group can also be a creative medium. Eight heads may be more resourceful than two when considering a problem from alternative positions. By simply encountering such a variety of views, the individual's horizons may be considerably expanded.

Where members contribute to one another in this way the group serves another important function in providing 'an opportunity for the client to disperse his dependencies at an early stage of therapy' (Kelly 1955, p. 1158). While dependency is not in itself a bad thing, too much dependency on one person, for example the therapist, may imply a long-term commitment to therapy. The person who functions optimally has well-dispersed dependencies, and the group as therapist facilitates this process.

There are, of course, disadvantages and difficulties associated with group therapy. Sheehan (1970) points out that a group is as good as its membership. It can be severely limited by members who are selfish, or who are destructive in the feedback they offer. It may be composed of members who have little or nothing in common, and the only reaction elicited is boredom. There are often more deep-seated reasons for boredom, which are time-consuming to unravel. A person may, for example, see himself as very different from all other 'stutterers' and therefore disclaim having anything in common with other members of the group. In fact, this person is probably finding the group very threatening, and a show of boredom may be an easy way of coping with this.

Other members may find themselves out of their depth in a group and feel unable to contribute to and interact with the rest. While some people may learn and change by listening, this is not the case for everybody. When a member thinks that he has little to offer the group, this can arouse feelings of inadequacy, of inferiority. It is likely that these feelings occur in situations outside the group, and that his negative view of himself has once again been confirmed by being exposed to group therapy.

There is also the danger that a person may become 'hooked' on group therapy. He may become too dependent on the group as the only place where he feels an equal person and may look to the group for friends and a social life. While this may be confidence-building in the short-term, if this setting becomes an exclusive source of relationships in the long-term, a new problem may have been created.

Group Therapists

The most important single variable affecting success in the treatment of stutterers is *the clinician* (Murphy & Fitzsimmons 1960, p. 27). Many therapists may feel that the opposite is equally true: that their success with a stutterer depends largely on the sort of person he is.

While some clients do seem more suited to work with particular thera-pists rather than others, it is still an important responsibility of the clinician to develop the expertise to deal with many adults who stutter. As a profession, we need to ask ourselves what these skills are and how we can set about acquiring them.

Van Riper (1975) has written an excellent account of the skills and qualifications of 'The Stutterers Clinician' (pp. 455-92), which is dis-cussed in the final chapter of this book. Sheehan (1970) has attempted to describe the group therapist suited to working with stutterers. He emphasises the dual task of the therapist in working with both feelings and stuttering behaviour. The therapist 'needs to be highly permissive on the feeling level, without being completely permissive or casual on the doing level' (p. 297). He points out the dangers of being too dominant a force in the group, and conversely how lack of leadership can divert the group from the task at hand. Different styles of leader-ship are important determinants of group functioning. An important series of studies conducted by Lewin, Lippitt and White (1938, 1939, 1953, reported in Heap 1977) investigated the effects of three styles of leadership.

Authoritarian leaders produced more work in less time, but evoked aggression, competitiveness and hostility. Originality was inhibited and dependence on the therapist stimulated. In stuttering groups this style of leadership is fairly typical of the very strict therapist who teaches a fluency technique within a behavioural model. To fulfil the role of an authoritarian leader, the therapist assumes all responsibility for monitoring speech, structuring activities and does not really allow the group as such to function. While much is achieved in the early stages, later the group may have to be weaned off the reinforcing effect of the therapist. In such groups, we find that stutterers have difficulty taking responsibility for their speech outside therapy, and certainly few challenge the therapist's judgement. The therapist's seeming com-petence and confidence can be inspiring to an anxious and sceptical group, but this increased dependence on the leader and not on the group may result in decreased individual autonomy in the long term, which seems to be an important issue in the maintenance of fluency. This style of group management seems very limiting.

Democratically led groups are initially less productive, but this improves once relationships between members and the leader have been cemented. Members show satisfaction with their achievement and use their resources well.

Democracy is difficult to achieve in stuttering groups, where the therapist is frequently cast in the role of 'saviour'. We have found that by honestly declaring that we do not possess any solutions to their stuttering problems, but are prepared to commit ourselves to a joint venture of exploration to find a solution, we set the right tone. A useful feature of trial therapy (Chapter 4), apart from the information it provides the therapist, is to give each person the feeling that if they can vary their speech pattern, they have choice and control over speech production. This is probably in direct contrast with feelings of loss of control when stuttering. We ask our groups to research in turn the effects of slowing down, whispering, shadowing, flow and many other possible techniques. Then we ask groups to suggest their own ideas for varying speech production, and as a result have seriously investigated the influences of shouting, reading backwards and singing, on fluency. It is doubtful that such 'research' has pushed back the frontiers of stuttering therapy, but such activity seems to stimulate curiosity and excitement. It cultivates an interest in why some techniques work better for some people and not for others. In this way our group members help to choose their route to fluency, and this seems to effect a lasting spirit of democracy in the group.

It is important to note that democracy does not imply lack of leadership. The therapist still has a responsibility to direct the group towards its goals, and if she can establish an atmosphere of shared effort, it is likely that the group will make full use of its potency.

Laissez-faire leadership generally results in less productivity than the two styles of leadership discussed above. Where the therapist plays no role in leadership and throws over all the choices to the group as to their aims and means of achieving these, the result is often lengthy discussions about what should be done and by whom. Stuttering groups left to their own devices will generate ideas about practising fluency techniques and suggest various possible activities, but unless someone assumes the leadership role, the group never gets off the ground. Having a leader seems to be an important determinant of the achievement potential of the group. Where the therapist does not assume the role of leader, group members soon become discouraged, perhaps even angry, and may leave the group.

Heap (1977) discusses two further qualities of successful leaders. The first is maturity, which the leader demonstrates by being sensitive to the needs of the group; sensitivity implies the ability to step momentarily into the shoes of the client and to view the situation from his position. This requires of the clinician the ability to listen to *what* the client says, to understand the *meaning* the experience has for him and the *feelings* they arouse in him (Rogers 1970, p. 53).

The second quality combines the instrumental and integrative functions of leadership. The instrumental function serves the purpose of achieving the aims of the group by direction. However, unless relationships in the group are fairly positive, little is likely to be achieved. This then is the integrative function of the therapist. Evidence of identification and support indicate that the group is knitting together. The therapist can test for identification by asking the rest of the group if anyone feels similarly on an issue raised by one member. For example, if one member discloses feelings of shame and guilt linked to stuttering, the therapist can ask if anyone else in the group has ever felt that way, or understands why someone might feel that way about stuttering. Usually replies to such enquiries are supportive and understanding. By opening a discussion around a personal disclosure, the therapist will also be reducing the amount of risk for any group member who wishes to share feelings or painful memories with the group. The sense of isolation is also diminished by these means and the purposes of integration further served.

The credibility of the therapist is important: the feeling that her experience and understanding of stuttering is valued by the group. To this end, the therapist should possibly test activities or techniques herself before recommending that group members try them. The willingness on the part of the therapist to share these experiences can serve to bridge the gap between a group of stutterers and a fluent therapist. Therapists need to be able to be themselves, to show their essential humanness. However, Barbara (1954) and Rogers (1970) agree that the group is not the place where the therapist should attempt to resolve her own problems. She should be aware of any difficulties in herself and attempt to ensure that they do not interfere with the constructive work of the group. Rogers does add that on occasion a therapist can help a group by sharing a personal experience. Where this is chosen as an appropriate tactic and for good reasons, self-disclosure can be useful.

Group therapy can be extremely demanding of the clinician and supervision in the case of an inexperienced therapist can be of great value. Co-counselling with colleagues may be useful for those with longer experience.

Selection of Group Members

In any speech therapy unit where group therapy is not the only form of treatment available, some form of selection of members will be used. Berne (1966) points out two different problems in selection: deciding which people are suitable for group therapy and, of these, deciding who should join a specific group.

For Whom Group Therapy?

We at the City Lit. have, over the years, used various criteria to select suitable candidates for group therapy. It is doubtful whether our intuitive procedures would stand up to the rigors of research. There do not appear to be any hard and fast rules for group membership selection, but rather a few trends in our selection procedures that have emerged over the years.

(1)   *Overall psychological stability*. It is advantageous if the person undertaking group therapy is in a reasonable frame of mind. It is up to the group leader to decide whether or not an individual is too disturbed or too depressed to participate meaningfully in a stuttering group. Further, if stuttering seems to be the person's least important problem, it may be wise to postpone group therapy. A person might, for example, be in the middle of a divorce, or be depessed after a bereavement, or be preparing for exams, etc. The likelihood that these external factors will distract the stutterer from the demands of therapy needs to be carefully discussed and evaluated individually. Where intensive group therapy is recommended, these influences can be particularly disruptive and should be taken into account before deciding on the dates for a course.

(2)   *Previous speech therapy*. For the adult who has had little or no stuttering therapy, a group may be inappropriate. The person may be unable to predict his feelings about the group situation, because he has no real idea of what speech therapy involves. Some preparation may be all that is needed.

(3)   The *very anxious client* who does not want to work in a group should not be forced into this situation. Sometimes a therapist has worked at great length with such a person, and feels that a group would now be helpful. This is a somewhat different matter and can be tackled directly with the client.

A Group, For Whom?

There is much controversy in this area where members are selected to join a specific group. Shames (1953) found that if the individuals in a group resemble each other in age, education, sex, socioeconomic level, type of speech problem, types of social and psychological difficulties, they will attain greater success than groups differing widely on these factors. Miele (1962) felt that homogeneity in terms of the speech problem is essential, but that heterogeneity of other factors was desirable. Fawcus (1970) supports this point of view. Working in an adult education institute, we have been constrained by a lower age limit of 18 years, but we have never set an upper age level. We believe that maturity is an important issue in terms of readiness for a group.

No member should be a conspicuous isolate, i.e. the only woman, the only mild stutterer or the only unskilled worker (Walton 1971). In selecting group members, Walton suggests that the 'Noah's Ark principle' be followed. We have taken this principle further and have experimented with separating the more severe stutterer from the essentially fluent, covert stutterer in our weekly group sessions. This has helped establish cohesion in the group in the early stages, because members find a common identity.

Selecting the Aims of the Group

A previous chapter deals at length with the various techniques currently thought to be effective in the treatment of stuttering (Chapter 4). Different techniques appear to adapt more or less readily to group vs individual therapy, and intensive vs non-intensive therapy.

Group vs Individual Therapy

Fluency techniques such as prolonged speech are very easily taught and maintained in the group situation. Group members can be 'programmed' through the talking speeds from 40 syllables per minute to their own comfortable level. The emphasis remains on fluency and all members know the rules whereby fluency is attained. This helps members of the group to assume responsibility for monitoring each other's speech, and leaves the therapist free to help each member refine his technique towards a normal-sounding pattern. The establishment phase of therapy is relatively quick and members are soon able to discuss 'the broader issues' fluently. Many people who stammer find talking in groups somewhat more difficult than on a one-to-one basis. The group can therefore provide a very useful setting for the first steps in transferring fluency to increasingly difficult situations. Teaching a fluency technique to an individual can be fairly tedious work without the variety of the group, although it is relatively easily accomplished.

The 'block modification' techniques of Van Riper (1973) and 'avoidance-reduction therapy' of Sheehan (1970, 1975) are more difficult to adapt to a group led by a single therapist. The emphasis of these approaches is, in the former case, on the individual nature of each person's stutter, and, in the latter, on his efforts to conceal it. Identification of these behaviours and issues can be a time-consuming process in a group situation. However, despite these drawbacks group members can gain considerable insight into each other's speech by sharing such a process and this then serves as an excellent basis for monitoring one another at a later stage in therapy.

Van Riper's desensitisation phase creates similar problems. Each member needs to be desensitised to different aspects of their problem. However, this can be worked around and the group turned to advantage by virtue of the variety of people present. This can, for example, be useful when desensitising members to feared listener reactions. Once the modification phase is reached, the group situation is easily managed. Each member may be using slightly differing techniques but the group is usually able to deal with this.

Both Sheehan and Van Riper's techniques are ideally suited to individual therapy where the depth of the exploration is not constrained by the demands of the other members, but as pointed out earlier, this type of therapy would achieve maximum effectiveness if both group and individual sessions were available to each member.

Intensive vs Non-Intensive Therapy

The teaching of a fluency technique with the emphasis on establishing a new pattern of speech is generally easily achieved in intensive therapy. It would seem that working intensively has distinct advantages over a non-intensive approach in that the tedious early stages pass quickly. Once fluency has been established, more interesting and challenging work can be tackled. There are, however, inherent disadvantages as Helps and Dalton (1979) have pointed out. Their research demonstrated that without adequate follow-up therapy, fluency attained on the course is difficult to maintain. We now generally do not accept people for intensive courses at the City Lit. if maintenance therapy cannot be provided.

It is doubtful that a person can change feelings and fears about stuttering in a lasting way on an intensive course. This throws into question whether or not block modification techniques can be successfully applied intensively. We have explored this possibility in a small way at the City Lit. and have been encouraged by results thus far. We have found that it is possible for clients to make solid beginnings on desensitisation and modification of the stuttering pattern. A most important component in determining the outcome is the extent to which the group members understand and appreciate the aims of such a course.

Block modification techniques adapt readily to non-intensive therapy such as weekly or twice-weekly sessions. Clients may be helped by a discussion at the outset of the successive stages involved so that they have a broad understanding of what is likely to happen in therapy. For example, many clients find the identification and desensitisation process initially causes their fluency to deteriorate between sessions. Later they may experience unfavourable reactions to easy stuttering. Understanding the rationale and aims of block modification techniques can serve to support clients in the periods between sessions.

Regardless of the technique chosen to bring about an easier speech pattern, non-intensive therapy has the advantage of facilitating gradual psychological change. New ideas which conflict with habitual ways of seeing things can be individually considered and incorporated if they seem useful. Such change is more likely to be meaningfully integrated into the client's understanding of self and others than if he were exposed to many new ideas within a short space of time. When therapy is set up on a weekly basis, clients can test the validity of the changes they are making between sessions. Intensive courses often lead to the client making changes in a setting removed from his normal life and this partly explains why such changes may be difficult to uphold after the course.

In summary, making a decision about the frequency of therapy sessions must take account of the changes each client wishes to make and how these changes will be best effected. Often combinations of approaches prove to be successful, such as commencing with weekly sessions to orientate the client, followed by an intensive course which can then be succeeded by weekly sessions to effect and maintain long-term change.

Principles of Group Therapy

Preparing the Scene

Physical Arrangements. The ideal setting for group therapy is a large, quiet room, that accords a degree of physical comfort and privacy to those attending. Although not all speech therapy units are equipped for group therapy, a reasonable setting is required if the aim of fostering self-acceptance and dignity is to be achieved. For example, a uniform set of chairs can create an atmosphere of equality.

Preparing the Client. Prior to the first group session, it is advisable that the group therapist meet with each client to assess his suitability for the particular group. It is useful to discuss the therapeutic goals and type of approach to be used. With stuttering, this is particularly relevant as many clients have expectations of a cure and have little idea of what to expect from speech therapy.

If the client is to be a late addition to an ongoing group, he can be informed about what has taken place so far and possibly be offered some individual sessions to catch up with the group. This is particularly important in stuttering therapy where sets of techniques are taught. It is desirable that the late arrival to a group should feel that he has every chance of becoming a full member.

Preparing the Therapist. The first task of the therapist is to familiarise herself with any data collected from interviews. On the basis of the group membership, the therapist may wish to define her aims and select techniques that will achieve these aims. As prepared as the therapist is before starting the group, it is also important to remember that every group evolves its own aims as members come to express their needs in a more articulate manner.

Where the therapist is inexperienced in group therapy and desires supervision, this should be arranged prior to the first meeting of the group. This should afford the novice therapist a chance to discuss her anxieties and to establish a supportive relationship with a colleague before the group gets underway.

Group Size. The optimal size of a group is approximately eight members plus a leader. Too small a group has the disadvantages of not providing enough variety of members for generating alternative ways of handling problems. If the group is too large, some members may not be inclined to contribute and may feel they are not receiving enough attention.

Duration. Depending on the task specified for the group to tackle, so the number and frequency of meetings will vary. Intensive therapy focusing on fluency skills can be extremely productive and can be the first step in lasting speech change. If the aim is for members to change in psychological terms, weekly meetings over a year would seem appropriate. One idea is to contract with each group to meet for, say, ten sessions and then review the aims of the group and determine the next set of meetings.

Group Structure

A group may be defined as an 'aggregation of individual human beings, who each bring to it their particular needs, motivations and resources' (Heap 1977, p. 44). No sooner is a group formed than it is faced with the task of resolving the discord bewen two opposing forces: that of *integration* of the individual into the group, and that of *differentiation*, the force expressing the needs of the individual (Heap 1977). In any stuttering group, the needs of the individual must inevitably be subsumed by the needs of the group as a whole. This can be viewed as a temporary measure, lasting as long as the group lasts. The ultimate autonomy of the individual members is possibly the most important long-term aim.

Integration into the group is brought about by two main influences. The first is the extent to which members come to mutually depend on each other. While too much dependence on the group may be regarded negatively as being counter-productive to change, Heap (1977) found that dependence on the group facilitated rather than hindered autonomy in outside situations. In stuttering groups, dependence is usually the result of the individual feeling accepted in his stuttering role, and is further able to share his feelings about stuttering knowing he will be understood. This is a unique experience for most stutterers, and it is not surprising that feelings of safety and acceptance bring about dependence on the group.

The second factor to influence integration is group cohesion. This is achieved once relationships between members have been forged, once there is a shared investment in the group aims and an established set of norms for behaviour. Smith (1980, p. 18) reports studies by a number of authors which show that group norms emerge as a result of the consensus of all the members, and not at the whim of the group leader.

In our groups at the City Lit. we have noted behaviours which are constructive to the group process. The more able a group member is to share impressions of his own and others' behaviour, the more useful this is to the process of change. Members are encouraged to take responsibility for the feedback they give, and to use appropriate pronouns, e.g. 'I stuttered badly' instead of 'it happened again'; 'you stuttered' instead of reporting to the therapist that 'he stuttered'. It is usually more helpful if feedback is given in descriptive rather than evaluative terms. When feedback is spontaneously asked for and given, this signals the development of trust in the self and others in the group. This paves the way for the expression of feelings, which members may seldom have put into words before.

It is of equal importance to note behaviours which are destructive to the group process. Irregular attendance of sessions is frequently a sign of lack of commitment to the group. Berne (1966) offers guidelines for judging the adequacy of attendance. He claims that if attendance exceeds 90 per cent, then the therapist is most probably doing a superior job. If it is below 75 per cent, something is wrong, and the matter should be investigated. When members begin to open up and express personal thoughts and feelings it can be very harmful to the group process if other members put them down or react unfavourably to the views expressed. Another signal that all is not proceeding well with the group is the development of subgroups or cliques. This is discussed in a later section.

Other features of group structure which are closely interrelated are those of role, rank (status) and relationships. Each of these merits more detailed discussion.

The new group faces the task of determining roles in relation to each other. It is inevitable that some conflict between group and individual needs will affect this process. However, as Heap (1977) points out, this is not necessarily negative, for growth seems inseparable from some degree of conflict.

In developing roles to cope with the various tasks of the group, members are often called upon to behave in new or unusual ways. The person who stutters may initially find it difficult to venture beyond the role of stutterer, which has provided a structure for his interactions over the years (Fransella 1972). Therapists will be interested in the extent to which the group members can develop roles that facilitate the group process and may find it useful to identify them. Some examples of group-building roles include 'the encourager' who praises and supports the other members, 'the harmoniser' who mediates between other members and 'the compromiser', who gives way in a conflict even though his own ideas are involved. Examples of individual roles which are detrimental to the group process include 'the aggressor' who attacks others, 'the blocker' who stubbornly disagrees without explaining and 'the self-confessor' who uses the captive audience to air personal issues outside the task of the group (Benne and Sheats 1948, reported in Heap, 1977).

Heap (1977) specifies other roles which seem to develop by mutual agreement of individual and group. These roles may be contested but once achieved they are difficult to shed. Some examples include the roles of leader, clown, scapegoat, newcomer and isolate. Roles assigned in this way to group members may be well-practised by the individual in situations outside the group and serve only to validate the person's view of himself. In stuttering groups the role of the 'incurable' can emerge and may exert a very negative influence on the group. The therapist needs to learn the extent of a client's investment in the role before any change can be effected.

While role relates to the function of each group member, rank or status is determined by 'the approval and influence accorded to members acting in their various roles' (Heap 1977, p. 169). Status is usually ascribed to a person by the rest of the group and is influenced by cues such as dress, bearing, age, profession and self-presentation. This process frequently involves stereotyping and can be detrimental to helping the group members to change.

Every group develops a network of personal relationships often referred to as the 'informal structure' of the group because it occurs spontaneously (Heap 1977). Tuckman (1965) proposed a model describing successive stages of the development of relationships in the group process: forming, storming, norming and performing. These stages cover the initial orientating process of the group, which is followed typically by conflict between group and individual needs. The third phase involves the setting up of agreed codes of conduct, while the final phase is characterised by the achievement of the group. Members use the group as a tool and channel energy towards attaining group goals.

Group structure is an important concept because of its implications for the achievements of each group member, because it offers a way of understanding and studying the group and hence influencing it in ways that serve the purposes of the group.

Group Dynamics

Brammer and Shostrum (1968) describe group dynamics as referring to 'the general principles of group interaction and communication' (p. 322). Communication and interaction can be differentiated as two separate, but related processes. The former involves the transmitting and receiving of information, while the latter is 'a process of mutual stimulation, response and influence between persons in contact with each other' (Heap 1977, p. 77).

Clear interpersonal communication is an obvious aim in stuttering therapy groups. When a group first meets, it is wise to assume that communication between members is likely to be distorted for a number of reasons:

(1)   Stuttering is a communication problem and as such exerts an influence on the choice of words available to the stutterer, when he will speak and the content he can cope with. If, as Sheehan (1975) claims, the stutterer is bent on presenting himself as a fluent speaker, then he is forced to assume a false role, and this may affect what he says.

(2)   Interpersonal communication is a two-way process, and unless a speaker is listened to, successful communication is not achieved. The person who stutters is understandably often a poor listener. He may be wrapped up in himself, planning his next utterance and be quite unaware of what is happening around him.

(3)   In a new group, it is also very easy to make false assumptions about the clarity of communication. Individuals may feel that they have been perfectly clear in what they have said, but because the group has not yet developed a system of shared meanings, much may be lost or misunderstood.

(4)   The person who has never had stuttering therapy may lack the words with which to define his difficulties. His theory about his problem may differ from others in the group, and he may err by assuming that everyone began stuttering in the same way, or has similar difficulties.

(5)   Non-verbal communication is an important aspect of information transmission. The person who stutters often transmits conflicting signals. Where the tension often linked with stuttering overflows from the mouth into the face and body, it is not surprising that there is often a lack of congruence between the content and visual impression of what is said.

The group therapist can set an important example by continually striving for clear communication. In the first instance, she needs to be very aware of her own professional functioning — how her own problems, biases and selective inattention may be acting as a barrier to communication. Van Riper (1975) recommends that every therapist should analyse video or tape recordings of their sessions, to achieve a clearer picture of how they present themselves. He raises for instance, an important issue about the speed of the therapist's speech. If it is rapid the difference between her and the group widens. Slower speech both evens things out and can contribute to a more relaxed atmosphere.

Although at times in keeping with the aims of a particular session, the therapist may allow the group to drift, to become silent or vague, it is often necessary for her to intervene to achieve definition and clarity. She might ask the sort of question suggested by Kelly (1955) to ensure that a member is understood by the others: 'Could you summarise what you've just said?' or 'You seem to be saying something different now, can you explain?' (p. 1069).

Nor can the therapist always assume that what she has said has been understood by the group. A useful tactic might be to ask some one to summarise what she has just said. Checking out in this way gives the therapist a chance to evaluate the effectiveness of her communication. We find that group members soon begin to use these strategies for making sure that they understand or have been understood by others.

Once communication networks have been established meaningful interaction can begin, which determines the ultimate success of the group. Bales (1950, as reported in Sprott 1977) developed a research instrument for studying interaction in groups. He postulates that interaction is affected by both the task of the group and the relationships between members. He devised a classification system that involves categorising the interaction attempts of each group member. He suggests twelve response categories which fall under two main headings: *task-oriented contributions*, covering the giving of and asking for information, opinions and suggestions, and *socio-emotional responses*, which exert either a positive or negative influence on group cohesion. Bales was primarily interested in group discussions centred around problems which the group members wanted to solve, which had alternative solutions and which involved evaluating decisions about how best to solve the problem.

Despite the fact that his classification system requires considerable expertise to be used effectively, the information generated by its use yields interesting results. For example, he found that the most active member appears to address the group as a whole more than anyone else, and also receives the most responses from the group. This model seems more useful as a research tool than as a system for speedy analysis of the group therapy process, but we find that our impressions about productive group members seem to coincide with those of Bales. Early on in group life, a member who is willing to take risks, initiate and lead discussions is often the most popular group member. As the group begins to function and becomes increasingly task-oriented, productive members become more important than popular ones.

It is apparent that without interaction, relationships cannot develop. Once people share a relationship they interact more with each other than people who do not. Thus the two processes become inextricably bound to each other. Relationships between a few members, or the formation of a subgroup can hinder progress in a stuttering group. Relationships often depend on playing a fairly fixed role in relation to each other. In time, this involves being able to predict each other's behaviour and reactions. If a close relationship is formed between two members of a group, this can considerably limit their development of role flexibility, which involves being able to vary roles in relation to each other. For example, the formation of a clique can lead to interfering comments such as, 'I can't imagine you being bossy, it just isn't like you'.

As Fransella (1972) points out, the stutterer starts therapy being limited to playing one major role in relation to people he cannot understand or who make him feel uncertain. Group therapy with stutterers focuses on developing new roles and the group is an excellent forum for such experimentation to begin.

Developing Communication Skills in Stuttering Groups

When a therapist speaks of fluency having been established, the implication is not that the stutterer can now speak fluently and sound like any other fluent speaker. Not only does the fluency thus achieved still require refining, but the stutterer also needs to learn to *use* fluency like a normal speaker. This involves both inner psychological change and external behavioural change. It is to this latter issue that this section is addressed.

In the development of communication skills within a stuttering group four major considerations must be taken into account. These will influence the structuring of therapy and help the therapist assess how each person is progressing.

(1) *Content*. What the person is attempting to communicate is likely to exert an influence on whether he can speak fluently. Usually, the more emotive a topic, the more involved the person becomes and he can no longer monitor his speech. In the early stages of therapy, it is advisable to keep the content level as simple and straightforward as possible.

(2) *Language*. Many severe stutterers have not had great experience of speaking fluently and find that without the long pauses for stuttering, they cannot plan sentences very easily. They may be inclined to use impossibly long, convoluted sentences and then wonder why they lose their listener. Alternatively, speech may sound telegrammatic and devoid of the prosodic features of speech.

(3) *Listeners*. Stuttering is usually a problem of communication and therefore listeners play an important role in determining whether or not stuttering will occur. Often the number of listeners present exerts an influence on the speaker, or the nature of the listener reactions. Each person needs to explore this with the therapist if accurate hierarchies are to be tackled.

(4) *Length of interchange*. Stutterers vary considerably on this issue. For some, the shorter the interchange, the easier it is for them. For others, a longer exchange provides more opportunity for settling down and watching the speech.

There are, no doubt, innumerable other determinants of difficulty in speaking situations, but the above have a generality to most people with whom we have worked.

In discussing the structuring of developing communication skills, we shall be referring in the main to groups where a fluency technique has been taught. However, we follow much the same schedule on our block modification courses. The graded activities are introduced in the early stages of variation and modification. For the purposes of this chapter the therapy process has been arbitrarily divided into three stages. These stages should not be regarded as mutually exclusive or as objectively 'real' phases in therapy. There is a great deal of individual variation which does need to be taken into consideration when planning such a programme.

The Early Stages

At this stage, when the group members are very unsteady in their use of techniques, we use prepared reading material. The language is simple, the content untaxing and the sentences short. The group is divided into pairs to reduce the listener effect. We limit people to talking in turns of approximately one minute each, so that they do not overstretch their newly-acquired monitoring skills.

Describing picture postcards is a typical example of the next step in the level of difficulty. Again we limit talking time, and ask for as accurate a version of the techniques as possible. The style and content of communication is not evaluated at this stage unless something bizarre intrudes.

Next we might ask the group to describe an object, a person or a book. Possibly talking time could be extended to two minutes. We then might progress to questions and answers, which involves some listening and moves away from monologue. If all is progressing smoothly, we would increase the subgroup size from pairs to threes and fours and work through the same sorts of exercises.

This type of structure serves the useful purpose of acting as a warm-up in the later stages of therapy. When people arrive at a group, rushed off their feet, going through this type of routine is a good way of re-establishing the target style of speech.

Group exercises are also important, both as an illustration of how the whole group works and as a base for learning to communicate in front of a group of people. Because listening skills in stuttering groups are often so poor, we have sought problem-solving exercises that involve attending to all that is said if the problem is to be solved. An example of such an activity is the murder game, described by Johnson and Johnson (1975). Each group member is given two or three clues to a murder. The group are instructed not to *show* anyone their clues. Their task is to find out who did the murder, when, where and how. The task requires a group effort rather than a competition between individuals. The therapist sets up the speech aims for each person, but does not participate in the ensuing discussion.

The group has to select a method for solving the mystery. Does each in turn read their clues? Do they read about one person at a time? Do they write things down? There is usually much confusion and members instinctively turn to the therapist for direction. It is important not to help, but to be with the group as an observer. Ultimately a leader (or two) emerges and the activity gets underway.

The discussion afterwards can refer to group dynamics. Did members say what they wanted to say? Did they feel they influenced anyone? Were they influenced by anyone? Could they interrupt each other?

How? Did they feel they were listened to? Did they feel they had a share in helping to solve the task? Because everyone has an equal amount of relevant information to start with the group interaction is fairly balanced. The group needed each other to achieve the goal and this can demonstrate optimum use of the group, as well as facilitating the development of communication skills.

Intermediary Stages

By now the group is able to take responsibility for monitoring each other's speech. Members are fairly fluent in the sessions and it is now time to increase the level of difficulty of group exercises. Sessions usually begin with a brief warm-up session as described in the previous section, first in pairs, and then in the larger group. The aims at this stage are to develop the prosodic features of speech, to emphasise the use of language as a tool and to develop listening skills. Nonverbal communication skills are also tackled now.

We have occasionally asked groups to try and communicate with each other using any channel of communication other than speech. Usually groups have reacted with horror at these instructions. (Sheehan (1975) has described the stutterer's fear of silence at length.) We may introduce a fluent speaker or two at this point, with the instruction to the group that they find out about them without speaking, of course.

The first things the group discover is that the fluent outsiders are not at an advantage in this exercise and so do not pose a threat. Eventually the group starts to become creative and develops signals to communicate. Eye contact becomes imperative, and body language is used and noted. People find themselves smiling at each other and touching. Video recordings can be so revealing when group members see how differently they communicate without speech. It is important that the therapist does not become anxious and stop proceedings too soon. A good time to stop is when the group are behaving spontaneously and creatively.

Exercises to develop listening skills might involve asking one group member to tell another a personal anecdote. Then the listener tells it back to the group as he heard it. The others listen for omissions, mutations and additions to the story. The group can practise this type of exercise until they feel they have improved.

We use a four-word exercise to increase listening skills. Each member is given a card with four unrelated words which he has to use in order over a two minute period. The group have to guess what the four words were. Some members use their imagination and tell wonderful tales peppered with red herrings, but the task always achieves its purpose.

To develop prosody we engage in script readings and play readings. It often seems easier for members to develop an 'interesting' voice when they are out of role, than in their own role. Video or tape recordings are important for giving the group a chance to evaluate their performances.

Working on the use of language is a complex matter. We do not aim to teach grammar or vocabulary on our courses. The way in which we work on the style of language is to emphasise what Stewart (1973) calls the principle of adaptation and what Kelly (1955) calls role construing. If the speaker can place himself in the psychological frame of reference of the listener, he can modify what he wants to say accordingly. We use role playing exercises where we ask a person to tell the same story to three different listeners (played by other members) such as an old person, a stranger, a child. Exchanging parts helps the person to understand both sides of the interaction.

We ask group members to prepare short talks in which they give a clear exposition on a chosen topic. Stewart's (1973) principles are useful guidelines for language usage.

(1) *Principle of parsimony*. Using only necessary words.
(2) *Principle of prior definition*. Define before developing.
(3) *Principle of single topic development*. One idea at a time. Communication should not be overloaded.
(4) *Principle of repetition*. Key points should be reviewed, difficult ideas stated more simply.
(5) *Principle of analogy*. Link the unknown to the known.
(6) *Principle of sequentiality*. Structure the transitions from one theme to the next.

These headings also serve as a structure for evaluating quality of communication.

Nonverbal communication is tackled largely through the use of video recordings. Stuttering groups can become very focused on fluent speech and we find it useful to turn the sound off when playing recordings back. Studying the ways people show agreement, disagreement, boredom or interest, etc. can be fascinating. We also look for congruence between content and nonverbal signals. This technique is easily adapted to a wide variety of activities and can be used to monitor the development of nonverbal skills.

Advanced Stage

By this stage, the group will be grappling with the issues of maintenance of fluency. Weekly attendance at a group seems to be vital to the
continued development of fluency in an ever-increasing variety of situations. The group will wish to deal with more specific situations such as
telephone conversations, dealing with time pressure in queues, inter-
rupting, and so on. There is often a gap between what a person believes
he should be achieving and what he is actually achieving. This causes
considerable frustration and despair, and the group serves a very
supportive function.

Our aims at this stage are to help the person to 'be the way he wants
to be'. This implies learning the skills of new roles, new ways of dealing
with people, learning to evaluate feedback from listeners, learning to
be constructive when things go wrong. Towards the end of therapy,
people seem to develop their own highly individual style and gradually come to rely less and less on the group and the therapist. Indeed,
many people terminate therapy by requesting a few individual sessions,
because the group no longer caters for their needs.

Techniques from the field of social skills training provide a powerful
adjunct to more traditional speech therapy techniques. Alberti and
Emmons (1978) describe the major facilitative components of assertive
training as being *covert rehearsal, modelling* and *behaviour rehearsal*.
In the group situation, the therapist or any group member can model
the scene for the person who brings the problem situation to the
group. Alberti and Emmons give a list of basic exercises: some examples
are: breaking into a group already busy talking, starting a conversation
with a stranger, returning defective items to a shop, saying 'no' to a
request for a favour, standing up for yourself with a dominant person.
Feedback is essential in the early stages of assertive behaviour training.
Later the group must learn to evaluate their own behaviour independently.

The group members usually bring a wealth of their difficult situations to therapy. We find it useful to set up two or three alternative ways
of handling them. These are modelled for the person who brings the
situation to the group, and he can then choose a way of dealing with it
that suits his needs. The whole notion of alternatives stimulates creat-
ivity and when the group enter whole-heartedly into the exercise, they
leave the session bubbling over with ideas.

Going outside on assignments in pairs is a good way of learning
about listener's reactions. One of the pair does the talking, while the
second person observes the listener's response. Feedback from the

listener can then be discussed and analysed.

Within the group there is now time for lengthy discussions on any stuttering issues. We do not usually structure these, but if they start to develop into a dialogue, it may be advisable to stop the discussion and check out why more people are not contributing.

We also set up more complicated group activities within the therapy room. We invite outsiders to the role play interviewing with the group. We have debates and also now introduce one of our favourite activities — heckling. The rules are very strictly adhered to. Each person chooses a topic which he feels very strongly about, e.g. nuclear disarmament. He is given 45 seconds to develop the topic before the heckling begins. Everyone in the group has to disagree with the speaker, whether they do so privately or not. No personal abuse is permitted. This gives the person the chance to see how he handles antagonism, interruptions and shouting. We find nonverbal communication always comes up for discussion in the post-mortem analysis. People who use eye contact and gesture do better than those who use only their voices.

The 'desert game' of Johnson and Johnson (1975) is very appropriate at this stage. Each member is given a briefing sheet which sets the scene, plus a position from which to argue. Each person has a different position in the argument and the task of the group is to reach a decision in a specified time on two issues: whether to stay near the wrecked vehicle or to walk to camp, and whether or not to hunt for food. People are advised that they can give way if they are convinced by other's arguments. The exercise involves eight people. This is the sort of exercise that leads to excellent group interaction. Everyone has to participate — their vote is needed. As a speech exercise, it excels because it is possible to become totally involved and this approximates 'real life'. A video recording is useful for later consideration.

Some of the ways in which a group can be utilised to develop communication skills have been discussed. People attending group therapy for any length of time seem to develop resources that make fluency seem a less important commodity than when they first arrived for therapy, in hot pursuit of a 'cure'.

Self-Help Groups

For a number of reasons self-help groups for adults who stutter have become increasingly popular in recent times. In Britain perhaps the most influential factor has been the founding (in 1978) and subsequent expansion of a British Association for Stammerers. This Association has attempted to put stutterers in touch with each other and has supported the notion of self-help groups both in principle and financially.

Unfortunately, many groups run by stutterers for stutterers have not survived long enough to achieve all of their initial aims. Some important lessons can be learned if we examine the reasons why these groups are not always effective. There are usually no selection procedures for such groups and anyone who is interested, regardless of their particular therapy experience or stuttering severity, is admitted. This can result in each person having substantially different ideas about which therapy techniques work and which do not. Groups often arise as a result of a lack of speech therapy services in the area. Members may regard the self-help group as second best and may not be very hopeful about its effectiveness.

Initially the organiser of the group may assume a leadership role, but may feel unqualified to direct the group. This can result in lengthy discussions to determine both aims and techniques to be used. Members may have strong ideas that methods which have helped them will help others, but if their initial plans do not succeed, they may not have enough experience to look for different techniques. Stuttering is an extremely complex problem and progress is generally slow and erratic. Many stutterers feel helpless victims of their speech problems and find it difficult to visualise ways of solving them. It is easy for a group to lose direction and collude with each other about how much of a problem stuttering is without coming up with any constructive suggestions about change. Members may not commit themselves wholeheartedly to the venture and erratic attendance can be disillusioning to those who attend regularly.

Groups appear to stand a greater chance of survival if they have some speech therapy assistance. If therapists could select people who are at similar stages in therapy or who are working on similar techniques, the group would probably be helped to a positive start. Perhaps a speech therapist could join early sessions to help the group plan their course of action. It seems that having a therapist to consult is an important determinant of the success of groups.

An initial investment of time and enthusiasm on the part of a speech therapist may have many long-term benefits to both stutterers and therapists. For stutterers, the feelings of independence and responsibility may be new and inspiring. The realisation that they can help each other may allow each person to gain confidence in his ability to help himself. For therapists self-help groups imply freedom to allocate services and resources elsewhere, quite apart from the rewards of participating in a project which increases the autonomy of stuttering clients. Although a speech therapist-supported self-help group sounds like a contradiction in terms, it would appear that this is a valuable undertaking.

Conclusion

Group therapy with adults who stutter can be directed towards more than the establishment of fluency: it can also bring about psychological growth. One of the most important ingredients determining the success of the group is the therapist who leads it. Although the emphasis in this chapter has been placed on helping group members extend themselves, it is also believed that a therapist should be willing to take risks, to do the unusual and to tackle the unexpected. Such a therapist will create a highly flexible setting in which constructive learning can occur. Formal training for speech therapists in the art and practice of group therapy seems warranted in the face of the increasing popularity of this approach.

There are many unresearched areas in relation to group therapy with stutterers. For example, consideration could be given to the timing of group therapy in the sequence of treatment. Apart from studies done some 20 years ago, there is little recent support for homogeneity in the selection of group members. It would be interesting to investigate how stutterers fare in more heterogeneous groups.

Personal construct therapy has only recently been applied to stuttering groups (see Chapter 7). Studies comparing this approach to more traditional speech therapy methods may yield important implications for tackling long-term group therapy. Personal construct therapy challenges the notions of establishment and maintenance phases of therapy, and implies instead the gradual elaboration of the meaning of fluency. This has been shown to be effective with individuals (Fransella 1972), but needs exploring in relation to stuttering groups.

The emphasis in stuttering therapy is gradually shifting away from fluency training. Group therapy with stutterers seems to be undergoing a similar transition as is evidenced by the numbers of groups being set up with other objectives in mind such as social skills training, relaxation therapy and personal construct therapy.

The group appears to be an adaptable, creative medium for facilitating change: its full potential has probably not yet been realised.

References

Alberti, R.E. and M.L. Emmons (1978) *Your Perfect Right: A Guide to Assertive Behaviour*, Impact Publishers, California

Barbara, D.C. (1954) *Stuttering: A Psychodynamic Approach to Its Understanding and Treatment*, Julian, New York

——(ed.) (1965) *New Directions in Stuttering: Theory and Practice*, Charles C. Thomas, Springfield, Illinois

Berne, E. (1966) *Principles of Group Treatment*, Grove Press, New York

Brammer, L.M. and E.L. Shostrum (1968) *Therapeutic Psychology*, Prentice-Hall, Inc., Englewood Cliffs, N.J.

Fawcus, M. (1970) 'Intensive Treatment and Group Therapy Programme for the Child and Adult Stammerer', *British Journal of Communication Disorders, 5*, 59-65

Fransella, F. (1972) *Personal Change and Reconstruction*, Academic Press, New York

Heap, K. (1977) *Group Therapy for Social Workers: An Introduction*, Holywell Press, Oxford

Helps, R. and P. Dalton (1979) 'The Effectiveness of an Intensive Group Speech Therapy Programme for Adult Stammerers', *British Journal of Communication Disorders, 14*, 17-30

Johnson, D.W. and F.P. Johnson (1975) *Joining Together: Group Theory and Group Skills*, Prentice-Hall, Englewood Cliffs, N.J.

Kelly, G. (1955) *The Psychology of Personal Constructs*, Volume Two, Clinical Diagnosis and Psychotherapy, Norton, New York

Miele, J.A. (1962) 'Group Psychotherapy with Stutterers' in D.A. Barbara (ed), *The Psychotherapy of Stuttering*, Charles C. Thomas, Springfield, Illinois, pp. 215-39

Murphy, A. and Fitzsimmons, R. (1960) *Stuttering and Personality Dynamics*, Ronald Press, New York

Rogers, C. (1970) *Encounter Groups*, Penguin Books, Harmondsworth

Shames, G.H. (1953) 'An Exploration of Group Homogeneity in Group Speech Therapy', *Journal of Speech and Hearing Disorders, 18*, 267-72

Sheehan, J.G. (1970) *Stuttering: Research & Therapy*, Harper and Row, New York

——(1975) 'Conflict Theory and Avoidance-Reduction Theraapy' in J. Eisenson (ed), *Stuttering: A Second Symposium*, Harper and Row, New York, pp. 97-198

Smith, P.B. (1980) *Group Processes and Personal Change*, Harper and Row, New York

Sprott, W.J.H. (1977) *Human Groups*, Penguin Books, Harmondsworth

Stewart, J. (1973) *Bridges Not Walls: A Book about Interpersonal Communication*, Addison and Wesley, Reading, USA

Tuckman, B.W. (1965) 'Developmental Sequence in Small Groups' in P.B. Smith (ed) (1970) *Group Processes: Selected Readings*, Penguin Books, Harmondsworth, pp. 322-51

Van Riper, C. (1973) *The Treatment of Stuttering*, Prentice-Hall, Englewood Cliffs, N.J.

——(1975) 'The Stutterer's Clinician', in J. Eisenson (ed), *Stuttering: A Second*

Symposium, Harper and Row, New York, pp. 453-92.
Walton, H. (ed) (1971) *Small Group Psychotherapy*, Penguin Books, Harmondsworth

7 MAINTENANCE OF CHANGE: TOWARDS THE INTEGRATION OF BEHAVIOURAL AND PSYCHO-LOGICAL PROCEDURES

Peggy Dalton

Echoing throughout recent literature on therapy for stuttering comes the sad refrain that, while short-term changes can be brought about through a wide variety of methods, maintenance of these changes over time is still far from satisfactory. An attempt will be made in this chapter to consider factors relating to the aims of particular approaches and the procedures developed within them to increase the possibility of maintenance in order to clarify some of the issues involved in this crucial therapeutic dilemma.

Evaluating Maintenance

First, the enormous difficulties encountered in any attempt to evaluate maintenance must be acknowledged. Apart from what Boberg (1979) refers to as the 'substantial logistic problems in both arranging for and persuading large numbers of clients to co-operate with evaluation procedures' (p. 94), clinicians and researchers inevitably disagree as to what exactly should be measured when long-term outcome is assessed (see also Chapter 2). To a few, percentage syllables stuttered and speech rate are the major focus of attention in presenting follow-up data. To many others (e.g. Ingham and Andrews 1971; Perkins 1979), the quality of that fluency in relation to normal speech should also be included. The question of what speech situations should be rated in order to give a comprehensive picture of the clients' performance in their lives as a whole and whether they should be aware of being assessed are still being debated. Even more controversial is the inclusion or otherwise of the measurement of attitudinal changes or changes in self-concept. There are many doubts as to the validity of 'objective' measures and even greater ones with regard to self-report data.

With the varying aims of different therapeutic approaches, how can we compare what one worker regards as success with the appraisal of another? And, above all, how can we evaluate the speaker's own sense of achievement or failure? Solutions to these problems are clearly something to work towards, but it is hoped that the issues raised in the following sections may throw some light on them.

Aims of Therapy

Reference has been made, particularly in Chapter 4, to what Sheehan has termed the 'great divide' (1979, p. 177) — the speak-more-fluently, vs stutter-more-fluently controversy. Most of the approaches outlined in earlier chapters can be seen to aim either at replacing stuttering with fluent speech or at a more gradual modification of the stuttering itself. As has been pointed out, the emphasis in programmes with the former aim is on changes in speech behaviour while with the latter far more attention is paid to anxieties about speaking, attitudes towards communication and self-concepts. Maintenance of *fluency*, therefore, is the primary focus of the so-called behavioural clinicians, whereas those labelled psychodynamic in their approach are actively seeking to bring about lasting psychological change, with changes in fluency seen as the secondary outcome. In practice, as has been suggested in Chapter 5, few therapists work firmly on one or other side of this dichotomy. It would seem impossible to separate speech behaviour from psychological processes and no one suggests that change takes place at one level and not at another. In reviewing some of the attempts of the last few years to extend our understanding of why some people who stutter are able to maintain change while others are not, we shall consider both behavioural and psychological procedures which seem to facilitate maintenance and factors which appear to relate to relapse.

Maintenance of Fluency

In 1979 an international conference was held in Banff in Canada and its proceedings published in *Maintenance of Fluency* (1981). The speakers and participants were largely those carrying out behavioural treatment, which ranged from Ryan's minutely structured Monterey Fluency Program to Perkins's work on the development of the normal speech skills of phrasing, breath-flow, use of voice and natural rhythm. There was no representative among the speakers of the stutter-more-fluently group of workers. Although there was much discussion as to how fluency should be measured, there was general consensus that the aim of therapy should be the total elimination of stuttering, that the resultant speech should be perceived as normal by the listener and that any treatment programme should include procedures for ensuring the speaker's ability to maintain fluent speech in all situations over time.

To Boberg (1981), who has been working for some years to develop effective maintenance programmes, such an achievement depends on the client's willingness to spend considerable time and energy in home activities and clinic visits. His original Plan A of speech activities included daily practice of prolonged speech alone and in conversation, plus five personal asignments, all of which were to be noted on a wrist-counter and then transferred to tables and graphs. These activities were estimated to take approximately one hour each day to complete and clients were asked to carry them out for a year after their intensive course. In order to sustain such a programme, the participants were encouraged to develop their own system of self-reinforcement, involving the help of family and friends and making use of natural reinforcers such as food, television, a period of recreation and so on. It soon became apparent that for many people this Plan A of home assignments was impossible to complete and two further plans, demanding rather fewer activities, were developed and the clients given the choice of which they felt to be the most compatible with their particular life-style.

Regular clinic visits were scheduled, initially once weekly, then reduced to fortnightly and eventually to once every twelve weeks. This was, of course, dependent on whether the client passed the criterion of less than 2 per cent disfluency at normal rate during the visit and in the recordings of his home practice presented on each occasion. A group session also formed part of the clinic visit to discuss any difficulties and plan for future activities.

Although unable to conclude from the results of this experimental programme which factors contributed most to the maintenance of immediate post-treatment levels of fluency, Boberg is able to demonstrate that, on the whole, those who carried it out showed only a negligible amount of relapse when they were assessed at 6 and 12 months after the intensive course, compared with a control group who did not have access to the maintenance programme and fared considerably less well. He admits to a number of unsolved issues emerging from his study. These include: difficulties in obtaining maximum client co-operation for such a programme; problems in determining the client's effectiveness in the post treatment environment; and both evaluating and improving the person's ability to self-monitor in his own environment. He also concedes that other variables such as personality, motivation and self-concept may affect and be affected by the clinical process and that these too should be measured.

In Chapter 4 of the *Maintenance of Fluency* proceedings Ryan (1981), also focuses on a study of the maintenance phase of his Monterey Fluency Program (discussed in some detail in Chapter 3). He makes the point that his results showed no difference in permanency effects, whether the establishment procedure used was GILCU, DAF or punishment. The maintenance programme was the same for all three. It consists, essentially, of periodic sampling of the client's performance in reading, monologue and conversation, together with reports from the client himself, a parent, teacher or spouse, as to the adequacy of his speech in a variety of situations. These procedures are repeated over a 22 month period: step 1 is conducted two weeks after completion of the transfer programme; step 2 one month after that; step 3 at three months; step 4 at six months and step 5 at a year. If the client continues to be fluent throughout this period, his treatment is regarded as completed. If, however, at any step he is not fluent or is reported to be stuttering outside the clinic, a recycling or retraining process is instituted until he is ready to start the maintenance programme again.

In fact, of the two groups studied, 23 of the 24 subjects did not complete maintenance and Ryan could only speculate that if they had, their follow-up re-checks would have shown even better results. As it was, he states that 62 per cent retained fluency at less than 1 per cent stuttering, and 83 per cent retained fluency at less than 2 per cent. This was almost three years after the completion of an average of 17.7 hours of therapy.

Pooling the results of both groups, Ryan points to a number of factors which seem to him to be important for maintenance of fluency. First, amongst the adults at least, the extent of stuttering pre-treatment emerged as significant. The more severe the original disfluency, the less likely the person was to maintain the fluency achieved during the establishment and transfer phases. Correlated with this pretherapy severity factor was that of hours of therapy undertaken. The longer the time required, which would include re-cycling when failing to reach criterion performance, the less satisfactory the outcome. Added to these was the finding that the younger clients, especially children, maintained fluency better than older clients.

Interestingly, there was no significant correlation between months in maintenance and permanence of fluency in either group. Nevertheless, despite the lack of evidence from this particular study of the importance of building maintenance procedures into a treatment pro-

gramme, Ryan advocates that this should continue 'if only to determine the dimension of their power and/or need' (p. 135). He even goes
so far as to pose the question whether 'maintenance programs at some
level should continue for the life of the client, similar to drug, alcoholism or weight-control programs' (p. 135).

While not confronting themselves with such a possibility, Helps and
Dalton (1979) concluded from their research that 'regular follow-up
therapy is desirable if the progress made on an intensive course is to
be maintained' (p. 28). Howie, Tanner and Andrews (1981), whose programme (described in Chapter 4) bears many similarities to Boberg's,
also advocate arranging 'continuing support for and practice of smooth
motion speech skills after intensive treatment is completed' (p. 108). It
should be noted, however, that Ingham and his colleagues (1981)
have achieved considerable success in maintenance with a programme
which contains no attempt at further therapy. The client's speech is
simply measured. 'Failure to achieve "criterion performance" results in
an increase in the frequency of clinic visits.' He regards this method as
providing 'a performance-contingent maintenance schedule in which
the consequence of maintained speech performance is a decrease in the
frequency of maintenance sessions' (p. 196).

It would seem from the focus so far on achieving and maintaining
changes in speech behaviour that considerable therapy time, continuous practice and vigilance are the major requirements for a speaker to
succeed. For Boberg, 'the rewards for such sustained efforts are substantial. The alternative, relapse, is unacceptable' (p. 111). Ingham, on
the other hand, in his contribution to the conference (1981), shows
how with characteristic honesty he admits to those with whom he
works that his rigorous programme is one which he himself might not
be willing to undertake and that it offers no guarantee of success, even
when meticulously adhered to. Keeping this point in mind, included in
Boberg's experimental group was a man who travelled two hundred
miles to the clinic, was very diligent in doing all that was asked of him
and yet, on post-therapy tapes, stuttered more severely than anyone
else.

Maintenance and Monitoring

It is Perkins (1981), however, who most firmly addresses the question
of the 'cost-effectiveness' of the need for continuous work on fluency
and the constant monitoring involved. He sees his own programme as
concerned with training speech actors, whose fluency is the result of
deliberately adopting the skilled management of all aspects of speech.

'The best outcome to be expected', he says, 'is to sound like a normal speaker'. And the cost of this 'can be measured in the number of skills that must be monitored and the frequency of monitoring required to maintain an approximation of normal-sounding speech . . . it is this cost that seems to stand between normal-sounding monitored speech and the stutterer's feeling of being a normal speaker' (p. 152). Clearly, for most severe stutterers, the demands will be too great, and even for the less severe, fluency would need to be of paramount importance in relation to their lives as a whole for them to devote the time and energy required of such attention to performance.

In his chapter 'Relapse in Stuttering' in the same volume, Shames briefly outlines the aims of his therapy programme, which take into account the problem of the need for self-monitoring. It involves, among other procedures, the gradual replacement of monitored stutter-free speech by unmonitored stutter-free speech. He points out that in the early stages of treatment most clients are capable of three ways of speaking: stuttering, deliberately monitoring their speech in a controlled way or speaking fluently without exercising control, depending on the particular circumstances of the moment. The therapy is designed first to strengthen monitored speech, then to weaken this type of utterance and strengthen unmonitored speech. As the client progresses, it has been noticed that the unmonitored speech becomes less rapid and takes on some of the characteristics of the monitored speech, which Shames sees as part of the speaker's developing sense of control. Depending on how far the stutterer himself feels it is safe to go, unmonitored speech may spread to all but the beginnings of phrases or all but pre-determined 'special events'. Some have eventually gone the whole way. They neither monitor nor do they stutter. (For a fuller discussion of the work of this author and his colleague, Florance, see Chapter 5.)

Self-responsibility

Self-reinforcement procedures are also included in the treatment described by Florance and Shames (1980) and have been referred to in the outline of Boberg's prgramme earlier. These form part of the approach of many clinicians towards transfer of responsibility for maintenance of changed behaviour from therapist to client. Other aspects of this transfer lie in the emphasis on self-evaluation and negotiation of aims and work schedules built into the early stages of a number of forms of therapy. For example, Cooper (1979) in his personalized fluency control therapy for children, stresses the need for young people to develop not only positive appreciation of their own progress but a clear appraisal of the amount of time and energy they are prepared to devote to it.

Owen (1981) draws on the general literature on behaviour modification when he suggests that 'Deliberate attribution of responsibility to the client's own efforts, rather than to external "treatment" agencies should also facilitate post-treatment maintenance'. He believes that 'an emphasis on personal activities that people believe to be under their own rather than external control' will contribute to the lasting effects of change. Where an increase in the sense of 'generalized personal efficacy' is achieved, the client has greater confidence in his ability to retain mastery over particular problem behaviours.

This brings us to a very important question about the presentation of a fluency technique in therapy. If it is seen by the client as something which will *make* him fluent if he sticks to it, rather than as a way of speaking which he chooses to assume as an acceptable alternative to the uncontrolled struggles of stuttering, then it remains as something external to himself, which he must follow faithfully or fail. Despite the fact that, as Shames points out, most people who stutter can speak fluently on many occasions, the strict adherence to a technique demanded by some programmes *can* serve to set up a belief that without it the only alternative is disfluency. It would therefore seem that part of the learning of speech control should, as Sheehan (1970) urges, entail the acknowledgement that both stuttering and fluency are the person's own behaviour, not something imposed from outside, whatever it may seem to the client at the beginning of therapy.

Throughout his writings over many years, Williams, whose work has been discussed in Chapter 3, has emphasised this point. And in a recent paper (1982) he elaborates on what he refers to as the 'learned-helplessness hypothesis' (p. 165). He takes to task those therapists who blame the clients for failure when they say 'if only they would continue doing what I taught them, they would maintain fluency' (p. 165). To Williams, that attitude ignores a huge dimension of the problem of some stutterers. To attempt to change simply by following the rules set by another will only reinforce the idea that the behaviour is uncontrollable from within and feed the sense of personal helplessness. Adams (1981), though more generally known for his work on the physiological and aerodynamic aspects of stuttering, also refers to this attribute in many clients: the sense of 'victimization'. He sees this as an important factor to be taken into account when we attempt to help the stutterer to change. Unless it is resolved in the course of therapy, relapse is inevitable.

Maintenance and Psychological Change

It will be clear from the preceeding section that the point made in Chapter 5 about the impossibility of splitting behavioural and psychological procedures is valid. Self-reinforcement may perhaps be placed under the behavioural heading by some. But once therapist and client turn their attention to the wider issue of self-responsibility in an effort to tackle this learned-helplessness factor, they are far beyond concern with speech alone. In fact, one of the most striking things about the Banff conference was the gradually increasing emphasis on the need not only for adequate measures of attitudes and self-concepts, but for building into maintenance procedures the psychological aspects of change. Perkins (1981), in his final address, points to the approach of Shames and his colleagues, with its emphasis on counselling, as having 'a lot more merit than the rather mechanistic solution that we've been looking at' and goes on to say 'we are indeed going to have to concern ourselves with a lot of the deeper, more private, intimate, important parts of the lives of these people if we are really going to solve their maintenance problems' (p. 259).

Also among the conference participants was a group of people who themselves stuttered and, when asked to summarise what for them had emerged as major issues, they left us in no doubt as to their order of priority. Among the factors significantly related to maintenance they pin-point: tolerance or desensitisation to fluency failure, the decision to assume responsibility for maintenance, confidence in therapy skills and control. For them, *control* has a specific meaning, described by Boehmler (1981) as 'having control over cognitive, attitudinal and feeling variables (such as avoidance versus approach set)' (p. 268), which in turn they feel, enables them to employ speech process control when necessary. Their ultimate goal is ease of communication, without significant need to control the process of speech production and they believe that they achieve this goal by monitoring attitudes, while only occasionally monitoring speech. They question the possible danger of fluency establishment therapy reinforcing cognitive patterns such as absolute fluency set or avoidance patterns.

It does seem, therefore, that this group at least, all of whom had undergone speech modification therapy of some kind, saw psychological change as the more important part of maintenance and were even questioning the fluency targets of the majority of clinicians present at the conference. They were clearly in agreement with Perkins (1981) about the cost-effectiveness issue involved in the demand for continual monitoring of speech processes. Their 'ultimate goal' is reminiscent of those expressed by a number of the stutter-more-fluently workers. For example, Sheehan (1970), sees *success* as having been achieved if the person can speak fluently much of the time and is not constantly forced to exercise vigilance and control. The way he speaks should not intrude conspicuously into any situation; the person should have reasonable freedom from anxiety about possible stuttering and a reasonably positive and well-integrated self-concept.

A Direct Approach to Psychological Change

Despite the successful outcome reported in the literature for some people following fluency programmes, then, it does seem clear that for many, as much if not more direct attention needs to be paid to the issues involved in maintaining attitude change. It is well known that in the first flush of achieving a substantial improvement in fluency, many people who have stuttered all their lives will confront stressful events with a new assertiveness. For a while, motivation to exercise control is maintained by the experience of success and the approval of others. With continued clinic contact, especially involving others on the same path, confidence and energy can remain high for some time. But the person's ability to speak to strangers, answer the telephone and express his opinion in front of a group may be dependent on this high level of confidence and energy. He may not have changed his view of these events as being special and challenging. His only alternatives are the old way of avoiding them, approaching them with dread or going into battle. There is no middle way of dealing with them as ordinary, more or less pleasant day-to-day situations.

Similarly, at a deeper level, having felt perhaps totally inadequate in relationships with others and unsure of his abilities in all directions because of his speech difficulty, he may have swung for a while to the opposite pole. Finding himself able to communicate freely with people whom he formerly regarded with awe, he may see this as all that is needed for friendship and love to be his for the asking. Having experienced what it is like to exercise authority in his job, he may assume that the world of work is his oyster.

However, no-one can remain confident all the time and all of us have periods when energy flags or something occurs to challenge our sense of being in charge of things. We need strategies for coping differently at different times and to recognise our own vulnerability. This is why it seems so important in the treatment of stuttering to work actively towards developing resilience in the face of old threats and a wider repertoire for responding to new challenges. Current programmes of speech modification are carefully planned in appropriate steps. It would seem equally vital for psychological change to be approached with the same thoroughness and structure. In the following section an outline is given of one maintenance programme which has these essential qualities.

Van Riper's Stabilisation Programme

The strategies developed by Van Riper (1973) for the stabilisation phase of his therapy are largely concerned with strengthening the client's ability to maintain the psychological changes brought about through the procedures described by Cheasman (Chapter 4) in the identification and modification stages. He points out how remarkably resistant to complete extinction anxiety-conditioned avoidance and struggle responses are. Though much of the work earlier on in therapy is undertaken outside the clinic, there are always limits to the amount of generalisation that can be hoped for. 'Under conditions of great stress or under fatigue or in those periods when the stutterer's self-esteem is low, the latent strength of these old reactions is very likely to manifest itself' (p. 350).

Van Riper pin-points a number of factors contributing to continued vulnerability, even after the achievement of a high level of improvement. The one which most directly threatens newly-established control is the inability of many people who stutter 'to express themselves in supramorphemic units' (p. 352). They do not yet have the experience of sequencing utterances of any length and the silences which occur as they search for words or the failure to handle the prosodic elements involved arouse some of the old anxieties and may lead to old coping devices. Work must be undertaken in this area, therefore, if relapse is to be prevented.

One method suggested for developing the integration of the longer sequences of speech is *free association*. The person trains himself intensively in continuous free association for increasingly longer periods of time, which is said to ease word-finding difficulty and facilitate the formation of verbalised thought. Another is *shadowing* someone else's speech, echoing it almost simultaneously. This can help the stutterer 'to get the knack of normal prosody' (p. 354) and give him the experience of longer stretches of fluent speech than he has been used to. Some also find it useful to practise a narration or exposition of the same material to different listeners until they can do it smoothly and continuously. Others employ immediate oral paraphrasing after reading material silently or set themselves targets of impromptu speaking which gradually increase in duration as they master the procedure. While such means are offered as suggestions, each person is encouraged to invent his own methods for developing this important communication skill, without which he is left very vulnerable to disruption and a return to negative reactions.

Van Riper also attempts in this stabilisation phase to extinguish residual fears of particular situations, words and sounds. Traumatic experiences from the past are reviewed in detail, verbalised or acted out, then retold using the slow-motion stuttering which they have learned (see Chapter 4, p. 97). This seems to have the effect of can-celling out these experiences and removing the threat from similar situations when they occur in the future. Word and sound fears are also directly confronted. Clients may pick out and analyse stuttered words from their own recordings, repeat them first in the disfluent way, switch to many repetitions using slow-motion stuttering and finally to saying them normally. Such massed practice results, for some stutterers at least, in the reinforcement of new models and the extinction of the old patterns and fears. It would seem, however, that the therapist's judgement should be used about suggesting such activity to a person who may already be obsessed by the details of speech performance to the detriment of a wider attention to communication as a whole.

Another procedure aimed at strengthening the client's ability to cope with stress is *buffering*. This is most effectively carried out within a group context, since it consists essentially of flooding each person with stress-provoking experience, until he is able to withstand the pressure without faltering. If interruption is particularly difficult for him to cope with, for example he is exposed to deliberate heckling. The group may produce noise for another to contend with, or fire questions at someone easily thrown by them. Where a person is especially vulner-able to loss of listener-attention he learns to deal with others' turning or even walking away. This buffering process is extended outside the clinic in deliberate confrontations with people, especially located as manifest-ing behaviours which create particular stress for many people who stutter — anger, impatience, sarcasm.

With these and other activities devised to extend work on communication skills and prevent regression to avoidance and struggle reactions, perhaps the most important feature of this stabilisation phase is re-integration of the self-concept. Van Riper describes the stutterer as beginning therapy with a conflict between the stuttering self and the very fluent imaginary self of fantasy. Through the earlier stages of his treatment programme he aims for his clients first to accept themselves as stutterers with a speech problem which is remediable, then to see themselves as fluent stutterers. He expresses himself content if someone leaves therapy with the self concept of a fluent stutterer, but he prefers to have him in a position where he can oscillate between this role and that of a normal speaker.

One way of achieving this end, he believes, is to give the person the opportunity to display his fluency in formal, public speaking situations. First, he is asked to speak before a friendly group with the aim of handling any residual disfluency so well that the audience does not recognise them and seems surprised when he points them out. Here he is exhibiting the self-concept of the very fluent stutterer. Then arrangements are made so that he can speak to groups of strangers, who do not know of his stuttering, and aims to present himself as a somewhat non-fluent normal speaker. These performances are video-taped in order to help the client in the task of self-definition in this new light.

These experiences are combined with the analysis of many day-to-day contacts. A client is asked to collect and classify the differing ways in which listeners may see him. He tries to judge whether he is viewed as a severe stutterer, a stutterer with some control over his problem, a fluent stutterer or even a normal speaker. He checks out these impressions and generally finds a mixture of reactions. At best, he comes to see that his role as a speaker can be a flexible one and that he does not have to choose between settling for the stutterer role or desperately trying to pretend that he is a fluent speaker. It is at this point that Van Riper sees maintenance of change as more assured and, therefore termination of therapy as appropriate.

The Contribution of Group Therapy to Maintenance

It will be seen that many of the procedures developed by Van Riper to facilitate maintenance of the changes brought about by his therapeutic approach are best carried through in the context of a group. In Chapter 5 Levy describes a number of group activities which are related to development beyond the establishment of improved communication in the clinic and the whole purpose of group therapy to her is that it should enable the participants to fend for themselves in the world outside. In the autumn of 1981 a course of weekly group therapy was initiated at the Centre for Personal Construct Psychology in London. Its aim was to test out the potential of a combined programme of speech modification procedures and personal construct psychotherapy for bringing about lasting change.

This course was in the nature of a pilot study, which posed a number of preliminary questions about combining a variety of procedures within a group. First, was it viable for the members to be working on different ways of modifying speech, chosen after trials as appropriate for each person's needs? Most groups reported in the literature focus on a single method. Second, was it possible for a group of people who stuttered to cope with and benefit from the highly individual nature of the reconstruction process implied by Kelly's approach? A programme such as Sheehan's, discussed in Chapter 5, seems to depend for its success on the group's agreement that the steps in therapy are the right ones for all to take, however much the pace may be varied for each participant. And, lastly, would this short-term course (presented as a commitment for three months) give us any indication of the suitability of such a group for people at varying stages in their attempts to overcome their problem?

Since the author was especially unsure as to the answer to the last question, no selection criteria were used when setting up the group. All the members joined because they had heard about personal construct psychology and its application to stuttering and felt that its attention to issues wider than fluency might have something to offer them. The original number was eight but one, unfortunately, became ill quite early on and another stopped attending because of pressure of examinations. Of the remaining six, two had mild disfluency, 'Alan' and 'Karen', the latter having had no therapy during her adult life. One, 'Veronica', had never before sought help because she could not bring herself to admit to anyone, apart from her parents, that she had a problem. The other three, 'Cynthia', 'Jennifer' and 'Guy', had all achieved considerable fluency on intensive courses at the City Lit. at some stage in the past few years. Although each had maintained some improvement both in speech and in their ability to cope with situations, all three had regressed since their courses and felt that they needed more than sheer practice to help them achieve the ease of communication they desired.

The initial assessment procedures on which individual aims were based consisted of a speech sample of reading, monologue and conversation, a rated grid and a self characterisation (see Chapters 2 and 5 for discussion of these procedures). The speech samples of the four who had had therapy recently could not be considered representative of their everyday levels as they acknowledged that they were used to being tape-recorded and could 'turn on' an assessment performance. All, including Cynthia, who could stutter very severely at times, showed only minor disfluencies in both reading and speaking. Karen was completely fluent during speaking samples, saying that disfluency only occurred occasionally out of the blue. It was for this reason she had joined the group, since these occasions shocked her and, she felt, other people, and caused disproportionate embarrassment. She read at a rate of 178 wpm and was clearly disturbed by the three instances of sound repetition which occurred. Veronica was fluent during speaking, where she admitted to many word changes and could not complete the reading after seizing up at the start.

These speech assessments, therefore, as with so many, can only be said to be of limited value in demonstrating the extent and nature of each person's stuttering. However, they did contribute in some cases to the more important purpose of setting up aims in relation to the type of modification which might be appropriate. Karen, for example, had not realised the impression of nervousness created by the excessive speed at which she spoke. She felt it out of character with the way in which she saw herself and wanted others to see her. A degree of rate control, therefore, was essential to her for reasons other than the prevention of disfluency. Alan was shown to adopt a monotone in order to ensure fluency and chose to work on greater variety and trusting to the natural fluency which was at his command. Although wanting to aim for more expressiveness, Cynthia felt that she needed to maintain the use of prolonged speech for the time being and only gradually risk using natural fluency when she had learned to approach speech generally in a less intense way. After a certain amount of negotiation, with one or two members trying to 'sell' their favoured approach to others, the group had no difficulty in accepting that each had his or her particular aims and needs with regard to speech work.

Individual aims were also set for the psychological aspects of our work, based on factors emerging from the grids and self characterisations. Cynthia's grid and character-sketch, for instance, showed a person who, despite a severe speech problem, was in many respects developing in the direction in which she wanted to go. Her major themes were related to achievement, making an impression on people, living life to the full and, above all, pitting herself against every challenge in order to prove herself. Although this had prevented her from being crushed by her problem in the past, it seemed that she could go no further unless she could approach events and people with less desperate intensity. She needed to find alternative ways of being someone people 'believe in and remember'.

Jennifer's grid showed her separating her 'self as a person' and 'self as a stutterer' from all other elements and one major construct expressed her wish to be 'on equal terms with others', rather than 'at a disadvantage', which was where she placed herself at the time. It seemed probable that she would need to find her commonality with others in her life and, at the same time, discriminate between them. She lumped them together as having the rather restricted range of attributes of being people she could 'communicate with easily' or not, 'felt at ease with' or the contrary, who found her 'amusing' or 'boring' and were 'critical' of her speech as opposed to not noticing it. Her self-characterisation consisted of a list of positive and negative attributes in a very precise manner and we found that she worked best when the experiments she was asked to make and the issues she wanted to take away to think about were clarified for her with equal precision.

It took several weeks for aims such as these to be developed and shared, but, with the exception of Veronica, one of whose major themes was the mistrust of others, the group members gradually learned to see things from each other's point of view and contribute more and more to evolving means for achieving individual goals. At the same time, there were procedures which, when modified to suit each person, were found to be useful for most of them. We worked to widen the focus on speech, for example, to more general communication and then expand to aspects of relationship. Where, in an early session, the members were asked to elaborate on the type of speech they wanted to achieve, this was later extended to descriptions of the person behind the speech and we experimented in role-play with alternative ways of relating to people in situations where formerly the 'stutterer' was the only role open to them.

As mentioned in Chapter 5 people in difficulty often construe those who threaten them in very limited ways. The group was asked to observe such people, listen to them more attentively and try to discover what they were like as a whole. If they continually had trouble it was usually because they approached the person in a particular way — apologetically, perhaps, or angry and defiant. We looked at as many different ways as possible and, having tried some of them out on each other, the members, on the whole, found that they could develop a more flexible repertoire. In some instances they noted a marked change in these people's behaviour towards them. Interviews or feared confrontations were prepared for by anticipating their outcomes in a variety of ways and elaborating more desired ones.

People varied in their willingness to relate what we were doing to past events and relationships, but some shared such reconstruing. One, for example, was able to put herself in her mother's shoes and see her apparent clumsiness in handling her problem as a child in a very different light. Another was able to look at an early trauma in the classroom from the point of view of the teacher at the time and thus free herself from a recurrent nightmare recollection.

It is not possible to give an impression of the wide-ranging discussions which occurred during our sessions. There was, however, a noticeable trend away from speech-related topics to those concerning what one member described as 'the really important business of living'. Another trend in most of the group was towards inventing their own independent experiments between meetings. An issue raised by one person would set up a train of thought or observation in another which more often than not led to action. As a whole, they became more and more interested in the Kellian notion of choice and perhaps the most important thing that came out of it for some was the idea that they were, to some extent at least, self-creating.

It is hoped that it has been made clear that this group experience was initiated, not as a controlled experiment to test specific procedures for their contribution to maintenance of change, but to pose some questions which might lead to such an experiment. The first question the author asked was easily answered. It is indeed viable for members of a group to be working on different ways of modifying speech. The second related to using the personal construct approach, with its emphasis on the individual, in a group context. Again, it was shown that, as with people with other problems, a group of stutterers can contribute to each other's reconstruing processes and benefit themselves from the experience.

The third question posed, the suitability of such a group for people at varying stages in their attempt to overcome their problems, is a more complex one. A sample of six can only suggest factors to be taken into account. Almost a year after the start of the course and six months after most of its members had left, five have obviously derived varying degrees of benefit. Alan and Karen, the two who presented with mild stuttering, report that they seldom think about their speech at all. To them, the most important feature of what we did together seems to have been the effect it had of putting their minimal disfluency into proportion in relation to other issues in their lives.

Guy, who could be very fluent and articulate and suddenly become locked in a spasm of severe blocking, is still working on the major task of taking his whole life less dramatically. He sees his speech as the least of his problems and probably gained most from recognising that his ability to contribute to the work of others was of great value. Having said initially in his self-characterisation that 'people make him agitated' and 'may be a little afraid of him', he proved to be the person in the group towards whom the others turned most for support. He rated himself very unfavourably on constructs such as 'whole-hearted . . . half-hearted', 'friendly . . . unfriendly', 'Involved . . . isolated', and yet he experienced himself as a central figure in the group. Partly as a result of this but undoubtedly also due to life experience outside therapy, he was able to say when asked on leaving for his comments on where he stood that he believed he would 'make out very well'.

Cynthia found that reducing intensity on both a behavioural and psychological level carried her forward in developing fluency and in dealing with life situations in a more flexible way. She of all the group made the most sense of the notion of choice. She learned to judge when she needed to exercise careful control and when she could trust others to be interested in her despite disfluency. She learned to manage people in threatening situations by focusing her attention on them and their concerns, rather than on her own speech performance. Above all, she came to recognise herself as having a great deal to offer, not in spite of her stuttering but unrelated to it. She is still working on conserving her energy and trying out new ways of approaching situations which were formerly only manageable if she 'psyched herself up'.

Jennifer, too, sees the course as one stage in an ongoing process of personal change. She left with a sense of knowing where she was going, but with more work to do. She had certain guidelines, which she crystallised in phrases such as 'life is an experiment', 'we all have choices' and 'communication is a two-way process'. She now comes to the present group occasionally when she is approaching something which she cannot construe in a 'positive' way or when she feels stuck in old ways of handling things.

Veronica was the exception. It was questionable from the beginning whether she would be able to use the group and contribute to it, but it seemed a possibility that she might, for the first time, find people whom she could trust. She warmed to Guy, whom she found understanding and almost believed he was genuinely concerned for her welfare, but any encouragement from the others was greeted with scepticism. She made no sense of the notion that it would be useful to relate her anxieties about speaking to any other issue and, at the same time, refused to experiment with any form of modification as an alternative to avoidance. Despite her edginess there was no doubt about the concern for her amongst the rest of the group by the time the course ended. They had all moved away from self-focus sufficiently to be able to understand something of her predicament.

Proposals for a Maintenance Group

Taking into account the factors which emerged from the Banff conference and later literature on maintenance, it would seem that what we learned from the group described above could contribute to maintenance of change. Such a group, with its flexibility of individual aims with regard to speech and its emphasis on self-development would seem potentially to encompass all the important needs from the clients' point of view. It can provide a regular boost to motivation for those who choose to continue monitoring speech performance as well as a setting where others who decide to experiment with trusting to their natural fluency can do so initially without too much at stake. While providing the peer support which has been shown to be of value (see Chapter 6), it also encourages self-responsibility and inventiveness. The focus of highly active work being placed on life outside the therapy sessions, there is no danger of the group's becoming a haven, where the people concerned commiserate with one another and become locked in the bondage of a shared problem. Above all, it should allow its members space to expand beyond the issues of speech performance and the opportunity to test out new self-concepts.

For such a group to form an effective part of the process of extending and maintaining whatever changes its members aim for, a number of selection criteria would seem to be essential. First, the participants should either have a fair degree of natural fluency or be able to achieve it through the use of a technique with which they are comfortable and confident that they are presenting an appropriate image of themselves. If they are to experiment with new ways of dealing with old difficulties, they must have access to the kind of speech behaviour they themselves find acceptable.

Second, they must have a genuine interest in being involved in their own self-development and aims beyond those of fluency for its own sake. The work in such a group is demanding and unless each person has some life-goal in mind, the incentive to continue will not last. Such goals do not need to be concerned with high achievement in the eyes of the rest of the world. One member of the group described wished, above all things, to reach a degree of serenity which would allow her to facilitate the development of her children's potential. All those who did well showed a willingness to reflect on how they were functioning and what they could do to further their own possibilities.

The third criterion concerns the members' ability to relate to other people. While it is essential for them to come with the incentive of their own demands, for the group to be truly creative they must be capable of developing an interest in the needs of others. Some may have been so swamped by their own difficulties that they have little experience of turning their attention outwards. There seems little doubt that, for many people, one of the major gains from any therapy group is the sense of being able to contribute, perhaps for the first time, to the well-being of another.

Preparation for the maintenance group proposed may take many forms. Someone with severe overt stuttering, for example, may benefit most from an intensive course of fluency training, with work on attitude change introduced gradually as he gains the means for dealing with more demanding speech situations more effectively. Longer-term individual treatment may be more suitable in the case of the client who is satisfied with the way he communicates in some situations but is disturbed by his failure to cope in others, where disfluency diminishes both his efficiency and his self-esteem. He may need the time and space offered by weekly sessions to try out changes in his interpretation of these events and his approach to them.

Direct work on fluency is contraindicated, initially at least, for the interiorised stutterer. The person who seldom or never stutters but who is haunted by the possibility has a very special problem, which is rarely understood either by the inexperienced therapist or other people who stutter. He or she may go to great lengths to prevent the occurrence of disfluency. Avoidance mechanisms are developed to a fine art, ranging from the refusal to become involved in threatening situations to skilful word-changes. Such clients are not suitable for a group in the early stages, unless it includes others dealing with their difficulties in the same way. They are generally not recognised as having a speech problem by the people they meet and often do not talk about it to those close to them. Nevertheless, to themselves they may be severely handicapped. Their whole lives may be governed by their apprehension about speech failure. Individual therapy along personal construct lines is suggested here, with transfer to a maintenance group when some of the major issues which have kept them locked in this unhappy position have been worked through.

It is emphasised that these are proposals only, based on some work currently in progress in London. A research project, carried out by a team of therapists from the Hertfordshire Health Authority in association with Fransella is nearing completion. Entitled 'An investigation of the effect on stuttering relapse-rate of a combined programme of training in speech technique and psychological reconstruction', it focuses on outcome for four groups of people who have been involved in intensive courses followed by weekly therapy. Two of the groups have only worked on prolonged speech and two on this technique combined with personal construct procedures. Results will be ready for publication in 1983.

Summary of Maintenance and Relapse Factors

The title of this chapter is 'Maintenance of Change', rather than 'Maintenance of Fluency' in order to encompass a wider range of goals than that suggested by the latter phrase. Some of the issues discussed have proved central only to those treatment approaches where the total elimination of stuttering is aimed at, while others seem of importance whatever change is desired. Focus on speech behaviour alone appears to be insufficient for many to guarantee continued speech improvement. Work on aspects of psychological change is seen as relevant by many workers, though researchers have so far been unable to pinpoint which among such treatment variables as self-reinforcement, group support or individual counselling may be responsible for permanency in particular cases.

It can only be suggested, therefore, that a number of factors should be taken into account when planning therapy for any individual who stutters if the effects are to be lasting. Assessment should be of such thoroughness that initial goals, whether they be for 100 per cent fluency or ease of communication, are set with every aspect of the speaker's personality and circumstances in mind, as well as the extent and nature of the disfluency. While it is the therapist's task to present treatment procedures with clarity and plan the steps involved with care, self-responsibility in the client is an essential development.

Although some stutterers *are* willing to go on practising and continue to monitor their speech in order to remain fluent, this does seem to be at the cost of learning to feel like a normal speaker. The gradual introduction of periods of unmonitored speech emerges as an important feature of work in programmes involving fluency techniques. Tolerance of fluency failure is also seen as essential by many clinicians and, certainly, in preference to a return to avoidance mechanisms.

Maintenance of attitude change has been shown to parallel maintenance of speech improvement. Direct work on a person's view of particular situations, people, and himself as a speaker is included in many approaches, though often in a somewhat unstructured way. The application of personal construct psychology is currently being tested as a means of helping those who stutter to extend their development of themselves in a wider context, the hypothesis being that planning speech change in relation to other changes is an important element in preventing relapse in the face of old threats.

Some factors relating to relapse must, of course, lie outside the person's control. Sudden termination of therapy through moving home or job or school is an obvious one. The inability to follow up intensive work with regular maintenance therapy is another. Although some people who stutter may rise to an unexpected challenge in life, others may be too vulnerable to meet say, the loss of someone close to them or the loss of a job, without losing their grasp of speech control. Others have found that the change in them is so unacceptable to the people round them that life is made easier by a return to stuttering.

Perhaps the most difficult factor within the people themselves, however, is to be aware of the recurrence of old anxieties and struggle behaviour and yet unable to acknowledge it. Wholly understandably, at such a time, many who have made great improvement fail to take immediate action and eventually either slip back to where they started or return to the clinic in considerable panic and disappointment. This last may well be the most common cause of relapse. It is for the therapist to prepare clients for such a possibility and work out strategies for rescue.

References

Adams, M. (1981) 'Aperçus' in E. Boberg (ed.), *Maintenance of Fluency*, Elsevier, Amsterdam, pp. 264-6

Boberg, E. (1979) 'Maintenance of Fluency: a Review', *Journal of Fluency Disorders, 4*, 93-116

——— (1981) 'Maintenance of Fluency: An Experimental Program' in E. Boberg (ed.), *Maintenance of Fluency*, Elsevier, Amsterdam, pp. 71-111

Boehmler, R.M. (1981) 'Aperçus' in E. Boberg (ed.), *Maintenance of Fluency* Elsevier, Amsterdam, pp. 266-8

Cooper, E.B. (1979) 'Intervention Procedures for the Young Stutterer' in H.H. Gregory (ed.), *Controversies About Stuttering Therapy*, University Park Press, Baltimore, pp. 63-96

Helps, R. and Dalton, P. (1979) 'The Effectiveness of an Intensive Group Speech Therapy Programme for Adult Stammerers', *British Journal of Disorders of*

Communication, 14, 17-30

Howie, P.M., Tanner, S. and Andrews, G. (1981) 'Short-and Long-term Outcome in an Intensive Treatment Program for Adult Stutterers', *Journal of Speech and Hearing Disorders, 46*, 104-109

Ingham, R. (1981) 'Evaluation and Maintenance in Stuttering Treatment', in E. Boberg (ed.), *Maintenance of Fluency*, Elsevier, Amsterdam, pp. 179-218

Ingham, R. and Andrews G. (1971) 'Stuttering: The Quality of Fluency after Treatment', *Journal of Communication Disorders, 4*, 279-88

Florance, C.L. and Shames G.H. (1980) 'Stuttering Treatment: Issues in Transfer and Maintenance', *Seminars in Speech, Language and Hearing, 1*, 375-88

Owen, N. (1981) 'Facilitating Maintenance of Behaviour Change' in E. Boberg (ed.) *Maintenance of Fluency*, Elsevier, Amsterdam, pp. 31-70

Perkins, W.H. (1981) 'Measurement and Maintenance of Fluency' in E. Boberg (ed.), *Maintenance of Fluency*, Elsevier, Amsterdam, pp. 147-78

—— (1981) 'Aperçus' in E. Bolberg (ed.), *Maintenance of Fluency*, Elsevier, Amsterdam, pp. 258-9

Ryan, B.P. (1981) 'Maintenance Programs in Progress – II' in E. Boberg (ed.) *Maintenance of Fluency*, Elsevier, Amsterdam, pp. 113-46

Shames, G.H. (1981) 'Relapse in Stuttering' in E. Boberg (ed), *Maintenance of Fluency*, Elsevier, Amsterdam, pp. 219-49

Sheehan, J.G. (1970) 'Role Therapy'in J.G. Sheehan (ed.), *Stuttering: Research and Therapy*, Harper and Row, New York, pp. 262-310

—— (1979) 'Current Issues on Stuttering and Recovery' in H.H. Gregory (ed.), *Controversies About Stuttering Therapy*, University Park Press, Baltimore, pp. 175-207

Van Riper, C. (1973) *The Treatment of Stuttering*, Prentice-Hall, Englewood Cliffs, N.J.

Williams, D.E. (1982) 'Stuttering Therapy: Where Are We Going – And Why?', *Journal of Fluency Disorders, 7*, 159-70

8 ADJUNCTS TO SPEECH THERAPY

Roberta Lees

Introduction

The concept of stuttering being alleviated by resort to 'outside agencies' has been popular with stutterers and those attempting to treat them for some considerable time. These outside agencies have taken many forms, from swallowing of various substances to using many types of mechanical or electronic devices. The popularity of these aids has often undergone changing fortunes, according to theories of aetiology and treatment principles in vogue during different decades. Nevertheless the stutterer himself often shows considerable faith in these aids, and the therapist, while recognising the importance of the interpersonal aspects of this disorder, may employ such aids as adjuncts to a more comprehensive treatment programme. If the aim of therapy is initially the achievement of fluency then the use of these adjuncts can be very beneficial.

Many such adjuncts have been described for the treatment of stuttering but only a few of those currently in use will be discussed in this chapter; these are considered to be representative of the machines, swallowing of substances, etc. used. The development of the Edinburgh masker has created interest in the use of auditory masking machines, while at the same time work on biofeedback machines has revived interest in the use of relaxation-based treatment approaches. The use of hypnosis and drugs has continued to intrigue stutterers and clinicians concerning their possible value in treatment. All of the aforementioned adjuncts will be discussed in this chapter.

Auditory Masking

One effect of the presentation of high intensity white noise on stuttering is that the frequency of disfluency is reduced. This use of noise in treatment is not a particularly new concept: Van Riper (1973) discusses accounts of 'therapeutic deafening' written half a century ago, although at that time its use was not confined solely to stuttering. Interest in the relationship of hearing and stuttering was aroused in 1912 by a report of Gutzmann (referred to in Wingate 1976) stating that the congenitally deaf never stutter. More recent reports are in general agreement with this finding, although these claims are now more modified. The presence of stuttering has been noted among the deaf and hard of hearing population but the incidence is much lower than amongst the normal hearing population (Harms and Malone 1939). Obviously, the explanation of this may be related to factors such as differences in social pressure or to some more obscure aetiology. However, it was clear that following this finding the next step would involve the experimental reduction of hearing level in stutterers.

Noise Characteristics

There has been general agreement concerning the characteristics of this noise which has an ameliorative effect on stuttering. Cherry and Sayers (1956) found that when a very loud masking noise was used, sufficient to overcome bone-conducted self-hearing, there was a very substantial reduction in stuttering. They eliminated first the high frequency components of the noise and then the low frequency components and concluded that the latter was more effective. As there have been a large number of subsequent reports on the frequency and intensity of masking noise, only a few, considered by the author to be representative, will be given here.

Ham and Steer (1967) masked frequencies of below 800 Hz and found increased fluency while Stromsta (1958) noted that disfluency was decreased when frequencies of below 500 Hz were masked. MacCulloch, Eaton and Long (1970) used a tone of 300 Hz and Parker and Christopherson (1963) varied the frequency but in general used the range of 150-200 Hz. More recently Dewar, Dewar and Barnes (1976) described the Edinburgh masker, which has a frequency range of 100-140 Hz (the frequency of vibration of the vocal cords). Certainly, it would appear that low frequency masking is necessary but there is no evidence that any specific frequency range is the most effective for stutterers.

Most reports on the intensity of masking noise conclude that the noise level must be sufficient to overcome bone conducted hearing. Maraist and Hutton (1957), using masking levels of 30, 50, 70 and 90 dB found a progressive decrease in stuttering as intensity of masking noise increased with considerable decreases above 50 dB. Ham and Steer (1967) returned the stutterers' speech signal at intensities of 30, 45, 60 and 75 dB above the individual speech reception thresholds and found that only the 60 and 75 dB increases were associated with a significant reduction in stuttering. Adams and Hutchinson (1974) have confirmed the general finding that stuttering decreased as noise level increased.

Continuous vs Contingent Masking

In most of the foregoing experiments, the masking noise presented to stutterers has been continuous and triggered by a manual switch which was under the conscious control of the subject. However, an interesting result was obtained by Sutton and Chase (1961) who used the stutterers' phonation to activate the masking noise. They created two conditions of masking, viz masking was presented only when the stutterer was phonating and masking was presented only during intervals of silence. They compared the results with those of the continuous masking and found that fluency was improved in all conditions and that masking during silence was just as effective as even continuous masking or masking only during phonation. These findings were corroborated by Webster and Dorman (1968). Subsequently, Dewar, Dewar and Barnes (1976) produced the Edinburgh Masker which incorporates a device for triggering the masking sound by means of a laryngeal micropohone switch. This masker is used only in the first of Sutton and Chase's two conditions, i.e. it is activated only when the subject initiates phonation and claims have been made that stutterers have obtained considerable benefit from this. Unfortunately, Dewar *et al* measured 'vocal errors' and showed that these decreased when the masker was worn, but these 'vocal errors' may incorporate speech characteristics not normally included in attempts to define stuttering.

Effect of Masking

The fact that the use of masking noise operated by a manual switch or triggered by the subject's phonation can produce a decrease in stuttering behaviour has aroused considerable interest amongst therapists. The effect of masking noise on stutterers can often be a very sudden and dramatic decrease in disfluency and thus much enthusiasm has been generated for this technique. However, it is by no means a panacea for all stuttering behaviour. Although Dewar *et al* (1976) did extol its virtues, their subjects used masking for only a short period of time. Garber and Martin (1974) attempted to determine the effect of a slightly longer period of exposure to masking noise. They asked three stutterers to speak for 50 minutes, during which time they received white noise presented binaurally in alternate five minute periods. All subjects experienced a decrease in stuttering frequency during the first five minute period, in which 100 dB noise was presented. Over longer periods of time while using a tone with an intensity of 100 dB, one subject increased and one subject decreased the frequency of stuttering slightly. The third subject showed a significant decrease in stuttering frequency. Ingham, Southwood and Horsburgh (1981) also attempted to evaluate the effects of masking noise over a longer period of time and they required four stutterers to read and speak spontaneously during eight 30 minute sessions, two hours with the Edinburgh masker and two hours without. Their findings showed that stuttering was virtually absent during masking for only one subject while another subject showed some improvement during spontaneous speech only. The remaining two subjects displayed only marginal reductions in stuttering during spontaneous speech or oral reading. These studies have utilised only a small number of subjects and would require to be replicated with large numbers in order to ascertain with some degree of certainty the percentage of stutterers who cannot maintain the initial dramatic decrease in disfluency. The fact that some stutterers can maintain some increase in fluency with masking noise has led to the development of portable masking machines to assist transfer of this noise-induced fluency.

Portable Maskers

One of the early reports on the use of portable masking units was that of Parker and Christopherson (1963) who designed the unit originally to assist stutterers to speak more freely during psychiatric examination, but later considered that this device could be useful for the treatment of the stutter itself. In the USSR Derazne (1966) produced the Derazne Correctophone which produced a very low frequency of 50 Hz with an intensity output of 60 dB. This machine was considered only as an adjunct to other types of therapy, e.g. sleep therapy, psychotherapy, etc. Gruber (1971) also found the masker to be useful when considered as an adjunct to therapy. She combined the use of the masker with a treatment technique described by Van Riper (1963) and trained her stutterers to activate the masker when learning to pull out of a block, her aim being to shift the stutterer's self-monitoring from auditory to tactile and proprioceptive channels. While using the masker none of the stutterers obtained stutter-free speech and although the frequency of stuttering remained approximately the same, there was a significant reduction in the severity of the block.

There have been variations on the type of masker used. Perkins and Curlee (1969) experimented with a masking device which generated a pulsing signal with variable rate and intensity and compared this with an unfiltered white noise unit. Their subjects were three stutterers who were in the final phases of conversational rate control therapy and agreed to use these devices to assist transfer of fluency to situations outside the clinic. All subjects reported that stuttering was decreased with both units, though two subjects preferred the pulsed noise to the white noise. A pulsed signal was also used by Donovan (1971) who developed a device which combines a pacemaker and masking sound. The masking tone is interrupted at regular intervals and the characteristics of the masking sound have been altered to make it resemble speech sound. Donovan claims that this device gives a degree of masking and at the same time provides a beat which is easier to synchronise with speech than the metronome beat (for further discussion on the metronome beat, see Wohl 1968). Further experimentation is required to determine whether a pulsed masking tone is more efficacious than a continuous tone in the treatment of stuttering.

Long-Term Effect

Although it is generally agreed that some stutterers do experience an increase in fluency while wearing such devices, the long-term effect on the stutterer is controversial. Trotter (1967), himself a stutterer, used a portable masker in difficult speaking situations over a period of 2½ years and found that the severity of stuttering was reduced while using the masker and for a short time afterwards, but within a day the stuttering had returned to its usual level. However, Dewar, Dewar, Austin and Brash (1979) followed the progress of 67 patients who used a masker from six to twenty-eight months and reported that 42 per cent considered the device to be of 'great' benefit; 40 per cent reported 'considerable' benefit and 18 per cent thought it to be of 'slight' benefit' They also reported that the masker produced some additional beneficial effects, viz reduction of tension and abolition of concomitant movements. Progress of patients was, however, monitored by questionnaire, phone conversation, individual correspondence and, where possible, by direct clinical observation. Although this follow up procedure failed to meet the basic experimental and statistical requirements, a point noted by Code and Muller (1980), it is still worthwhile to consider the viewpoint of the patient concerning any therapeutic technique.

Subgroups?

The fact that masking noise is effective for some stutterers merits further investigation into the possible subgrouping of patients with this disorder. One interesting finding in relation to this concept was that of Conture and Brayton (1975) who studied the effect of masking noise on the type of disfluency. They identified seven disfluency types and found that the only significant difference between the control and noise conditions was in part word repetitions. The difference in prolongations approached but did not reach statistical significance at the 5 per cent level of confidence. Part-word repetitions and prolongations accounted for 77 per cent of the total disfluency behaviour during the control condition and 71 per cent during the noise condition. They thus concluded that noise had a significant influence only on the types of disfluency that occurred relatively frequently during the control condition. Silverman and Goodban (1972) have also noted that when normally fluent speakers read in the presence of noise, only part word repetitions and revisions were significantly reduced. This may relate to the frequency of these behaviours in normally fluent speech. It is possible that, in the future, one of the conditions used in the selection of patients for treatment with a masking device will involve consideration of the type and frequency of disfluency.

Difficulties

Like so many devices, difficulties have been reported in the use of masking units for treatment of stuttering. Wingate (1976) has commented that stutterers do not adapt to the use of this device even on an intermittent 'as needed' basis, or sometimes inappropriate reactions are elicited from others who may erroneously believe that the stutterer is deaf and shout to him. Van Riper (1973) has also noted that some patients tended to press the switch to activate the masker either too soon or too late and even when the therapist turned on the noise, his reaction time delayed the contingent sound. Voice-activated masking devices would seem to be useful here, except for stutterers whose greatest difficulty lies in the initiation of phonation. One of the greatest sources of concern, however, must be the long-term effect on the stutterer's hearing. Garber and Martin (1974) assessed two stutterers for temporary threshold shift during a 50 minute session and found no systematic change in auditory thresholds following exposure to 100 dB white noise during alternate 5 minute periods. Dewar *et al* (1979) have found no evidence of temporary threshold shift. They have also monitored sixteen stutterers for periods of up to three years and found no evidence of any deterioration of hearing acuity in the frequency range 125-128 k Hz. Further studies on the hearing acuity of stutterers monitored carefully for the total exposure time to masking noise and the intensity level of this noise would allow for more confidence in stating the limits, if any, of 'safe' use of masking over an extended period.

The Role of Masking Noise in Therapy

Despite these difficulties, much use has been made of auditory masking, often as an adjunct to therapy rather than as a treatment *per se*. There have been many case studies of patients reporting an increase in fluency when using a masking device for difficult speech situations (e.g. Perkins and Curlee 1969). Its use in the prison setting has also been reported by Walle (1980) who found that prisoners obtained increased fluency when speaking at Review Boards and recommended its use at court hearings. Others have used the masking device, again as an adjunct to other forms of therapy, but specifically to shift the stutterer's attention from auditory to tactile/proprioceptive monitoring of speech (Gruber 1971). Thus, masking devices could be regarded as useful adjuncts to therapy either to encourage the stutterer to monitor speech without recourse to the auditory channel or to give him confidence or the feeling of fluency in difficult speaking situations. Dewar *et al* (1976) have noted that masking noise may also help to reduce concomitant movements of stutterers. The use of auditory masking units has also been found to be effective with children, the effect being maintained after the device was removed (MacCulloch, Eaton and Long 1970). There is, however, a paucity of information on the long-term effects of auditory masking on child stutterers.

Rationale

Any treatment technique seems to have more validity if some explanation can be given of its effect but, unfortunately, no single rationale can be found for auditory masking. Attempts to explain the effects of masking on the basis of distraction have been discussed by Boers-Van Dijk (1973) who considers that the benefits are not due entirely to distraction. She bases her reasons for this conclusion on the grounds that masking is just as effective during silence as during speech (Sutton and Chase 1961), low frequency masking is more effective than high frequency masking, and the effect of masking can continue for a short time after the noise has been removed. Thus, although it is possible that some element of distraction is implicated, it would appear unlikely that this is the sole explanation for the ameliorative effects of noise on stuttering. Shane (1955) considered that the less the stutterer hears of his speech, the less basis he should have for making a critical and possibly negative evaluation of it. Shane's findings are similar to others from the

Iowa school concerning the beginnings of stuttering. Using palmar sweat measures of anxiety Adams and Moore (1972) found no evidence of reduced anxiety during noise conditions when the subjects experienced a significant reduction in stuttering. One obvious explanation for the effectiveness of masking noise lies within the cybernetic theories of stuttering. If there is some disruption in the auditory feedback mechanism of stutterers (for a discussion of this, see Van Riper 1971) then the use of masking noise forces the stutterer to monitor his speech by means of some other channel, i.e. masking noise circumvents the use of a possibly defective channel. The evidence for the existence of a disorder of auditory feedback is controversial as it is difficult to explain certain aspects of stuttering within such a theory. Stuttering often occurs at the initiation of an utterance but in this instance no auditory feedback is operative.

The natural reaction of speakers deprived of auditory feedback is to increase volume (the Lombard effect). Adams and Hutchinson (1974) have noted a reduction in stuttering frequency which accompanied a rise in vocal intensity while others found that masking still increased fluency when stutterers spoke quietly (e.g. Cherry and Sayers 1956). Wingate (1976) commented that one could deduce that such changes in manner of speaking as are encountered by normal speakers in masking conditions might explain the reduction in stuttering. He quotes a number of studies on the effects of masking noise on norms which would generally indicate a rise in vocal intensity and vocal frequency with a reduced rate of articulation. Wingate (1981) pursued his vocalization hypothesis and showed by recourse to spectrographic evidence that when a stutterer attains fluency there is minimal variation in fundamental frequency and concentration of energy in the lower harmonics. Unfortunately this study investigated the ameliorative effects of four influences on stuttering, but masking was not one of them. The hypothesis would, therefore, require more investigation. Ingham *et al* (1981) attempted to ascertain if there were perceptually evident changes in speech quality during masking conditions and found that there were perceptual differences between some stutterers' speech in masking conditions, though this did not apply to all stutterers. They write of one subject who improved considerably in their study that when improved fluency occurs during masking, it is associated with a perceptibly altered speech pattern. A greater understanding of the fluency characteristics of stuttering may explain the apparent effectiveness of various treatment techniques and may contribute to the reason why some stutterers resist the transfer phase in therapy.

Thus, as with so many treatment techniques for stutterers, although reasons for its effectiveness are still unclear, it remains a useful adjunct in therapy. It would certainly appear to reduce stuttering for a considerable amount of speaking time for some stutterers. Its value as an adjunct in therapy would be enhanced if the complex interrelationship between noise and stuttering were more fully understood, with observation of the intensity and frequency of the noise and whether or not the tone should be pulsed or continuous. Subject variability in relation to speech symptoms and attitudes towards the use of such devices must also be considered before a more definitive statement on the role of auditory masking noise in stuttering therapy can be made.

Biofeedback

As struggle behaviour plays an important role in stuttering, the use of relaxation techniques in the treatment of this disorder has enjoyed a long history. Indeed many stutterers ascribe their problems to tension and certainly training the stutterer to speak under relaxation has been known to produce fluency , for whatever reason. Nowadays biofeedback machines, which objectively measure the degree of relaxation attained, may be used as adjuncts in therapy. These machines not only aim to inform the patient of the degree of tension present in the muscle groups studied, but also of the effectiveness of his strategies for reducing this tension; obviously they are not concerned with its cause. The most widely used biofeedback machine for the treatment of stuttering has been that utilising electromyographic evidence. In this instance, electrodes are placed over the muscles being studied to pick up their electrical signals and these signals are then electronically amplified, processed and finally displayed, by either auditory or visual means, to the patient. Alternatively some biofeedback machines are dependent on psychogalvanic skin response and thus give a measure of generalised tension rather than that of specific muscle groups. Other methods of assessing degree of tension would include measurement of heart rate, laryngography, etc. Although monitors utilising EMG feedback have been most widely used, recourse to other types of monitoring may reveal additional information on physiological changes occurring before and during the stuttering instance.

Stuttering and Increased Muscle Activity

Biofeedback machines have been used to demonstrate that increased muscular activity does exist either before or during the audible or obvious moment of stuttering. Shrum (1967) measured surface electrical activity of facial, neck and chest muscles in stutterers and found that stuttering was preceded by an early and sustained rise in signal amplitude in almost all muscles studied. Platt and Basili (1973) placed surface electromyographic electrodes on the masseter and suprahyoid muscles of three adult stutterers and showed that both the frequency and the amplitude of tremors from the two muscles were similar for stuttering and isometric contractions. If stuttering is accompanied by a spasm of the laryngeal muscles it would be difficult to prove this by recourse to EMG as it is impossible to measure the action of the intrinsic laryngeal muscles. However, Hanna, Wifling and McNeill (1975) have shown that EMG spikes from the throat differentiate periods of stuttering from periods of normal speech, though it can not be assumed that this is a singular representation of activity from any one largyngeal muscle or well-delineated muscle group. This change in activity of muscle groups may occur before the listener perceives stuttering and raises the question of a definition of the moment of stuttering and the role of anticipation. Knox (1974), using spectrographic analysis, found increased fundamental frequency, inappropriate transitions and slow rate of articulation in the seemingly fluent syllables preceding the obvious moments of stuttering. The results were interpreted as evidence of excessive laryngeal muscle activity.

Thus, evidence does exist of excess tension in various muscle groups required for speech production and so many clinical reports have ascribed considerable importance to voluntary tension reduction in stuttering therapy (e.g. Azrin and Nunn 1974).

Biofeedback in Treatment

Electrode Placement. One of the major problems in the use of biofeedback techniques is the site of electrode placement, as no single site has yet been delineated as optimal for all stutterers. Many muscle groups have been used, mainly, and perhaps not surprisingly, in the facial and throat regions. Guitar (1975) placed pairs of electrodes over the orbicularis oris superior, under the chin and above the thyroid cartilage, while Kalotkin, Manschreck and O'Brien (1979) placed electrodes bilaterally over the masseter muscle area. Some have varied the site of electrode placement according to the symptoms with which the patient presented. Lanyon, Barrington and Newman (1976) attached two surface electrodes to a location on the stutterer's face and jaw area where muscle tension was thought to be high during stuttering: this location being determined from the subject's own report and tactile examination by the therapist. Stromer (1979), having also concluded that there was no reason to assume that a single most effective site for electrode placement existed, commented that clinical experience had demonstrated the great intersubject locus variability of stuttering and secondary behaviours. He suggested that choices for relaxation site specification would thus involve, (a) choosing the site showing the highest EMG level during blocks, or (b) noting the voice quality break-downs or airflow deviations during observed blocks. This may also involve an analysis of those sounds that seem to be most often blocked, e.g. if the patient showed most difficulty with /pbmw/, electrodes would be placed on the lips. Although it may seem natural to utilise the patient's obvious symptom to infer the locus of excess tension, this too is open to question. Guitar (1975) found that the effective sites did not necessarily correlate with sound production, e.g. he found that by placing electrodes on the lips, stuttering was reduced on lingual consonants.

It would seem that for each stutterer there is an optimal site for electrode placement, but a means for ascertaining this has not yet been systematically developed and it thus seems likely that this decision will be based on trial and error for some time.

Type of Feedback Display. The stutterer is given feedback of his degree of tension either through the auditory or visual channel. Auditory feed-back may involve a series of audible clicks which are increased or decreased according to a rise/fall in tension, or tension may be repre-sented by a constant sound, rising in pitch. Visual feedback often takes the form of a modified voltmeter. There is little evidence to suggest that one form of feedback is more effective for some/all stutterers.

Possible Technique. Biofeedback techniques may be used as an adjunct to some other form of therapy or may be used as the sole treatment. The application of these techniques has varied, but, in the writer's opinion, the following method may be regarded as being representa-tive.

Electrodes are attached to whatever group of muscles the therapist or experimenter considers relevant and the patient is given an initial period of training in reducing tension levels of these muscles by attend-ing to the biofeedback machine. When the patient has learned to relax these muscle groups he is given a criterion level to reach, often 4-5 μV (Lanyon *et al* 1976), or the criterion level is determined by averaging the integrated EMG activity during base line segments (Moore 1978). In the latter situation, if the patients' tension levels rose beyond the criterion level they received a blast of white noise with an intensity of 65dB, but if the patients remained below the criterion level 85 per cent of the time over at least two 5 minute segments, then the criterion voltage was decreased in either 2.5 or 5μV steps.

Patients are then instructed to look at the first word of the speaking task and, by utilizing the biofeedback machine, ensure that the criterion level has been reached. If it has, they can proceed to say the first word of the task. The same procedure is used for every other word until gradually the length of the task is increased. The speaking tasks vary from reading graded material (Lanyon *et al* 1976), to reading prose passages (Cross 1977), to more spontaneous speech (Hanna *et al* 1975). During the time the patient practises this speaking task, he learns to attend to somaesthetic cues. Thus he initiates speech only when his tension levels reach a specific criterion and he associates fluency with this 'new' somaesthetic feedback.

Transfer. As with most treatment techniques, when fluency is achieved the transfer to other situations has proved difficult. In order to assist this transfer a period of indirect feedback may be given, such as that used by Lanyon (1977). As Lanyon utilised visual feedback this involves turning the feedback monitor to face the therapist who requests that the stutterer does not begin to speak until he has reached the criterion level already practised with direct feedback. If the patient speaks too soon (the more common fault) or too late after the criterion level has been reached, the therapist then indicates to the patient that he should initiate speech. Thus the stutterer is trained to attend to somaesthetic cues without relying solely on biofeedback instrumentation. Interestingly, the criterion for relaxation chosen by the therapist is not always the same as that chosen by the patient. Patients indicated that they started to speak when they felt they had relaxed the muscles sufficiently to do so without stuttering, regardless of whether or not they had reached the formal relaxation criterion (Lanyon 1977). Perhaps a more appropriate way of finding a suitable criterion level for each patient will be found in the future, but there is no reason to suggest that one criterion level exists which is appropriate for all stutterers.

The results of most studies employing this technique have shown that stutterers were able to achieve increased fluency when using the material given to them in the laboratory or clinic conditions. Although this fluency was achieved in a 'safe' environment, the mechanism or mechanisms by which this was achieved may assist understanding of factors required in any fluency instatement phase of therapy.

Rationale

As with many techniques, the concept of distraction has been mooted, i.e. if the stutterer's attention is directed almost entirely towards achieving and maintaining a certain criterion level of relaxation, he does not think solely of his speech. However, in a single patient study (Hanna *et al* 1975) the stutterer received both true and false feedback of his tensions levels and results showed that he experienced considerably more fluency when on true feedback, but he was slightly more fluent on false feedback than on no feedback at all. This study requires replication with larger numbers before any firm claims about the possible role of distraction can be made. The fact that the patient was slightly less disfluent on false feedback than on the no feedback condition would indicate that distraction may be implicated, but is not the sole explanation for the achievement of increased fluency. It seems possible that some patients may be influenced by the use of 'machines' and may therefore respond favourably to them at least for a short time.

The fluency effects of these techniques may also result from the biofeedback equipment acting as a vigilance device ensuring that 'the stutterer pays more attention to the planning and execution of his utterances' (Cross 1977). This vigilance device may assist the stutterer to produce changes in vocalisation such as soft attack, reduction of volume and intonation range, slowing of rate, etc. — all factors sometimes recognised as assisting fluency. If this is so, the patient, by attending to somaesthetic cues rather than to speech *per se*, is assisted in achieving fluency, albeit 'artificial' fluency, initially. In some studies discussing the efficacy of various treatment techniques in stuttering, particularly those aimed at 'speaking fluently', the quality of the fluency obtained is rarely discussed. Recent work has suggested that the perceptually fluent utterances of stutterers show differences, when analysed by means of high speed cineflurographic techniques, from the fluent utterances of non-stutterers (Zimmerman 1980).

In a similar vein, if stuttering is regarded as an anticipatory disorder, biofeedback training may be effective, as it trains the stutterer to lower or eliminate covert pre-utterance activity (Guitar 1975). The stutterer may have some form of discrete awareness of types of physiological behaviour involved in his disfluencies and therefore learn strategies which help to reduce these. These strategies may not be entirely relaxation-based as shown by an interesting result obtained by Pachman, Oelschlanger, Hughes and Hughes (1978), who trained two stutterers to both raise and lower EMG levels of the frontalis muscle and found that the frequency of part-word repetitions was decreased in both conditions. Again, replication with larger numbers would allow more certainty on comments concerning the implications of these results. (Similarly, Moore (1978) in a three patient study, found that although there was a relationship between EMG activity and disfluencies, this was far from perfect.)

Value of Biofeedback Training

The technique of using biofeedback training could be very useful and helpful to all involved in the treatment of stuttering. One of the main advantages of this technique is that it is unobtrusive as the stutterer does not noticeably modify or alter his speech, but rather provides for himself the pre-utterance reduction of tension and/or pre-utterance strategies which assist fluency. Obviously there is a considerable discrepancy between saying specific material in a laboratory or clinic situation and speaking spontaneously in a hitherto feared situation, thus the ability of the patient to retain the appropriate somaesthetic cues and to reproduce these cues under stressful situations must be considered. In this connection more studies on the long term effects of biofeedback training would be particularly beneficial.

Some may criticise the use of instrumentation on the grounds that this could destroy or weaken the therapist-patient relationship, yet Stromer (1979) comments thus; 'biofeedback work implies a close harmony among the client, the clinician and the instrumentation'. Provided that the therapist understands the uses and limitations of the instrumentation, the patient-therapist relationship should not be adversely affected. Silver and Blanchard (1978) consider that, for many of its applications, biofeedback has not been shown to be superior to relaxation training. However, Lanyon (1977) lists the advantages of instrumentation as:

(1)   A greater degree of experimental precision is possible;
(2)   Objective criteria for relaxation are continually available, and
(2)   Immediate and continuous feedback is present.

Although a greater degree of precision is possible concerning relaxation criterion, some allowance must be made for day-to-day changes in stutterers' tension levels. In relation to this, further information is required on the intra- and inter-subject variability of tension levels in the non-stuttering population when speaking in different situations.

It would therefore seem that biofeedback training could be helpful, particularly in the initial stages of a fluency instatement programme, but would be most effective if regarded not as a single treatment technique, but as part of a wider therapeutic programme designed to meet the requirements of each individual stutterer.

The use of biofeedback techniques has also extended to the diagnostic and prognostic role, although at present there is little information on this area. Kalotkin *et al* (1979) attempted to discover if electromyographic measures could differentiate severe and mild stutterers from norms, and found that during conversational speech the difference was significant, though this difference did not obtain during relaxation with no speech. Of interest was the additional finding of no correlation between EMG level and stuttering severity rating, suggesting that factors other than tension levels differentiate severe and mild stutterers.

It has been noted that stutterers manifesting laryngeal blocking tended to have a poorer prognosis (Van Riper 1973) and this has been confirmed by Guitar (1975), who found that subjects showing great amounts of laryngeal tension were less successful when using biofeedback techniques. It seems possible that the future use of biofeedback techniques will be limited to the early stages of therapy with the stutterer, i.e. diagnostic and fluency instatement phases.

Hypnosis

It was not until 1890, when hypnotism was approved by the British Medical Association, that it became 'respectable' in this country. Rockey (1980) described how some physicians attempted to treat stuttering by hypnosis at that time. She reported the results of two physicians: Kingsbury, who claimed to have successfully treated one stutterer by hypnosis, though no evidence was available on how many stutterers he hypnotised; and Tuckey who, from his experience of twelve patients, considered it to be the best remedy for young adults. Rockey (1980) also describes how James Braid, a Manchester surgeon, began his investigations into mesmeric phenomena in 1841 and made claims that in this 'natural state of heightened sensibility', patients were 'therapeutically receptive'. He claimed to have treated many conditions, including deafness and aphonia, by this means, but claims on the treatment of stuttering were notable by their absence.

This state of 'heightened sensibility' is still not fully understood. Under hypnosis the person is not truly asleep as EEG studies have shown that his cortical brain waves are undistinguishable from those recorded in his waking states when his eyes are closed.

Post-Hypnotic Suggestion

Many patients request the use of hypnosis in the form of post-hypnotic suggestion as an 'answer' to their stuttering problem. This use of suggestion implies a very passive treatment where the patient is no longer an active participant in his own therapy and would seem to be ill advised. Van Riper (1958) found that fluency could be attained when the patient was deeply hypnotised, but there was only a momentary transfer of this fluency, when the post-hypnotic suggestion was used, that the stutterer would be able to speak without stuttering. However, increase in fluency was noted when hypnotic training was used to induce relaxation while speaking and then the post-hypnotic suggestion was given that the stutterer could speak in the same relaxed way upon coming out of the trance. No mention of stuttering was made throughout. Unfortunately these fluency effects wore off and patients required more and more hypnotic session boosters to maintain the relaxed way of speaking.

Hypnosis and Speech Therapy

Van Riper did succeed in inhibiting the instrumental behaviours of three stutterers by means of hypnosis. He found that the stutterers seemed to unlearn these behaviours much more rapidly than would have been expected. This raises the issue of whether or not the instrumental coping behaviours have a different origin and pattern of development from other aspects of stuttering behaviour. Starkweather and Lucker (978) have already proposed that the concomitant movements do have a different history from the speech symptoms of stutterers, as they found that punishment decreased these concomitant movements but did not consistently decrease the repetitions and prolongations of their stutterers. If this is so, hypnosis, in the form of post-hypnotic suggestion, may be useful for inhibiting these extraneous movements and would thus be a valuable adjunct in treatment.

A few reports are now available on the use of hypnosis either to assist the patient in achieving success with a speech symptom treatment or to desensitise him to various feared situations and the attendant anxiety. One of the early reports on the use of hypnosis to aid treatment of the speech symptom was that of Richter (1928), who hypnotised stutterers and told them, while in an hypnotic trance, to repeat simple words and sentences speaking slowly and carefully. Moore (1946) also used hypnosis as a supplementary method to other systems of therapy and found that the relaxation obtained by stutterers under hypnosis persisted during subsequent performances in complex speech situations according to introspective reports of the subjects. More recently, Lockhart & Robertson (1977) combined hypnotherapy and block control in separate sessions for some of their stutterers. Under hypnosis patients were given suggestions to improve awareness of tactile feedback and to associate block control with calmness, confidence and relaxation. Twenty-three patients were given this form of treatment and ten had been discharged as fluent with some evidence of maintenance of fluency at the time of the author's writing. Eleven of the remaining patients showed some improvement but final reassessment figures were not available. Lockhart (1982, personal communication) reports that a few of the original twenty-three stutterers have now been re-referred to speech therapy, but after very few treatment sessions involving only re-teaching of block control techniques, these patients have regained at least clinical fluency, with some evidence of transfer of this fluency beginning to take place.

An individual case study on the use of hypnosis and specific speech exercises has been discussed by Dempsey & Granich (1978). They quote one patient who started to stutter at 22-years-old following a traumatic incident and found that hypnotherapy allowed the patient to supply information which seemed largely unobtainable in a waking state and provided him with an abrupt and significant reduction in the speech symptom. In conjunction with hypnosis the patient was requested to look in a mirror and stutter for varying periods of time to diffuse some of the anxiety associated with being disfluent, and to show him that he was in control. Treatment lasted approximately four months and the patient produced a significant change in speech fluency across several dimensions: increased word output, fewer repetitions per word and reduced duration of blocking. The patient himself reported feeling considerably less anxious and much more confident and relaxed about his ability to speak in a fluent manner. Although this was a single case study it is worthwhile noting that both objective assessment of the speech symptoms and introspective reports of the subject were in agreement that improvement had occurred.

Elicitation of Aetiology

The aetiology of stuttering has attracted interest for many centuries and the possibility that hypnosis would help to elicit the cause or causes of this disorder has interested a few researchers. Obviously, they were assuming that the aetiology was related to some emotional trauma. Most workers who have investigated the possible causes in this way claim that such an approach is helpful only if the patient is informed of the cause. It has been argued that if the stutterer knows the cause of his disorder he is then able to overcome it. Vogel (1934) typifies much of the work in this area. He hypnotised hospitalised marines who stuttered and in the trance they were told they would remember the incidents which caused the onset of their disorder and on waking they would thus be able to overcome their stuttering. It is assumed that the stutterer requires no further assistance once he knows the cause of his disorder, but it would seem likely that he would still benefit from further therapy to help him to make the necessary adjustments in his life to accommodate his new-found fluency.

Van Pelt (1975) has produced an interesting theory on the aetiology of stuttering. He considers that patients suffering from nervous and allied disorders, e.g. asthma, migraine, stuttering, must be regarded as being acccidentally self-hypnotised. He believes that emotion concentrates the mind and superconcentration of the mind is hypnosis; therefore patients who have experienced a severe emotional shock are often left with foolish and irrational ideas which cause them to act as if hypnotised. Fear of these symptoms creates more tension and establishes a vicious circle. He cites seven case histories but gives no indication of whether or not these were specially selected. One of these cases is of a stutterer, 'Mrs E. complained of stammering. Investigation revealed it had started after her father had put her across his knees and spanked her. She had never spoken properly to him or anybody else since then. Hypnotherapy enabled her to adjust her mind, adopt an adult point of view and speak perfectly'.

Hypnosis and Psychotherapy

Lesser claims have been made of hypnosis than of eliciting the aetiology of stuttering. Some authorities have used it during psychotherapy at points where resistance becomes particularly severe (Hubbard (1963), but results are variable and inconsistent. Morley (1957) also mentions the use of hypnosis during psychotherapy with the severe stutterer who is unable to speak with sufficient fluency to explain his thoughts and feelings to the psychiatrist. However, hypnosis does not seem to have been widely used, or at least no great claims have been made of its use in this connection with stutterers.

Treatment of Children

In the last century, claims were made of the value of hypnosis with children and more recently Silber (1973) has investigated this in some detail. He has used hypnosis with children who present with various speech disorders including stuttering. He sees the goals of hypnosis with children as (a) the restoration of damaged self-esteem and bolstering of self-confidence, and (b) the vulnerable area, which has given way, must be healed and strengthened. He stresses the importance of rapport being established almost completely on terms compatible with the child's understanding, imagination and needs. In effect, there must be an unconditional commitment of the child and the hypnotist to an interpersonal relationship stressing participation and co-operation. Silber then teaches the children to imagine themselves in fairy tale situations with two notional aides to bolster self-approval and to ward off pain and evil respectively. This use of fairy tales is intended to heighten the effectiveness of the hypnotic approach. Silber claims to have successfully treated a number of children with a 'variety of speech defects', including stuttering.

Long-Term Effects

Although hypnosis does seem to produce an almost immediate change in the speech and non-speech symptoms of stuttering, consideration must also be given to the long-term effects of this technique and unfortunately these are not so promising. Morley (1957) has commented that although hypnosis does produce greater relaxation and the hypnotic suggestion of easy speech can be maintained for a short while, in general, it has failed to produce a permanent cure. One study involving larger numbers of subjects was that of Gottlober (1953) who conducted a series of experiments with fifty stutterers aged 14-47 years over a two year period using hypnotherapy. All patients were co-operative and participated in group and individual sessions for an average of 120 sessions. The stutterers showed no blocking during the trance state and for short periods following this, but all resumed their usual patterns soon after coming out of the trance. Obviously increased understanding of the difficulties faced by stutterers in the transfer and maintenance of fluency would assist results using many different treatment techniques, including hypnosis.

Value of Hypnosis

It is difficult to make any generalised claims on the value of hypnosis with stutterers as there is a paucity of objective evaluation. Although promising results have been claimed in single case studies, it is unfortunate that often there is no indication of whether these are representative of the authors' results using hypnosis or are examples of 'successful' patients with no information on how many patients have been unsuccessful. Much of the research also fails to describe the type and frequency of stuttering, type of trance, data on follow-up particularly long term follow-up.

The use of hypnosis with stutterers would seem to merit much further and more detailed research to discover the true extent and limitations of this technique. It is possible that its value lies in the treatment of non-speech symptoms or in providing the patient with a feeling of deep relaxation and enhanced fluency, though the patient should be cautioned that this is not a 'cure'. It is also likely that only a limited number of stutterers will respond positively to hypnosis and, interestingly, much of the reported successes of hypnosis has been with patients who began to stutter relatively late in childhood or in adulthood, many of these cases apparently experiencing some traumatic incident. Hypnosis then requires much further investigation as it could be a useful adjunct in therapy for at least some stutterers.

Drugs

The concept of stuttering being controlled by means of the patient swallowing certain substances has been popular for centuries. Rieber and Wollock (1977) quote Hieronymus Mercurialis, who suggested dietary techniques to control stuttering, recommending aromatic, salty and sharp food, while advising abstinence from pastries, nuts and fish. They also refer to Sir Francis Bacon's belief that the stutterer's tongue was cold and dry and noted that more difficulty was experienced at the beginning of sentences. His explanation of this differed from that of today, as did his remedy, viz he suggested that the stutterer should drink hot wine to heat the tongue. Many folk remedies for stuttering also suggest this willingness to rely on outside agencies to relieve the stuttering symptom. Van Riper (1973) gives examples of Bantu stutterers chewing garlic, while those in Japan were forced to swallow raw eggs or to eat charred shrikers' or frogs' tongues. Rockey (1980) describes the use of drugs for the treatment of stuttering in Britain during the nineteenth century; the choice of drugs apparently being related more to its popularity at that time than to its actions. Thus, stutterers have been treated to dietary control, swallowing of unpleasant substances and the use of drugs which seem to have had varying effects, including purgatives, tonics and analgesics.

In the twentieth century the choice of drug has been related to various viewpoints on stuttering. The effects of various drugs and placebos on the stutterer have been investigated. In general, the tranquillising drugs have been popular as these have a calming effect and do not appear to alter the state of consciousness.

Reserpine

Reserpine would seem to be a useful drug for anxiety reduction but its effects on stuttering are still unclear. Meffert (1956) in a single-case study found that the stutterer's speech showed a reduction in disfluency during administration of reserpine. However, assessment in this instance was subjective. Objective assessment was used by Hollister (1955) to determine the effects of reserpine on six subjects, but the results were very variable, i.e. two improved, two were unchanged, one improved equally on reserpine and on the placebo and one improved only on placebo. Subjective assessment was used and it is possible that the experimenter may have been influenced by the subject's attitudes as much as by the overt speech symptoms. Thus, Mitchell (1955), in a study of sixteen stutterers being treated with reserpine, found that no change occurred in the severity or frequency of the stuttering block but there was a tendency toward easier and more overt blocks, with the subjects reporting that they were in more control of these blocks than previously. Mitchell also noted an 'improved attitude' by the subjects towards their stuttering. Kent (1963) cites personal communication with Glasner who administered reserpine to children aged 4-8 years and found that in six of them there was a change in non-verbal behaviour, viz they were reported to be more relaxed and to sleep better. The other child showed no change in either verbal or non-verbal behaviour.

Thus, the effect of this drug on stutterers can at best be described as variable and although there is little evidence to suggest that it produces much change in overt speech symptoms, it does seem to help the stutterer to become generally calmer with a more relaxed attitude towards his speech.

Chlorpromazine

Chlorpromazine is another of the tranquillising drugs which has been used with stutterers, but as yet insufficient data exist to allow for confidence in any statement about its value in reducing stuttering behaviour. Lang (1954) reported the use of this drug on a 15-year-old mentally handicapped boy who stuttered. An 'improvement' in speech was noted, but the methods of speech assessment were not indicated. Kent (1963) quotes an experiment by Heaver, Franklin and Arnold who gave four groups of ten stutterers either reserpine, reserpine-placebo, chlorpromazine or chlorpromazine-placebo over a period of nine weeks. They reported that on the speech assessments used the drug groups could not be differentiated from the placebo groups. If chlorpromazine has a similar effect to reserpine, i.e. anxiety reduction, it should have a beneficial effect when used in conjunction with speech therapy. Beech and Fransella (1968) quote Hackett, Hoffman, MacLeod and Surtees (1958) who studied the effects of chlorpromazine in conjunction with speech therapy on a group of child stutterers. All children were given a placebo for six weeks and chlorpromazine for a further six weeks, after which time they were divided into two groups, those on placebo and those on chlorpromazine, for another twenty-four weeks. At the end of this time 'speech improvement' was noted in 80 per cent of the active drug group, while only 30 per cent of the placebo group showed similar improvement. An additional finding arose from this work which might be particularly relevant when considering this drug as a treatment or as an adjunct to therapy. One year following the study it was found that the drug group tended to maintain its 'speech improvement' whereas the placebo group tended to relapse. Further information on the long-term effects of chlorpromazine or chlorpromazine plus speech therapy would be particularly helpful.

Meprobamate

This is another of the tranquillising drugs, but its effects on the speech of stutterers are still uncertain, though the work of Katz (1957) would attest to its efficacy. Katz randomly assigned three groups of stutterers to meprobamate, placebo or no medication and found that those on meprobamate showed a 'substantial reduction' in the mean number of stuttered words, while those on the placebo showed a 'significant increase' in the number of moments of stuttering. The non-medicated group showed no change. Di Carlo, Katz and Batkin (1959) replicated the work of Katz with thirty patients and the results over a six week period showed a 'substantial reduction' in the mean number of stuttered words for the meprobamate group, though this reduction was not significant at the 5 per cent level of confidence. However, somewhat unexpectedly, there was a statistically significant increase in stuttering for the placebo group and a very slight increase in stuttering for the no-treatment group. The reasons for the increase in stuttering in the placebo groups are unclear. Although these experiments would suggest that this drug held some promise in the treatment of stutterers, Kent and Williams (1959) found that meprobamate had no particular benefits. They compared a group of college students receiving meprobamate with a group receiving a placebo over a fourteen-week period and found no differences between the two groups on the four assessments used. It seems likely that this drug also has an anxiety-reducing influence and may have an effect on the speech of stutterers, though anxiety reduction *per se* may ultimately affect the speech symptom. After working with eighteen stutterers who were receiving meprobamate, Maxwell and Paterson (1958) concluded that this drug was 'of value in restoring speech confidence, facilitating treatment and shortening the period of speech therapy required'. It may thus have a valuable role as an adjunct in therapy.

Pentobarbitone

This belongs to the barbiturate group of drugs and its effect on stuttering has also been investigated. Love (1955) attempted to determine the influence of a depressant drug (pentobarbitone) and a stimulant drug (benzedrine) on stuttering. Twenty-two stutterers read a different 200 word passage at the same hour on four consecutive days. During these four days the stutterers were given pentobarbitone, benzedrine, placebo or no capsule – not necessarily in that order. Results showed that a relatively large dose of pentobarbitone, a rather potent sedative drug, had no significant effect in decreasing the number of stuttered words in oral reading. Furthermore, benzedrine, a strong central nervous system stimulant, also produced no signficiant effect. The placebo failed to produce a statistically significant difference from the no-capsule control condition. While the drugs used in this experiment failed to have any significant effect, it would be inadvisable to make a generalised statement on the effects of barbiturates or stimulant drugs on stuttering based on so little evidence.

Haloperidol

In the nervous control of the locomotor system of the brain, two particular chemical transmitters are involved – acetylcholine and dopamine. The main drug used with stutterers in recent years has been haloperidol, which is thought to block dopamine receptors and so increase the turnover rate of acetylcholine. In general, dopamine, which is stored in presynaptic neurones, has an inhibitory effect on the locomotor system of the brain, while acetylcholine has an excitatory effect. Interest in the use of haloperidol arose because of the resemblance of stuttering to the tics, habit spasms, and movement disorders of Gilles de la Tourette syndrome. Certainly, abnormalities of central dopaminergic systems have been implicated in a number of disorders involving rhythmic locomotor activity and speech. Dinnerstein, Frigyesi and Lowenthal (1962) have commented on analogies between parkinsonism and stuttering. They consider that the tremor in parkinsonism is superficially similar to the syllable repetitions often found in stuttering, while the slowness in movement in parkinsonism is somewhat analogous to the slowness and tense pauses in stuttering. In parkinsonism there is an abnormality in the basal ganglia, which causes an imbalance in acetylcholine and dopamine; there being a shortage of dopamine, giving the acetylcholine undue effect. Although the analogies between stuttering, parkinsonism and Gilles de la Tourette syndrome are superficial, the possibility of a locomotor system disorder has aroused interest and so the drug haloperidol has been used in a number of experiments with stutterers.

Much of the experimentation with this drug has used a double-blind crossover design involving a placebo similar in appearance to the drug. This type of design allows each subject to serve as his own control, though the presence of some fairly well-documented side-effects can make this difficult. The side-effects most often reported with haloperidol are lethargy and drowsiness, weakness and pain in the legs, blurred vision, nausea, nervousness and restlessness, dizziness, increased urinary frequency and dry mouth. The dosage is 0.5-4.5 mg daily, the most common dosage being 3 mg daily. However, to obviate the possibility of these side-effects, encouraging results have been obtained from a single low dosage injection of haloperidol. In one study (Burns, Brady and Kuruvilla 1978) nine of the twelve subjects were significantly more fluent after a single injection of haloperidol, but information is not given on the length of time the drug had this effect. Nevertheless, much more work is required on the effects of chronic low-dosage drug administration.

Patients' Attitudes. Any drug-administration programme should consider the patient's viewpoint on whether or not he has benefitted from the drug and there would seem to be some discrepancy between the therapist's measurement of improvement and that of the patient. This problem is exemplified by Wells and Malcolm (1971) who gave haloperidol along with orphenadrine to avoid the side-effects of haloperidol, to twelve stutterers. Although ten subjects showed significant improvement on objective speech measurements after the first four-week period, four of those 'successful' patients failed to return for a second four-week period. Those who did return for the second four-week period of drug administration failed to show any further significant changes. Similar results have been obtained by Murray, Kelly, Campbell and Stefanik (1977). This would serve to highlight an area of concern for the researcher in stuttering in that there may be a considerable discrepancy between the clinician's measurement of improvement and that of the patient. If the latter does not consider that sufficient change has occurred he may cease medication despite the clinician's assessment results.

Changes in Fluency. It is difficult to compare the results of different experiments using haloperidol, as many variables have been involved, e.g. drug dosage, period of time the subjects received the drug, methods of speech assessment, etc. It is clear, however, that some stutterers have shown an increase in fluency while receiving haloperidol, although the percentage is still uncertain. The percentage of stutterers who have shown a reduction of at least 50 per cent in stuttering frequency has varied from approximately 22 per cent (Quinn and Peachey 1973) to approximately 40 per cent (Andrews and Dozsa 1977).

Subgroups. This variability of results is puzzling and could suggest a subgroup of stutterers who do respond positively to this drug when objective speech measurements are considered, but the patient's attitude towards the drug and its side-effects must also be taken into account. Controversy exists concerning the possibility of a subgroup of 'haloperidol responders' being unambiguously delineated. No demographic differences have yet been noted but Quinn and Peachey (1973) indicated that their more severe stutterers did tend to show disproportionally greater improvement than the others, and this finding was corroborated by Rosenberger (1980).

Effects of Haloperidol. If haloperidol is effective for some stutterers, the question still remains of whether the effect of haloperidol is attributable to the drug's anxiolytic potency or to some other pharmacological action, e.g. does it have a specific effect on motor function? In the light of studies previously mentioned on the use of tranquillising drugs, it seems unlikely that the drug's main effect is anxiolytic, although some patients did experience a tranquillising effect. It is thus thought likely that the beneficial effects of haloperidol on some stutterers may be specific and not secondary to sedation or relaxation.

Burns *et al* (1978) have hypothesised that the beneficial effect of drugs like haloperidol alter dopamine metabolism in the brain in a fashion that suggests that these drugs block dopamine receptors and, to a lesser extent, norepinephrine receptors. If this is so, it leads to interesting hypotheses being formulated concerning the aetiology of stuttering, at least for some stutterers. If stuttering is in some way related to parkinsonism then it is anomalous that a dopamine-blocking drug should produce an improvement in symptoms. Use of the drug apomorphine, which is thought to stimulate dopamine receptors, has also produced an increase in fluency for some stutterers while reading but not in spontaneous speech (Burns *et al* 1978). Nevertheless, it seems paradoxical that patients should experience some increase in fluency during reading after receiving a drug which is thought to stimulate dopamine receptors. For this reason the role of the dopaminergic system on stuttering must remain uncertain.

It may also be hypothesised that this drug is beneficial for some stutterers because it slows speech rate, but Burns *et al* (1978) have shown that many stutterers who were more fluent after administration of haloperidol spoke more rapidly, whereas a slowing of speech was frequently associated with non-responsiveness to haloperidol. It thus remains to be proven whether or not speech rate before administration of haloperidol is a prognostic indicator for its use in treatment.

Thus, although results with this drug are so far very variable, more work on elucidating possible prognostic indicators for its use would be helpful. Also, further studies with other agents affecting the dopaminergic system would be useful to assist understanding of a possible aetiological factor in stuttering.

Conclusions

It would appear that these adjuncts do contribute towards the gaining of fluency for some stutterers, but it is still unclear whether the same stutterer would benefit from all these adjuncts, with the obvious corollary that some stutterers will benefit from none of them, or whether the therapist must choose them on a more selective basis. It would be unrealistic to ignore the possibility of the existence of subgroups of stutterers, with the logical conclusion that there may be a selective response to these adjuncts. The concept of sub-groups of stutterers is by no means novel. Ssikorski (1889) raised the question of whether stuttering is 'a single disorder or a number of disorders which have been grouped together because they have been insufficiently analysed'. More recently, the work of Riley and Riley (1980) would suggest that subgroups do exist, but as yet there is no definitive evidence to show that a clearly delineated subgroup responds perfectly to a specific treatment aid. Nevertheless the description of possible subgroups would seem to be an area worthy of further investigation to aid understanding of this enigmatic disorder and to assist in choosing the treatment technique most suitable for each stutterer.

This raises the further problem of the therapists' ability to prescribe these aids. Therapists can and do prescribe the Edinburgh masker for stutterers who, after initial trial with the machine, are considered to benefit from it. A similar situation exists for biofeedback machines. However, under no circumstances are therapists permitted to prescribe drugs. This therefore means close co-operation between therapist and physician if it is considered that drug therapy would be the treatment of choice for any stutterer. The problem of the stutterer being treated by two different clinicians also appertains to the use of hypnosis. Currently the speech therapist would be required to refer the stutterer to a qualified hypnotist. As speech therapists frequently utilise deep relaxation procedures in their treatment programmes, it would seem reasonable to train them in the use of hypnosis, particularly as the dividing line between deep relaxation and hypnosis is ill-defined. This problem remains to be solved in the future.

Nevertheless these adjuncts are by no means the sole consideration in the treatment of stuttering. If fluency is achieved, it must be transferred to situations outside the place of treatment, with the stutterer learning to perceive himself more positively concerning his ability to speak fluently. It is possible that in some instances the use of any of these adjuncts alone will produce fluency, with the necessary attitude change to allow this to be maintained. In those cases the adjunct has functioned as a complete treatment programme. The reasons why this can happen with some stutterers is worthy of further investigation. No doubt in the future many new devices will be found, each claiming to 'cure' stuttering, but each must be objectively evaluated to determine its true role in the treatment of this disorder.

References

Adams, M. and Hutchinson, J. (1974) 'The Effects of Three Levels of Auditory

Masking on Selected Vocal Characteristics and the Frequency of Disfluency of Adult Stutterers', *Journal of Speech and Hearing Research, 17*, 682-8

Adams, M. and Moore, W.(1972) 'The Effects of Auditory Masking on the Anxiety Level, Frequency of Disfluency and Selected Vocal Characteristics of Stutterers', *Journal of Speech and Hearing Research, 15*, 572-8

Andrews, G. and Dozsa, M. (1977) 'Haloperidol and the Treatment of Stuttering', *Journal of Fluency Disorders, 2*, 217-24

Azrin, N. and Nunn, R. (1974) 'A Rapid Method of Eliminating Stuttering by a Regulated Breathing Method', *Behaviour Research and Therapy, 12*, 279-86

Beech, H. and Fransella, F. (1968) *Research and Experiment in Stuttering*, Pergamon Press, Oxford

Boers-Van Dijk, M. (1973) 'Distraction in the Treatment of Stuttering' in *Neurolinguistic Approaches to Stuttering* Mouton, The Hague, pp. 1-7

Brady, J. Burns, D. and Kuruvilla, K. (1978) 'The Acute Effect of Haloperidol and Apomorphine on the Severity of Stuttering', *Biological Psychiatry, 13* 255-64

Cherry, C. and Sayers, B. (1956) 'Experiments upon the Total Inhibition of Stuttering by External Control and Some Clinical Results', *Journal of Psychosomatic Research, 1*, 233-46

Code, C. and Muller, D. (1980) Comments on Paper: 'The Long Term Use of an Automatically Triggered Auditory Feedback Masking Device in the Treatment of Stammering', *British Journal of Disorders of Communication, 15*, 141-2

Conture, E. and Brayton, E. (1975) 'The Influence of Noise on Stutterers: Different Disfluency Types', *Journal of Speech and Hearing Research, 18*, 381-4

Cross, D. (1977) 'Effects of False Increasing, Decreasing and True Electromyographic Biofeedback on the Frequency of Stuttering', *Journal of Fluency Disorders, 2* 109-116

Dempsey, G. and Granich, M. (1978) 'Hypno-behavioural Therapy in the Case of a Traumatic Stutterer: A Case Study', *International Journal of Clinical and Experimental Hypnosis, 26*, 125-33

Derazne, J. (1966) 'Speech Pathology in the U.S.S.R.' in R. Rieber and R. Brubaker (eds.), *Speech Pathology*, North-Holland, Amsterdam, pp. 613-18

Dewar, A., Dewar, A.D. and Barnes, H. (1976) 'Automatic Triggering of Auditory Feedback Masking in Stammering and Cluttering', *British Journal of Disorders of Communication, 11*, 19-26

Dewar, A., Dewar, A.D., Austin, W. and Brash, H. (1979) 'The Long Term Use of an Automatically Triggered Auditory Feedback Masking Device in the Treatment of Stammering', *British Journal of Disorders of Communication, 14* 219-29

Di Carlo, L., Katz, J. and Batkin, S. (1959) 'An Exploratory Investigation of the Effect of Meprobamate on Stuttering Behaviour', *Journal of Nervous and Mental Diseases, 128*, 558-61

Dinnerstein, A.J., Frigyesi, T. and Lowenthal, M. (1962) 'Delayed Feedback as a Possible Mechanism in Parkinsonism' in D. Legge (ed.), *Skills*, Penguin, Harmondsworth, pp. 188-99

Donovan, G. (1971) 'A New Device for the Treatment of Stammering', *British Journal of Disorders of Communication, 6*, 86-8

Garber, S. and Martin, R. (1974) 'The Effects of White Noise on the Frequency of Stuttering', *Journal of Speech and Hearing Research, 17*, 73-9

Gottlober, A. (1953) *Understanding Stuttering*, Grune and Stratton, New York

Gruber, L. (1971) 'The Use of the Portable Voice Masker in Stuttering Therapy', *Journal of Speech and Hearing Disorders, 36*, 287-9

Guitar, B. (1975) 'Reduction of Stuttering Frequency Using Analog Electromyographic Feedback', *Journal of Speech and Hearing Research, 18*, 672-85

Ham, R. and Steer, M. (1967) 'Certain Effects of Alteration in Auditory Feedback', *Folia Phoniatrica, 19*, 53-62

Hanna, R. Wifling, F. and McNeill, B. (1975) 'A Biofeedback Treatment for Stuttering', *Journal of Speech and Hearing Disorders, 40*, 270-3

Harms, M. and Malone, J. (1939) 'The Relationship of Hearing Acuity to Stammering', *Journal of Speech Disorders, 4*, 363-70

Hollister, L. (1955) 'Advantages of Placebos and the Double-Blind Method for Evaluating Drugs Used in Psychiatry', *Proceedings of the Academy of Psychosomatic Medicine*, New York

Hubbard, O. (1963) 'Hypnotherapy of a Patient Complaining of a Speech Defect (following Lindner's Method of Hypnoanalysis)', *American Journal of Clinical Hypnosis, 5*, 281-94

Ingham, R., Southwood, H. and Horsburgh, G. (1981) 'Some Effects of the Edinburgh Masker on Stuttering During Oral Reading and Spontaneous Speech', *Journal of Fluency Disorders, 6*, 135-54

Kalotkin, M., Manschreck, T. and O'Brien, D. (1979) 'Electromyographic Tension Levels in Stutterers and Normal Speakers', *Perceptual and Motor Skills, 49*, 109-110

Katz, J. (1957) 'The Effects of Meprobamate on Stuttering', MA Thesis, Syracuse University

Kent, L. and Williams, D. (1959) 'Use of Meprobamate as an Adjunct to Stuttering Therapy', *Journal of Speech and Hearing Disorders, 24*, 64-9

Kent, L. (1963) 'Use of Tranquillizers in the Treatment of Stuttering: Reserpine, Chlorpromazine, Meprobamate, Atarax', *Journal of Speech and Hearing Disorders, 28*, 289-94

Lang, F. (1954) 'Un Cas de Guérison de Bégaiement par la Chlorpromazine, Chez un Garçon de 15 Ans, Débile Mental', Abstracted in *Annales Medico Psychologies, 129, 233*

Lanyon, R., Barrington, C. and Newman, A. (1976) 'Modification of Stuttering Through E.M.G. Biofeedback: A Preliminary Study', *Behaviour Therapy, 7*, 96-103

Lanyon, R. (1977) 'Effect of Biofeedback-Based Relaxation on Stuttering During Reading and Spontaneous Speech', *Journal of Consulting and Clinical Psychology, 45*, 860-6

Lockhart, M. and Robertson, A. (1977) 'Hypnosis and Speech Therapy as a Combined Therapeutic Approach to the Problem of Stammering: A Study of Thirty Patients', *British Journal of Disorders of Communication, 12*, 97-108

Love, W.R. (1955) 'The Effect of Pentobarbital and Amphetamine Sulphate on the Severity of Stuttering' in W. Johnson and Leutenegger R. (eds.), *Stuttering in Children and Adults*, University of Minnesota Press, Minneapolis, pp. 298-310

MacCulloch, M., Eaton, R. and Long,E. (1970) 'The Long-Term Effect of Auditory Masking on Young Stutterers', *British Journal of Disorders of Communication, 5*, 165-73

Maraist, J. and Hutton, C. (1957) 'Effects of Auditory Masking Upon the Speech of Stutterers', *Journal of Speech and Hearing Disorders, 22*, 385-9

Maxwell, R. and Paterson, J. (1958) 'Meprobamate in the Treatment of Stuttering', *British Medical Journal 179*, 873-4

Meffert, M. (1956) 'The Effect of Serpasil (Reserpine) on the Severity of Stuttering', MA Thesis, University of Virginia

Mitchell, B. (1955) 'An Analysis of the Effect of Reserpine on Adult Stutterers',

MA Dissertation, Western Michigan University

Moore, W. (1946) 'Hypnosis in a system of Therapy for Stutterers', *Journal of Speech Disorders, 11*, 117-22

Moore, W. (Jnr.) (1978) 'Some Effects of Progressively Lowering Electromyographic Levels with Feedback Procedures on the Frequency of Stuttering Verbal Behaviours', *Journal of Fluency Disorders, 3*, 127-38

Morley, M. (1957) *The Development and Disorders of Speech in Childhood*, E.S. Livingstone, Edinburgh

Murray, T., Kelly, P., Campbell, L. and Stefanik, K. (1977) 'Haloperidol in the Treatment of Stuttering', *British Journal of Psychiatry, 130*, 370-33

Pachman, J., Oelschlaeger, M., Hughes, A. and Hughes, H. (1978) 'Toward Identifying Effective Agents in the Use of Biofeedback to Decelerate Stuttering Behaviour', *Perceptual and Motor Skills, 46*, 1006

Parker, C. and Christopherson, F. (1963) 'Electronic Aid in the Treatment of Stammer', *Medical Electronics and Biological Engineering, 1*, 121-5

Perkins, W. and Curlee, R. (1969) 'Clinical Impressions of Portable Masking Unit Effects in Stuttering', *Journal of Speech and Hearing Disorders, 34*, 360-2

Platt, L. and Basili, A. (1973) 'Jaw Tremor During Stuttering Block: an Electromyographic Study', *Journal of Communication Disorders, 6*, 102-109

Quinn, P. and Peachey, E. (1975) 'Haloperidol in the Treatment of Stutterers', *British Journal of Psychiatry, 123*, 247-8

Richter, P. (1928) '*Das Stottern und Seine Heilung Durch Hypnotische Suggestion*', Rudolph, Dresden

Rieber, R. and Wollock, J. (1977) 'Historical Roots of Theory and Therapy' in R. Rieber (ed.) *The Problem of Stuttering*, Elsevier, Amsterdam, pp. 3-24

Riley, G. and Riley, J. (1980) 'Motoric and Linguistic Variables among Children who Stutter: a Factor Analysis', *Journal of Speech and Hearing Disorders, 45*, 504-514

Rockey, D. (1980) *Speech Disorders in Nineteenth Century Britain*, Croom Helm, London

Rosenberger, P. (1980) 'Dopaminergic Systems and Speech Fluency', *Journal of Fluency Disorders, 5*, 255-67

Shane, M. (1955) 'Effect on Stuttering of Alteration in Auditory Feedback' in W. Johnson and R. Leutenegger (eds.), *Stuttering in Children and Adults*, University of Minnesota Press, Minneapolis

Shrum, W. (1967) 'A Study of the Speaking Behaviour of Stutterers by Means of Multi-Channel Electromyography', *Dissertation Abstracts, 28*, 825

Silber, S. (1973) 'Fairy Tales and Symbols in Hypnotherapy of Children with Certain Speech Disorders', *International Journal of Clinical and Experimental Hypnosis, 21*, 272-283

Silver, B. and Blanchard, E. (1978) 'Biofeedback and Relaxation Training in the Treatment of Psychological Disorders: Or Are the Machines Really Necessary?' *Journal of Behavioural Medicine, 1*, 217-39

Silverman, F. and Goodban, J. (1972) 'The Effect of Auditory Masking on the Fluency of Normal Speakers', *Journal of Speech and Hearing Research, 15*, 543-6

Starkweather, C. and Lucker, J. (1978) 'Tokens for Stuttering', *Journal of Fluency Disorders, 3*, 167-180

Stromer, J. (1979) 'Some Comments on "Biofeedback in the Treatment of Psychophysiologic Disorders: Stuttering" ', *Biofeedback and Self Regulation, 4*, 383-5

Stromsta, C. (1958) *The Effects of altering the Fundemental Frequency of Masking on the Speech Performance of Stutterers*, Technical Report, National Institute of Health, Project B-1331

Sutton, S. and Chase, R. (1961) 'White Noise and Stuttering', *Journal of Speech and Hearing Research, 4*, 72

Trotter, W. and Lesch, M. (1967) 'Personal Experiences with a Stutter Aid', *Journal of Speech and Hearing Disorders, 32*, 270-2

Van Pelt, S. (1975) 'Hypnotherapy: not merely a Treatment, More a Way of Life', *Journal of the American Institute of Hypnosis, 16*, 44-5

Van Riper, C. (1958) 'Experiments in Stuttering Therapy' in J. Eisenson (ed.) *Stuttering: A Symposium*, Harper and Row, New York, pp. 275-390

—— (1963) *Speech Correction*, Prentice Hall, Englewood Cliffs, N.J.

—— (1971) *The Nature of Stuttering*, Prentice Hall, Englewood Cliffs, N.J.

—— (1973) *The Treatment of Stuttering*, Prentice Hall, Englewood Cliffs, N.J.

Vogel, V. (1934) 'Stuttering Cured by Hypnotism', *Scientific American, 151*, 311-13

Walle, E. (1980) 'Masking Devices and the Edinburgh Masker-Clinical Applications Within a Prison Setting', *Journal of Fluency Disorders, 5*, 69-74

Webster, R. and Dorman, M. (1968) 'Decrease in Stuttering Frequency as a Function of Continuous and Contigent Forms of Auditory Masking', *Journal of Speech and Hearing Research, 11*, 219-23

Wells, P. and Malcolm, M. (1971) 'Controlled Trial of Treatment of 36 Stutterers', *British Journal of Psychiatry, 119*, 603-604

Wingate, M. (1976) *Stuttering Therapy and Treatment*, Irving Publishers Inc. New York

Wingate, M. (1981) 'Sound and Pattern in Artificial Fluency: Spectrographic Evidence', *Journal of Fluency Disorders, 6*, 94-118

Wohl, M. (1968) 'The Electronic Metronome – An Evaluative Study', *British Journal of Disorders of Communication, 3*, 89-98

Zimmerman, G. (1980) 'Articulatory Behaviours Associated with Stuttering: A Cinefluorographic Analysis', *Journal of Speech and Hearing Research, 23*, 108-121

9 MAJOR ISSUES FOR THE THERAPIST

Peggy Dalton

Considerations in the Approach to Treatment for Stuttering

Stuttering is a phenomenon which has attracted the interest of philo-
sophers, psychologists, clinicians and the speaking world at large for
centuries. Thousands of books, papers, articles have been written about
it, a multitude of methods suggested for its alleviation. The contributors to this volume were given no directives as to the lines they should
take in their discussion of approaches to treatment, nor were they
asked to emphasise particular aspects of the areas designated to them.
Nevertheless, certain themes have emerged throughout these chapters as
important if we are to attempt to improve the help we have to offer to
disfluent children and those responsible for them, and to the adults
whose speech difficulty may severely limit their lives.

First, all agree that stuttering should not be approached as if it were
a single disorder. Each client will manifest not only an individual
pattern of disfluency but different reactions to it. These reactions, the
devices developed to cope with them and the effect disfluency will have
on the developing person will similarly be varied according to other
aspects of their personality as a whole. The attitudes of significant
people in a child's life will have their effects in later years. The environment in which the child grows up and the adult lives and works will
vary in the demands and pressures exerted on speech. And, not least,
the theories that children, parents and older people who stutter have
about the problem and their expectations of therapy will be highly
idiosyncratic and, initially at least, govern their approach to the treatment which is offered.

It will be clear, therefore, that the second major theme to recur,
that of the need for a thorough and broadly-based assessment, is crucial
for the therapist. Hayhow (Chapter 2) has discussed the assessment of
the speech itself in terms not only of instances of disfluency but the
quality of fluent speech and general linguistic skills. She also presents
a range of procedures for the assessment of attitudes towards communication. Rustin and Cook (Chapter 3) seek information on every aspect
of the child's development and personality and the family and school
environment before they embark on the choice of an appropriate pro-

216

gramme of treatment.Cheasman (Chapter 4) sees much of the work done on the intensive courses for adults as a process of continuous diagnosis. Dalton (Chapter 5) urges the importance of spending sufficient time in the exploration of the client's view, not only of his problem but of himself as a person and the events and people that make up his life.

The third theme of this book comes naturally out of this emphasis on wide-ranging and thorough assessment. Implying as this does that each client will be found to have his own special needs, the authors agree that there is no one 'right' approach to the treatment of stuttering. A range of procedures and programmes have been described and evaluated for their appropriateness in particular cases. Suggestions have been made for combining certain aspects of different approaches which might be of value to the individual client or group. This is not a haphazard matter of trying out one technique after another, with a stab at social skills training and a bit of counselling thrown in. It is more a question of what Kelly (1965) has described as the 'orchestration of techniques' in order to provide a coherent programme which covers every aspect of the problem as it emerges.

Is There a 'Stutterer's Clinician'?

The issues raised in the preceding section ask a great deal of the therapist involved in the treatment of stuttering. Van Riper (1975), in his description of the skills and attributes needed by the 'stutterer's clinician' wonders at one point 'why any clinician would ever want to work with a stutterer. The therapy can be incredibly demanding, the investment of time and energy seems excessive; one's successes are soon forgotten; one's failures continue to haunt the remote corners of the cranium.' (p. 487) And yet, he says, he would not have traded this experience for any other. He regards it as exciting, challenging and rewarding.

The first proposal he makes, which seems a crucial one, is that the clinician should assess her own beliefs about the nature of the problem. This is not to suggest that the newly-trained therapist makes up her mind once and for all what stuttering and its treatment are all about. Van Riper himself has modified his own beliefs and developed his approach over a long period of time. Many of the workers whose programmes have been referred to have changed with the advancement of our knowledge. What he is saying is that the therapist should work from the basis of clearly thought-out notions of what she is dealing with and what she and her clients are aiming at. Therapy then will have the structure, purpose and clarity that are essential if it is to be effective.

He also stresses the importance of the clinician's competence. He sees clients, especially those who have been through many previous attempts to overcome their problem, as 'probing and testing us, searching for evidence that we understand the nature of their difficulties and how they can be resolved'. They must be convinced the therapists 'know their professional stuff' (p. 469). This will not be taken for granted, but needs to be demonstrated. He makes some specific suggestions for beginning clinicians to gain this competence: first, they must acquire a solid foundation of information about the nature of stuttering; second, they must come to know a number of people who stutter personally; and third, they should assume the role of a severe stutterer for long enough and in enough situations to enable them to experience the 'frustrations, anxiety, shame and other negative emotions that constitute the context of the stutterer's daily life' (p. 470).

While in full agreement with the first two points, this author would question the third. The experience of a whole series of such assignments in training certainly proved useful in some respects. It was possible to understand more about the variety of listener reaction. Some of the feelings of apprehension and frustration were indeed there, but there was always the sense that it was 'not real', that there was a choice as to whether to continue with the experiment. What was missing, too, was the very personal concept of the self as a stutterer and all that this implies in the approach to people and situations. Though we can generalise in terms of the experience of the negative emotions described by Van Riper, taking on the role of a stutterer will only give us *one* view of what it may be like – and a transient, limited view at that. If we extrapolate from this and make assumptions as to what it is like for stutterers-in-general, we are likely to tune in less sensitively to the meaning of stuttering to the particular client.

Perhaps a more fruitful suggestion is found in Lay (1982). He set up a project with the members of a graduate seminar in fluency disorders where they were asked to develop and maintain a programme of personal behavioural change for a period of four weeks. Through this, they all had direct experience of what may be involved in the various aspects of attempting change: the problem of setting appropriate goals and sub-goals, difficulties with maintaining motivation, the importance of the people and other factors in their environment.

Their personal reflections on the experiment showed them to have increased their understanding of the practical issues involved in setting up a programme of change for people who stutter. They also recognised the importance of regular support for their endeavours, without which a number of them felt they would not have continued..They became aware of the repercussions that change in one area might have for other aspects, not only of their own lives, but those of other people. Most importantly, however, Lay felt that they had all developed 'an empathetic perspective' (p. 68) towards what their clients were undertaking.

Van Riper dwells at some length on the need for empathy in therapy. More specifically, he refers to *accurate empathy*, described as the ability to imagine how it feels to be inside another person's skin. He emphasises that this does not entail full identification with the client. The therapist must be able to step into another person's shoes, but not find herself unable or unwilling to step out of them again. He sees this attribute as developed through a combination of careful observation and inference, but stresses that the therapist should be aware of the difference between the two. The more sensitive and wide-ranging the clinician's observations, the more likely the inferences are to be appropriate and the hypotheses based on them to be fruitful for treatment.

Van Riper links *personal warmth* with this empathetic attitude towards clients and refers to Rogers' (1957) notion of unconditional positive regard. He speaks of the need for non-possessive warmth and acceptance of clients as persons in their own right, though pointing out that acceptance need not mean indiscriminate agreement or approval.

Kelly (1955), in his 'credulous approach' in treatment, also stresses the need for the therapist to see things through the other person's eyes. He too would concur with the idea that clients should be accepted as they are, but he goes further than Van Riper in distinguishing between acceptance and approval. He sees acceptance as involving 'not so much the approval of the client's view of himself as it does the readiness to utilize the client's mode of approach' (p. 587). He expands on this idea when he says of the therapist:

> He should attempt to anticipate events in the way the client anticipates them. He should try to employ the client's vocabulary in thinking about the issues which the client sees himself as facing. He should give words the meanings that the client gives them, rather than the meanings the dictionary gives them, or the personal and professional meanings he has himself customarily given them (p.587).

He too warns against the therapist's surrendering his own professional overview of the client's problems in his earnest attempts to put himself into his client's shoes.

When Van Riper discusses the need for *genuineness* in the clinician, he does so in terms similar to those used by Levy (Chapter 6). While not burdening clients with their own problems, therapists should be open, willing to admit to mistakes and misunderstandings. Defensiveness with regard to one's own frailties he sees as unnecessary, 'What stutterers cannot bear is the smell of fraudulence' (p. 469).

Throughout his chapter on the stutterer's clinician, Van Riper refers to the clinician's need for continual self-observation and evaluation. He suggests video- and audio-recording of sessions, not only for students in training but also for experienced therapists. He has clearly evaluated his own personal approach in therapy constantly and continued to learn from the experience. Having outlined the attributes of a good therapist he produces a 'bipolar adjective checklist' (p. 472) containing 67 constructs relevant to the clinician's conduct of a treatment session. The three headings under which they fall are *Evaluative*, with such constructs as 'enthusiastic . . . phlegmatic', 'organized . . . disorganized'; *Activity oriented* including 'controlling . . . permissive', 'effective . . . ineffective'; and *Strength*, including 'secure . . . insecure', 'committed . . . uncommitted'. In evaluating his own or a student's therapeutic role a mark is placed between the two poles of each construct to indicate the therapists' position on any particular occasion. While not presenting this procedure as in any way scientifically valid he has found it a useful means of scrutinising clinical behaviour.

Along similar lines and equally 'unscientifically', a group of therapists and counsellors working with this author set up a 'Therapy' grid (see Chapter 2), where the elements were factors in clients which we chose as representing a range of ease or difficulty in our dealings with them: 'passive'; 'anxious', 'violent', 'depressed'. The constructs agreed upon were to do with our attitudes and feelings when confronted with such attributes: 'makes me feel anxious . . . doesn't make me feel anxious', 'feel relaxed with . . . don't feel relaxed with', and so on. This too gave us food for thought in considering aspects of our therapeutic approach and led to some useful sharing of alternative means of coping with the difficulties.

The Therapeutic Relationship

Van Riper gives a clear account of the kind of clinician he sees as working effectively within his own approach to treatment. The therapeutic relationship implied by all he says is central to the work undertaken. Florance and Shames, too, (1980), while carrying out a highly structured programme of behavioural procedures, also lay great stress on this relationship. They see it as the ' "human dimension" which breathes life into the behavioural tactics and strategies' (p. 386).

Kelly (1955) devotes much thought to the therapeutic relationship, which he has likened to that between a PhD student and his supervisor. Both are 'experts' in their own way — the student on the subject he is studying for his thesis, the supervisor on the processes involved in research. Thus the client is the expert on himself, the subject of the experiments for change, while the therapist's task is to see that he sets up reasonable hypotheses to test and evaluate his results in a productive way. Although a paper on the therapeutic relationship (1965) describes this relationship in psychotherapy as he sees it, his summary at the end would seem equally to apply to speech therapy:

'I have tried to indicate that the task of psychotherapy is not to produce behaviour, but rather to enable the client, as well as his therapist, to utilize behaviour for asking important questions. In fact, the task of psychotherapy is to get the human process going again so that life may go on and on from where psychotherapy left off. There is no particular kind of psychotherapeutic relationship — no particular kind of feelings — no particular kind of interaction that is in itself a psychotherapeutic panacea. The relationships between therapist and client and the techniques they employ may be as varied as the whole human repertory of relationships and techniques' (p. 223).

The Training of Therapists

It is hoped that the earlier discission of some of Van Riper's ideas about what is needed for a therapist to work with people who stutter has not given the impression that she must be superhuman. This is not what he or Florance and Shames or Kelly imply, although clearly they expect a good deal of those they work with. Most therapists do not specialise in the treatment of stuttering initially at least, and many of the skills demanded in this area are mainly developed through later experience. Certain basic requirements, however, should be included in the training period and, if they are not, the newly-trained therapist should be prepared and facilitated by her seniors to fulfil them.

The thorough knowledge of the nature of stuttering referred to by Van Riper is clearly essential. The assessment procedures described by Hayhow, Rustin and Cook need to be carried out with competence, for which supervision and practice are needed. If a technique is to be taught, the therapist herself must be skilled in its use in a wide variety of situations and able to sustain it over time and maintain it under pressure. Where a structured programme is to be followed the student needs to know and understand it so well that she can move through it with ease and focus most of her attention on the client.

Even more important than the development of these practical skills the student needs both supervised experience in working with people who stutter and the opportunity to observe sessions run by those who specialise in this area of treatment. Participation in a group, especially, can be a very useful learning experience, where it is possible to gain some direct knowledge of the wide range of problems which may be encountered.

Perhaps the greatest lack in our training at present relates to the counselling aspects of our work in all areas of speech and language difficulty. One theme throughout this book has been the need to go beyond disfluent behaviour and concern ourselves with the effects it may have on the person and those he is involved with. We have suggested that the speech therapist, unless she chooses to restrict herself to programmes such as those described by Ingham and Ryan and Van Kirk (1978) should be prepared to approach the client's stuttering in the context of his personality as a whole and the life-style which is peculiarly his own. In order to do this she must have some understanding of interpersonal and intrapersonal difficulties which may arise and some means of helping the client to cope with them, beyond sympathetic listening and encouragement (valuable as these may be), to press on with working for fluency. Whether this be called 'work on attitudes', 'counselling' or 'psychotherapy', these skills too need to be learned and provision for their learning should be made part of a therapist's basic training.

References

Florance, C.L. and Shames, G.H. (1980) 'Stuttering Treatment: Issues in Transfer and Maintenance', *Seminars in Speech, Language and Hearing, 1,* 375-88

Ingham, R.J. (1981) 'Aperçus' in Boberg (ed.), *Maintenance of Fluency,* Elsevier, Amsterdam, pp. 260-2

Kelly, G.A. (1955) *The Psychology of Personal Constructs,* Norton, The Hague
—— (1965) 'The Psychotherapeutic Relationship' in B. Maher (ed.) (1979) *Clinical Psychology and Personality,* Krieger, New York, pp. 216-23

Lay, T. (1982) 'Stuttering: Training the Therapist', *Journal of Fluency Disorders, 7,* 63-9

Rogers, C.R. (1957) 'The Necessary and Sufficient Conditions of Therapeutic Personality Change', *Journal of Consulting Psychology and Psychiatry, 21,* 95-103

Van Riper, C. (1975) 'The Stutterer's Clinician' in J. Eisenson (ed.), *Stuttering: A Second Symposium,* Harper and Row, New York, pp. 455-92

INDEX